W9-AXR-697

Glory,
Darkness,
Light

Glory, Darkness, Light

A HISTORY OF THE UNION LEAGUE CLUB OF CHICAGO

James D. Nowlan

Northwestern University Press
Evanston, Illinois

Northwestern University Press
Evanston, Illinois 60208-4170

Copyright © 2004 by the Union League Club of Chicago.
Published 2004 by Northwestern University Press.
All rights reserved.

All photos courtesy Union League of Chicago Archives
unless otherwise indicated.

Frontispiece: Union League, 1885
Page 3: "Long John" Wentworth
Page 99: Unidentified fashion-show participants
Page 143: Frederick C. Ford, Union League president, 1985–86

Printed in the United States of America
10 9 8 7 6 5 4 3 2 1
ISBN 0-8101-1549-2

Library of Congress Cataloging-in-Publication Data
Nowlan, James Dunlap, 1941–
Glory, darkness, light : the Union League Club of Chicago, a history / James D. Nowlan.
p. cm.
Includes bibliographical references and index.
ISBN 0-8101-1549-2 (hardcover : alk. paper)
1. Union League Club of Chicago—History. 2. Chicago (Ill.)—History. I. Title.
HS2725.C4 U69 2004
367'.977311—dc22 2003025436

The paper used in this publication meets the minimum requirements
of the American National Standard for Information Sciences—
Permanence of Paper for Printed Library Materials, ANSI Z39.48-1992.

CONTENTS

PREFACE

Roman baths may have been the ancient forerunners of city clubs, where select groups of like-minded men gathered, away from the hustle-bustle of the Forum to relax, socialize, and do business. In more modern times, English taverns and coffeehouses provided the settings for the first men's social clubs. "We now use the word *clubbe*," wrote an observer in 1659, "for a sodality [brotherhood, fraternity] in a tavern."

Sir Walter Raleigh organized a club in the Mermaid Tavern in London that included Shakespeare among its members. The Mermaid, Apollo, and other clubs formed for the purpose of eating, drinking, and discussing literature or politics. The clubs grew so large that all but members were excluded from the taverns, which in effect became clubhouses.

Early in the nineteenth century, clubs were owned by the members rather than, as earlier, by the tavern keepers. Many of the early English clubs were based on politics, where those who shared political affinities met and discussed the issues of the day (Carlton [Tory], Liberal, and Reform clubs), although this tradition has mostly disappeared. Other clubs were based on old-school ties (Oxford and Cambridge clubs) or the armed services (army and navy clubs) or the world of acting (the Garrick). The nineteenth-century clubs symbolized the English elite who had conquered much of the world. At "the club" men could discuss the challenges of running the empire, meet former schoolmates and friends, pick up information, and exchange opinions.

In a book about gentlemen's clubs in London, Anthony LeJeune noted that two hundred such clubs existed in that city at the beginning of the twentieth century, a number that declined to forty by 1979.

A good club, contended LeJeune, is much more than a mere catering establishment. "It should be a refuge from the vulgarity of the outside world, a reassuringly fixed point, the echo of a more civilized way of living, a place where (as was once said of an Oxford college) people still prefer a silver salt-cellar which doesn't pour to a plastic one which does."

An English club man observed that a club ought to have only two rules: First, that every member should pay his subscription; and second, that he should behave like a gentleman at all times.

American city clubs drew from the English model, but only in part. The grand hotels of the world provided another inspiration. Gathering places for the wealthy, the lavish hotel ballrooms and dining rooms offered glittering settings for social events. Overnight sleeping accommodations and athletic facilities represent other dimensions of American city clubs that were not generally part of the English clubs.

City clubs in Chicago followed the models of those established earlier in the East, such as the Union Club of Boston and the Union League clubs of New York and Philadelphia, all of which incorporated and had club-houses during the Civil War. (These clubs have no ties to the club about which this book is written.)

The 1911 *Chicago Blue Book*, a directory of prominent Chicagoans published periodically, listed ten city clubs: the Chicago, Chicago College, City, Germania, Hamilton, Iroquois, Marquette, Standard, Union League, and University clubs. Since then others, such as the Covenant Club and Illinois Athletic Club, have come and gone.

Today there are five major city clubs in Chicago: The Chicago, Chicago Athletic, Union League, University, and Women's Athletic clubs. The others are no longer. A "major" city club is distinguished from many other dining clubs, such as Chicago's Metropolitan, Mid-day, and Tavern clubs, by the more extensive facilities and offerings as well as the free-standing clubhouses of the former.

After country clubs, city clubs are the second most common of private clubs, numbering more than two thousand in the United States. According to Joe Perdue in *Contemporary Club Management* (1997), there are about a thousand members in the typical club. Average initiation fees are $2,500 and monthly dues are typically $100–130.

City clubs are not generally so exclusive as outside impression might hold. An up-and-coming business or professional person with self-confidence and sociability is probably eligible (or "clubbable," as the English say) for a club.

But why belong to a club?

Young businesspeople are often encouraged to join. In Chicago, bankers and law partners often encourage their bright associates to look into either the Union League or University clubs. The young professionals take the tour of a clubhouse, or of several. They might like the energy of the

Rendezvous Room bar or be impressed by the athletic department or by the special qualities another club emphasizes. Clubs have personalities. Prospective members can discern as much rather quickly and decide if there is a match.

There are practical reasons for belonging. "It was a jungle out there" in the 1880s when men took refuge in the Club from the muck of the unpaved streets, the stench from the meatpacking plants, the noise, and the crowds in the public restaurants.

It's still a jungle out there. When members come through the front door today, whisk snow off their coats, or stomp the rain off their shoes, they also sigh in relief at the warmth and quiet of the setting and the friendly staff who call them by name and await their every need.

For out-of-town, or nonresident, members the overnight accommodations are comfortable and reasonably priced. The nonresident member can entertain his in-town friends or business associates in splendid surroundings. The member is also assured of being the host (the member always signs the checks; no money changes hands in the Club).

Inside the Union League Club of Chicago, and most clubs, members are accorded great space. Tables in all the Club's restaurants are widely separated; conversations are your own. The waiter often has your favorite glass of wine ready to pour before you are seated. The library is expansive, the carpeting deep. Fine art is everywhere. It is one's mansion in the city.

A mansion in the city, but in the case of the Union League Club, a club and its house with special missions! The three conditions of membership in the 1879 Articles of Association are about the use of moral, social, and political influences to encourage unconditional loyalty to our federal government; to inculcate an appreciation for the sacred obligations of American citizenship; and to resist and expose corruption. (See Appendix.)

Heavy stuff. Not fully appreciated by new members, nor by many longtime members, but taken to heart by those who become Union League Club leaders.

These responsibilities are restated every year in clarion tones at the Club's annual Washington's Birthday celebration dinner. In February 2001, Club president Robert Fitzgerald declared, "The spirit of the 1879 charter is as relevant today as when written. . . . No other institution in the city commits to the city and country as this club does."

That's a lot to live up to.

The original Club members focused so much on their political mission that they debated whether even to offer a dining facility for members. Other, less political, members convinced the founders a dining room was a necessity to sustain a broad membership.

The value and responsibility of American citizenship has been an enduring value of the Club leaders. For decades, the Club participated in the ceremonies in Chicago that bestow American citizenship. Without fail since the 1920s, inner-city boys and girls at the Club's summer camp begin each day with the raising of the American flag and the Pledge of Allegiance.

When the American flag was being dragged through the streets, and American servicemen spat upon during the Vietnam War, the Club organized the Armed Forces Council of Chicago. During Armed Forces Week, the Club coordinated patriotic and military celebrations in the major plazas of the city.

In 1946, Sam Witwer began his quest to create a modern state constitution. In 1970, the Club held a victory dinner to celebrate the adoption that year of the controversial new state constitution. Constitutional Convention president Witwer, Governor Richard B. Ogilvie, and unrelenting advocate Bob Bergstrom, active Club members all, received most of the applause; the Club, which put its name and money behind the long effort, deserved some as well.

Its leading members characterize the Club as more of a giving, than a taking, institution. In the early 1920s, thirty members gave $1,000 each to found the Club's first Boys Club. In 2000, the Boys and Girls Clubs' trustees gave an average of $30,000 each for the $6.4 million capital campaign that was fulfilled by Club members in less than a year.

Yet the Club has not been perfect, as readers will learn.

The Club president is the custodian, for one year, of the spirit of the Club. He or she must infuse the activists with energy, purpose, and focus and keep the corpus of members content. "My presidency was the greatest year of my life, bar none," declares Everett Barlow, for four decades a Club activist. "When I was thirteen, we lived in a working-class neighborhood in Rock Island[, Illinois]. Armistice Day was a big day. The commander of the army arsenal there put on a big pyrotechnics display.

"Being boys, two brothers from the neighborhood and I foolishly watched from the bluff where the fireworks sometimes landed. The brothers were killed in an explosion. To bring me out of my grief, my minister convinced me I had to do something for other people—but I had to do it for three people, the two brothers and me."

Barlow has given the Club and its missions more even than that.

"A decade ago," Barlow continues, "George Sinka learned of a volunteer program at Cabrini Green [a problem-plagued public housing project]. Sinka, you know, was originally a poor boy himself, and he's the only member to have been president of the Club and also of all three of our Club foundations—the Boys and Girls, Civic and Arts, and Engineers foundations. Anyway, seven of us decided to help—three past presidents, two directors, and two nonresident members. For one year, we went up there and helped renovate apartments."

Though not a Club activity, nor ever mentioned in the Club magazine, that is the spirit many Club presidents try to pass on.

The Union League Club is part of the warp for the weft that is Chicago, and this is the story of that Club and its city.

SOURCES

Buckingham, George. *The Spirit of the Union League Club*. Chicago: Union League Club of Chicago, 1926.

LeJeune, Anthony. *The Gentlemen's Clubs of London*. New York: Mayflower Books, 1979.

Perdue, Joe. *Contemporary Club Management*. Lansing, Mich.: Educational Institute of the American Hotel and Motel Association, 1997.

ACKNOWLEDGMENTS

I am indebted to many for the development of this book. The Club history subcommittee of the public affairs committee commissioned me to write this book. Members include Robert Sharp and Paul Wisner, successive chairs, Michael Chioros, Ken Meuser, Everett Barlow, Robert Fitzgerald, Matt Iverson, John Scully and Jack Wiaduck. Both the committee and I insisted upon telling an honest story of the Union League Club of Chicago; the contract provided complete editorial independence for the author. Not once in the course of almost three years has any member of the committee tried to insist that I change a single sentence. At the same time, I learned a great deal from committee members about the present and historical Club, and the book is richer for that knowledge.

Robert J. (Jay) Pierce served as president of the Club for the 2002–3 Club year. Jay and his lovely wife Cathy were in the Club every day that I was at work in the clubhouse, or so it seemed. Like other Club presidents and spouses, they took seriously, and with apparent enjoyment, their responsibilities to other members and to the fine presentation the Club makes to all who enter the clubhouse.

Diana Nelson, the public affairs director for the Club while I was at work on the book, is a longtime friend and associate from our days as liberal Republican activists. She assisted the committee and proved of invaluable support and counsel to me as well. Pat Summers of the public affairs office saw to it that I was provided everything I needed. I am grateful for her assistance.

Club historian and archivist (and former club president) Everett Barlow provided both insights and inspiration. Consulting archivist Jane Kenamore and her associate Alla Tamarkina of Kenamore and Kinkow, professional archivists, devoted two years prior to my arrival on the scene in retrieving, organizing, and cataloging a remarkably rich record of the Club and thus of Chicago. The work and counsel of these three fine people has enriched the book a great deal. Club librarians Jill Postma and Joy Ronstadt while I was doing research were also of great assistance with the Club's fine collection of Chicago and Club books.

Chicago writer James Merriner, and James C. Cornelius, a historian at the University of Illinois at Urbana-Champaign, read the final draft of the manuscript and displayed a knowledge of the subject matter that was deeper than mine in several respects. The two improved the final product significantly. Sam Gove and Paul Green, both veteran writers of Illinois and Chicago history and politics, read an early draft of the manuscript and offered helpful insights. Henry Pitts, the oldest living past president of the Club, did the same at an early stage. He is a distinguished Chicago attorney and civic leader who now lives in Roswell, New Mexico. His knowledge of Chicago and the Club proved invaluable. The same goes for Frank Whittaker, a former director of public affairs at the Club, who was available with answers whenever I had questions.

Roger Henn, director of public affairs for the Club from 1956 to 1978, wrote an unpublished history of the Club from which I drew extensively. I owe Roger a significant debt for his earlier fine work and for the hospitality he and Mrs. Henn afforded me at their home in Ouray, Colorado.

I interviewed most of the living past presidents of the Club and tried to arrange meetings with all, which proved not to be possible in a few instances. Those interviewed are listed in the bibliography. Milton F. Darr, Jr., Fred Ford, Don Harnack, Robert Bergstrom, Jack Wiaduck, Robert Rylowicz, and Tony Batko gave me extensive amounts of time. Other Club members, staff, and outside observers whom I interviewed are also listed in the bibliography. Their time, knowledge, and perspectives are all appreciated.

Senior staff of the Club provided information and perspective that richly informed the writing. These include General Manager Jonathan McCabe, Carl Madsen, Lee Ramirez, Betsy Buckley, Debbie Lee, Jim Krautsack, Tracey Schmidt, and Jim Lynch. Marianne Richter, curator of the art collection, was patient and of immense help in preparing the chapter on the collection, as was Joan (Mrs. Clark) Wagner, who has written a fine history of the art collection. Director of Admissions Marsha Pender read the chapters that deal with membership and corrected me on several important points.

Lois McCullagh offered valuable perspectives and information on both the role of women in the Club prior to their election to membership and of the development of the Boys and Girls Clubs, in which she played a major role over many years. Similarly, I am indebted to Rose Ann Grundman and Jack and Angie Higginson for their insights and counsel regarding life in the Club generally and in the Civic and Arts Foundation specifically. William Barnard produced important files about the life of his father, Harrison B. (H. B.) Barnard. These files and Bill's remembrances provide original information about both the Club and the city in the 1920s. Paul Stack and Tony Batko provided similarly valuable recollections of the Club's battle against putting a new central public library in the former Goldblatt's department store.

The history of the Union League Boys and Girls Clubs is central to the Club. I am grateful to executive director Mary Ann Mahon-Huels and her colleague Gerry Gersey for their assistance and observations. Further, the staff at the four clubs and also at the summer camp in Wisconsin, all of which I visited, were generous with their time.

The Illinois Historical Survey at the University of Illinois at Urbana-Champaign, directed ably by John Hoffmann, provided excellent support and information. This proved true as well for the Chicago Historical Society, Newberry Library, University of Illinois at Chicago Library, and the Chicago Public Library. All are acknowledged here for their fine collections regarding Chicago and for their gracious and helpful staff.

Over the past three years, I have lived much of my life at the Club. Sleeping rooms and dining services provided by the Club have allowed me to develop an intimacy with the facilities that informs my writing in many ways. From the archives in the first of three basement levels to the five floors of athletic facilities at the top of the clubhouse, I have roamed at will and at all hours.

This provides entrée for what may be the most important acknowledgement that I can make—to the staff of the Club. Paul Palmeteer handled room reservations flawlessly; Bobby Richmond and his fellow bell captains answered endless questions about the city. Chef Michael Garbin and his fine team are appreciated for all my great meals and for delightful, impromptu seminars on the finer points of selections on the Club's wine list. The staff at the front desk are noted for good work in registering me in and out of most of the nonsmoking sleeping rooms in the clubhouse.

The housecleaning crew, the terrific waiters in the Rendezvous and Wigwam Rooms, and the administrative team on the ninth floor have been universally gracious, warm, professional, and have indeed become my friends. The staff are part of the Club family and they are key to the vaunted reputation the Club has among city clubs around the world.

Finally, I want to thank my assistant Vicki Moutoux, who suffered—and met—my often outrageous demands with a generally pleasant smile.

I take full responsibility for any errors that appear in the pages that follow.

Jim Nowlan
TOULON, ILLINOIS

Glory,
Darkness,
Light

Glory

Chapter 1

THE UNION LEAGUES VERSUS
THE KNIGHTS OF THE GOLDEN CIRCLE

The Union League of America was founded in 1862 in Pekin, Illinois, to battle conspiracy on the home front.

The Civil War began ominously for the Union. The Confederate army humiliated Union forces at Bull Run and dashed naive hopes for a short war. The dreary Peninsula campaign, the bloody sacrifice at Fredericksburg, and the defeat at Chancellorsville dampened the spirits of Union loyalists.

Neither freedom for the African American nor the oncoming war had been popular causes in Illinois except in the northern part of the state. In 1860, voters rejected a new Illinois Constitution but approved two "Black Laws" by 2–1 margins. The "Black Laws" restated earlier Illinois policy that "No negro shall migrate or settle in the State" and that "No negro shall vote or hold office in the State."

Southern sympathizers were found throughout Illinois, in the heart of the northwestern states. Large numbers of southerners had migrated to Ohio, Indiana, and Illinois from Virginia, Tennessee, and Kentucky. "Egypt," the southernmost region of Illinois, recruited two companies for the Confederacy.

The important North-South trade on the Mississippi generated Confederate hopes that the northwestern states could be broken away from the East and into the southern cause.

The early Union defeats also bolstered the honest opposition of Peace Democrats in Illinois and the Northwest who wanted both union and a cessation of hostilities.

In 1862, Union success was anything but guaranteed. Anxiety ran high among fervent Republican war supporters such as firebrand editors Joseph

Medill at the *Chicago Tribune* and William Penn Nixon at the *Chicago Inter-Ocean*.

Radical southern sympathizers in the North plotted violent insurrection in Lincoln's home state. Union men imagined conspiracies hatching wherever two or more men gathered in evening shadows. Rumors flew; facts were few.

The reminiscences of Union League Club of Chicago member Oscar Dinwiddie are illustrative. A farm boy during the war, Dinwiddie lived near Lowell, Indiana, a busy crossroads to Chicago and the interior of the Hoosier State. On market days in Lowell, young Dinwiddie overheard outspoken rebel sympathizers and rumors of their plans to release Confederate prisoners from Camp Douglas in Chicago. Their braggadocio objective—to carve a swath of destruction all the way to the Ohio River.

A handful of Confederate prisoners did escape from Camp Douglas on July 23, 1862. Located on the south edge of Chicago, between Thirty-third and Thirty-fifth streets and Cottage Grove Avenue and Lake Michigan, the prisoner-of-war camp contained up to eight thousand rebel prisoners guarded by one captain and, at best, four hundred untested Union troops. Only twenty-five rebels escaped, however, and no one was hurt. But the sound of gunfire and the thunder of Union cavalry on State Street had the effect, as a Chicagoan recalled, of causing her and visiting friends "to change into walking suits and sit in the dark, stunned and stupid with fear."

Fear and excitement were frequent companions to residents throughout the Northwest, generated in large part by a secret society called the Knights of the Golden Circle and its offshoot proslavery secret societies. In Illinois and Indiana, the Knights and their more militant arm, the Sons of Liberty, developed an impressive organizational structure. Following a secret initiation ritual similar to that of the Masonic fraternity, "Sons" could seek elevation to three degrees of commitment, each more binding than previous oaths. County lodges were called temples; district leaders called major generals met in "castles."

One-time Democratic Congressman Clement Vallandigham of Ohio, banished by Lincoln to the South but operating in exile from Canada, headed the Sons. He claimed four hundred thousand members at the high point in 1864, with sixty-five thousand from Illinois. Such numbers are suspect in retrospect but invoked fear at the time. Sons were sworn to aid and protect deserters, disseminate antiwar literature, and aid Confederates in destroying government property.

In Charleston in eastern Illinois in 1864, one hundred Sons attacked a group of Union soldiers on furlough there, killing three and wounding twenty; strong military force was needed to rout the rebel collaborators. Guerilla proslavery bands, supported by local Knights, operated near Hillsboro in south-central Illinois where six Union supporters were killed by the marauders.

Early in the war, the Knights were particularly strong in Tazewell County along the Illinois River opposite Peoria. To counter the influence of the Knights, a group of eleven men gathered on June 25, 1862, in Pekin, the county seat of Tazewell, to establish the first council of the Union League of America.

One of them, a Union refugee from Tennessee, brought with him the simple rituals and language of patriotic obligation from the Union Club of Knoxville, Tennessee, formed in 1861 and active during the war in the border states. Other Union Clubs and Union Leagues had also been organized earlier in Maryland.

The organization started in Pekin spread rapidly. Union supporters had longed for an organization to rally round. The Union League of America (ULA), like the Knights of the Golden Circle, drew inspiration from Masonic lodges for ritual and passwords for their society.

Typical of fraternal organizations of the day, colorful regalia bedecked the leaders. Officers wore broad red, white, and blue scarves, brought over the right shoulder to extend across the breast and back to the left hip. Insignia for the officers were of silver or a white metal. For the president, an eagle; the vice president, a star; the herald, a bugle; and the sentinel, an open eye. All members other than officers wore a rosette of red, white, and blue with the letters "ULA." in white on a blue center, worn over the left breast during any public meeting or patriotic demonstration.

The Chicago Council of the ULA was organized August 19, 1862, by newspaper editors Joseph Medill and William Penn Nixon and by Colonel F. A. Eastman, Ira Buell, and Alfred Cowles. Former Chicago Mayor John Wentworth also became active in the Chicago Council. In 1863 in Cleveland, Medill chaired the first national convention of the Union League of America.

Late in 1862, separate Union Leagues organized in Philadelphia and New York. The New York League was created by leaders of the U.S. Sanitary Commission, headquartered in that city. The commission was a private war relief organization, similar to the Red Cross of today, headed by city patricians such as the city planner Frederick Law Olmsted and operated largely by women such as social reformer Dorothea Dix, who served as superintendent of women nurses in the Civil War.

These primarily Unitarian and Episcopalian men and women raised medical supplies and directed the training and supply of nurses for the war. They also wrote and distributed influential tracts. Equality for the slaves was a natural outgrowth of their liberal views. These Union Leagues worked closely with the much larger Union League of America, which grew to two million members by the end of the war.

The Lincoln administration encouraged and provided behind-the-scenes financial support to the various Union Leagues. According to William Stoddard, a private secretary to the president, Lincoln feared "the fire in the rear" more than that on the battlefield. Lincoln funneled money to army contractors who in turn became liberal contributors to the Union League efforts and to their Union League agents who spread out over the North organizing councils.

The elections of 1862 were a disaster for the Union cause. In Illinois, both the legislature and a state constitutional convention fell into Democratic hands. The strident *Chicago Tribune* declared the convention to be "under the control of the Knights of the Golden Circle." Peace Democrats in the legislature thwarted Governor Richard Yates in his attempts to help the Union effort.

Support for peace grew across the North following the early Union defeats. Increasing numbers of citizens became convinced the South could not be defeated on the battlefield. Lincoln's policies also caused deep misgivings among those in the North more interested in Union than in freedom for the African American. The Emancipation Proclamation, suspension of the writ of habeas corpus, and the arrest without warrant of many peaceful war opponents went too far for many moderates.

The Union Leagues fought back. The Union League in New York and the Union Club in Boston took the lead in raising recruits for the army, including the first black regiments. Most New Yorkers were at first resistant to the idea of black soldiers. But when prominent men of the Union League provided the escort, city residents turned out in force to cheer black regiments that paraded down Broadway and off to duty. An observer declared, "No more distinguished company of ladies ever honored a regiment than the ladies on the balcony of the Union League Club, handing their colors to that first negro regiment."

Union League representatives also crossed the Atlantic with a strong message to the British government that its possible support for the South would never be forgiven and redress would be claimed later. But the most important contribution of the Union Leagues came through force of growing numbers and the Leagues' prominence in the elections of 1864, the make-or-break year for the Union cause.

Fortunately, the tide of battle had turned to the Union's favor. In the summer of 1863, Lee spent much of his force at Gettysburg; Vicksburg capitulated to Grant. In the spring of 1864, Union forces looked toward Atlanta.

Confederate president Jefferson Davis became desperate. He listened to strategists who had long looked covetously on Illinois. The great, long state reached fingerlike into the Confederacy, commanded two great rivers, and blocked overland routes from east to west. Illinois was a keystone of the Union. The leader of the Confederacy initiated a plan to dislodge Illinois from the Union.

Davis dispatched two of General John Hunt Morgan's border raiders to Canada, reportedly with three hundred thousand dollars in gold, a huge sum from a nearly depleted southern treasury.

This Great Northwest Conspiracy planned to storm and free the eight thousand Confederate prisoners at Camp Douglas; march west to Fort Armstrong at the Mississippi River town of Rock Island, Illinois, to free additional thousands; and hurry down the state to more congenial territory.

In Toronto, Major John Castleman and twenty-year-old Captain Thomas Hines gathered seventy picked Confederate soldiers. They plotted to smuggle arms and ammunition into Chicago and rouse an expected five thousand Knights and Sons against Camp Douglas.

There were not, however, five thousand ardent sympathizers in Chicago and whatever number existed, they had no stomach for battle. The plan was postponed time and again in the summer of 1864 for lack of local support. An attempt on Camp Douglas was finally set for November 7, the day before the national elections. By that time, a Union spy had learned of the plan. Federal officers and Union Leaguers swept down on the ringleaders and their caches of weapons, stopping the mischief in its tracks.

Desperate measures are so named for good reason.

While the Confederates plotted, Union League councils and their members became the foot soldiers and precinct captains in Lincoln's reelection battle. Even with the tide of battle turning against the Confederacy, the unpopular Lincoln was in trouble. The war had dragged on years longer than expected. Maimed soldiers had returned to their hometowns to remind citizens of the toll. Secretary of the Treasury Salmon Chase and pathfinding general John C. Frémont surfaced as opponents to Lincoln's renomination.

Union Leagues across the country swung into action. Councils evaluated political candidates from the national down to the local level; politicians began to seek out League endorsements. Radical Republicans who favored full equality for African Americans dominated the National Council of the League. Like smart politicians, however, they played down their extreme positions and focused instead on themes of patriotism and union.

In keeping with the theme, the Republican Party became, for 1864 only, the Union Party. The strategy was to appeal for votes from northern Democrats and—Union Leaguers liked to think—draw upon the popularity of the Union Leagues and its 2 million members in 1864, 125,000 in Illinois alone.

Working closely with the Republican Party, Union Leagues held rallies across the country. Joe Medill and the Illinois Council repeatedly drew fifty thousand to a rally in Springfield which included torchlight parades, fireworks, marching bands, and seven speakers stands—one for German Union Leaguers, in their language.

The Union League Grand Council met in national convention in Baltimore on June 7 of election year, the day before the Union Party held its convention in the same city. Two-thirds of the League delegates carried similar credentials for the Union Party presidential nominating convention. Lincoln was assured nomination, yet dissatisfaction with him lingered.

The Democrats met in Chicago to nominate former Union General George McClellan. Exiled Knights leader Vallandigham slipped into Chicago. The ex-congressman gave a stirring speech in the heart of the city. Following his remarks, Union League member John Wentworth rose to his full six-foot-six stature. "Long John" rebutted his former congressional colleague point by point and then some, according to partisan Chicago onlookers.

Between the conventions and the November election, Union forces claimed victories at Mobile Bay and under Philip Sheridan in the Shenandoah; Sherman captured Atlanta. The Union League and Republican leaders took no chances with the election, however, and coordinated efforts throughout the campaign. Big supplies of political tracts, largely paid for by the wealthy Leagues in New York and Philadelphia, flowed through local councils and into voters' hands across the country. Even so, Lincoln defeated McClellan in Illinois by just 30,000 votes, 190,000 to 160,000.

Union League members took pride in their roles in that election, justifiably.

After the war, Union League chapters became a force in the liberated South as well, at least for a short period. Voting rights and the advancement of African Americans to full citizenship had always been at the heart of the agitation of the radical Republican leadership of the National Council of the Union League of America. In the South, both whites and blacks were members of local Union Leagues. The two races met and paraded together, shouting for "Bread, Wages, and Schools."

Southern white leadership and the hooded Ku Klux Klan moved quickly, however, to reassert their mastery through Black Code legislation, bondage, and terror. Mississippi enacted a law aimed at Union Leagues and Republicans: groups "unlawfully assembling" were declared vagrant as were "white people usually associating with freedmen, free people, or mulattoes." Klan violence was particularly ferocious when Union League members and African Americans were found together.

In the North, most local Union Leagues, including that in Chicago, faded away, their primary mission of preserving the Union fulfilled. The rosette of the Union Leagues of America became a badge of honor and a continuing reminder that patriotism and civil order were imperative values for the young country. The Union League clubs of New York and Philadelphia, which had enjoyed clubhouses from the first, continue to this day.

This "spirit of the Union" also provided the rationale for two men who felt a need to start a men's club in Chicago.

SOURCES

Former Union League Club of Chicago director of public affairs Roger Henn wrote an unpublished manuscript, "Lincoln's Loyal Legions," which synthesizes effectively the scholarship on the creation and efforts of the several Union Leagues during the Civil War. In addition, the reminiscences of Frank Aldrich, a charter member in the Union League Club of Chicago and the club's first historian, and those of fellow early members proved illuminating as well. All are found in the comprehensive and well-organized archives of the Club.

The following sources were also drawn upon:

Bateman, Newton, and Paul Selby. "Secret Treasonable Organizations." In
    Union League Club of Chicago (hereafter abbreviated as ULCC),
    Men & Events, April 1962.
Boss, Henry. "Founding of the Union League of America." May 4, 1863.
    Reprint, *Men & Events,* April 1962.
Buckingham, Colonel George T. "The Projected Sack of Chicago." 1939.
    Reprint, *Men & Events,* April 1962.
Buckmaster, Henrietta. *Let My People Go.* New York: Harper and Brothers,
    1941.
Dinwiddie, Oscar. "Reminiscences." ULCC archives, 1925.
Haight, George I. "History of the Union League of America." Chap. 1 in
    History of the ULA. ULCC Archives. N.p. Circa 1946, #2001–18.
Hamilton, E. Bentley. "The Union League: Its Origin and Achievements
    in the Civil War." *Transactions of the Illinois State Historical Society,*
    1921 (Springfield, 1922), 110–15.
Hofer, J. M. "Development of the Peace Movement in Illinois during the
    Civil War." *Journal of the Illinois State Historical Society* 24:1 (April
    1931): 79–83.
Lawson, Melinda. *Patriot Fires.* Lawrence: University Press of Kansas,
    2002.
Levy, George. *To Die in Chicago.* Evanston, Ill.: Evanston Publishing, Inc.,
    1994.

McAdams, Benton. *Rebels at Rock Island.* DeKalb: Northern Illinois University Press, 2000.

Also:

Atkins, General Smith D. "Patriotism in Northern Illinois." *Transactions of the Illinois State Historical Society,* 1911 (Springfield, 1913).

Benton, Elbert J. "The Movement for Peace without a Victory during the Civil War." *Collections of the Western Reserve Historical Society,* Cleveland, 1918.

Cochran, William C. "The Dream of a Northwestern Confederacy." State Historical Society of Wisconsin, Separate No. 175, from the *Proceedings of the Society for 1916.*

Fesler, Mayo. "Secret Political Societies in the North during the Civil War." *Indiana Magazine of History* 14:3 (September 1918).

Stoddard, William O., Jr., ed. *Lincoln's Third Secretary.* New York: Exposition Press, 1955.

Walton, Clyde C. "Illinois in the Civil War." *Men & Events,* April 1962.

Chapter 2

OWEN NEEDS A JOB;
"LONG JOHN" SEEKS A MARCHING CLUB

Owen Salisbury did need a job. And John Wentworth needed a political "marching club" for his last political battle. These are the practical reasons for the creation of the Union League Club of Chicago. Their timing could not have been better. In 1879, Chicago capitalists and up-and-coming young businessmen longed for a refuge from the hurly-burly on the crowded, muddy streets. Inside clubrooms, men could relax among their own kind and do business in a comfortable setting over a glass of wine at lunch or with some Kentucky bourbon and water when the day's work was done.

The 1870s were tempestuous times for Chicago. Chicago became the fastest-growing city in the world. Fire and anarchy blazed.

The Fire of 1871 burned four square miles in the heart of the city. The morning of the second day of the fire, at the Chicago Club, the town's wealthiest businessmen lifted glasses of champagne over breakfast to mock the fire's efforts to bring them down. Then, with flames licking at their club-house, the members carried the club's red sofas down to the lakefront, where they finished breakfast.

The next day many of these men had reopened for business, some from their mansions on Prairie Avenue to the south, which was spared. Before the ashes were cool, merchants Marshall Field and his competitor J. V. Farwell were also again serving the public.

The national depression of 1873 to 1879 followed, igniting discontent among laborers who lost their jobs or saw their wages cut. This sparked the harrowing Chicago labor riots of 1877. Over three days, anarchy reigned in much of the city.

Two-thirds of the workers in manufacturing companies were foreign born. Among the unskilled, the percentage was higher. The Irish congregated in Bridgeport, the Germans around Goose Island, and the Bohemians along the south branch of the Chicago River. More than others, the Germans were spreading the gospel of socialism and communism. These newcomers were also outraged by efforts of the Protestant middle class to reform the drinking habits of the workingman by limiting the number of taverns and closing them on the Sabbath.

The railroad strike that began in the East reached Chicago on July 24, 1877. Crowds of workingmen left their jobs and gathered on street corners to hear anarchists like Albert Parsons hector them to action. Three men who would become Club members left their top hats at home and listened to the numerous "rabble-rousers" from the edges of the crowd. What they heard scared them.

"We fought for the Negro and brought him up to the level of the white man," declared one. "Now let's do something for the workingman!" And from the crowd, "Let's kill those damned aristocrats." An Irish boat hand joined the chorus: "We know what we're fighting for and what we're doing. We're fighting those God damned capitalists. That's what we're doing, ain't we?" And another: "Bring the big bugs down to our level!" The plain-dressed businessmen, not feeling like very big bugs, slipped away unnoticed.

For three days, rioters rampaged through the streets of Chicago with police unable to contain them. Three thousand militia and army regulars augmented the constabulary. When mobs failed to disperse, they were fired upon.

The "Battle of Halsted Street" took place on July 26 at Sixteenth Street. Five thousand angry workingmen, many of them teenagers, refused to break up. The police emptied their revolvers into the mass. As men dropped, they were carried away at an instant.

Nor was it just men who took up the laborers' cause. On Twenty-second Street between Fisk and May, hundreds of Bohemian women gathered at a door and sash manufactory. Nixon's *Chicago Inter-Ocean* described it thus: "Dresses were tucked up around their waists . . . and brawny sunburned arms brandished clubs torn from the factory fence." When police arrived to protect the factory in what became known as the "Outbreak of the Bohemian Amazons," the women stood firm and stoned the hated blue coats.

The local newspapers talked of civil war. After three days, however, the force of the mobs was spent. Eighty-eight rioters had been killed; half were teenagers. A majority of the slain were Irish, the rest German, Bohemian, or Polish.

Though the price was staggering, the riots "worked." Manufacturers restored a number of wage cuts. In the fall of 1877, the first socialist candidates were elected to office in Chicago, drawing their support from the eight key wards of the 1877 strike. By 1879, Chicago had reportedly become the most important site for socialist activity in the nation.

The riots scared Chicago manufacturers and businessmen to their souls. Socialism or capitalism—that was the issue.

Corruption in local government added outrage to anxiety within the capitalist community. Following the 1871 Fire, from which many leading businessmen were protected by good insurance policies, a tremendous need arose for great public improvements—reconstruction of public buildings, wooden pavements, water mains, sewers, bridges, and viaducts. In the eyes of the business community, the Irish ward politicians saw nothing but boodle and pelf, today called political pork and corruption.

Joseph Medill became mayor after the fire but resigned before his term ended. A rigid man, Medill lacked the temperament for the give-and-take of politics. Harvey Colvin followed Medill as mayor, and his allies on the city council included Ed Cullerton, Tom Foley, Jimmie O'Brien, Mickie Ryan, Bart Quirk, and Jake Lengacher. They stole elections with the brazenness of the ladies of the night down in "the Levee" district just south of the business district. In 1874, taxpayers fought adoption of a new city charter that gave the boodlers more opportunity for fraud. But Colvin and his henchmen stuffed the ballot boxes and then certified the outcomes as proper. In the first ward, there were 1,655 votes for the charter and just 97 against—in a ward with fewer than 500 legal voters.

Patience was no longer a virtue for the good citizens of Chicago.

The 1870s created conditions ripe for the establishment of the Union League Club and of numerous civic and social clubs for upright, law-abiding businessmen, as they saw themselves.

A decent enough chap but past his prime, Owen Salisbury had been active in the Union League of America. When the Chicago council of the ULA closed its office in 1877, Salisbury had trouble finding congenial employment. Owen felt there was a real need for more men's social clubs in the burgeoning city. Further, he would make a fine manager of clubrooms. But Salisbury lacked the standing to start one on his own

Love him or hate him—many did both—John Wentworth personified the city. Wentworth arrived barefoot in Chicago in 1836, his boots and a jug of whiskey under his arms (to hear him tell it). John had a degree from Dartmouth College, so he was not just anybody. Chicago was a swampy frontier town, incorporated just three years earlier.

Wentworth became a newspaper editor, mayor twice, police commissioner, and congressman for eight years. With stovepipe hat always on, the six-foot-six, three-hundred-pound Wentworth appeared to scrape the sky when he stood erect, as he always did. "Long John" posed like a monument waiting to be gilded.

Leadership meant everything to Wentworth, friendship little. A cold man, he had scant sympathy for the underdog. In 1857, the territory north of the Chicago River and east of Clark Street had become infested with the shacks and hovels of degraded men and women, it was said, a hiding place for criminals. These squatters defied the authorities, frequently driving police out of their district. As mayor, Wentworth personally led the police and firemen in an attack on the poor folks, burning their shacks to the ground, scattering men, women, and children to the four winds. This had to be done, upstanding citizens said, but only John Wentworth had the stomach for the job and they respected him for it. The land was also ripe for business development.

In the summer of 1879, former president Ulysses Grant toured the country, gauging support for a third-term candidacy. John Wentworth was sixty-five and the parade was passing him by. Some say it was fear for the country, prompted by the recent bloody conflicts between labor and capital, that roused Wentworth to become a staunch, vocal supporter for a third term for Grant. Maybe he just saw an opportunity for one last political battle.

Owen Salisbury also saw an opportunity. He convinced Wentworth that a patriotic men's club in Chicago, site of the 1880 Republican National Convention, would make a fine "marching club," as politicians called them, for Grant. Marching clubs were bands of partisans who worked—and paraded—for their favorite candidates. "Long John" liked the idea. With Salisbury as his aide-de-camp, Wentworth recruited a dozen loyal old associates from his Union League days to organize a club.

Alas, the convention took neither Grant nor Wentworth seriously. The credentials committee even denied Wentworth and several other Illinois Grant delegates their convention seats (including Stephen Douglas, son of the famous Democratic U.S. senator). The real battle for the nomination was between James G. Blaine of Maine and Roscoe Conkling, the upstate New York boss, "two charming and corrupt rivals," as a contemporary described them. To break a deadlock between the charming rivals, the convention turned to James A. Garfield of Ohio. But by then, a now venerable club had been launched.

"We need the League as much today, men, as we did two decades ago," Wentworth boomed to a prospect. Few dared dispute old John. That was the clarion call Wentworth and the other Club founders put to young Republican capitalists they wanted in the new Club, and it worked.

James Bradwell was the president of the incorporators of the Club in 1879. Born in England in 1828, he came as an infant to the United States. He worked his way through Knox College in Galesburg, Illinois, and was admitted to the bar in 1852. That same year he married Myra Colby, who was also trained in the law.

A county judge throughout the Civil War, James Bradwell fought the Copperheads, or Southern sympathizers, strenuously. He forced those with doubts about the war to come to his office to take the oath of allegiance before he would give them their mail. President of the Chicago and Illinois bar associations, Judge Bradwell also actively sought women's suffrage. As a state legislator in the 1870s, he authored bills to make women eligible to hold school offices.

Myra Bradwell may have been behind these initiatives. Even better known than her husband, Myra Bradwell struggled to become a member of the bar. The Illinois Supreme Court denied her a law license, declaring that the profession was "too stressful" for a lady. Possibly in retaliation, she founded the *Chicago Legal News* in 1868 and chronicled the good, bad, and the ugly of the early legal profession in Chicago. Bradwell did, finally, become the first woman in the United States admitted to the bar. She represented Mary Todd Lincoln at her insanity hearings and secured her release from the insane asylum at Batavia, Illinois.

Men who wore Union blue in their twenties or younger were in 1880 just in their forties. Many early Club activists had served. The architect Major William LeBaron Jenney had been with General W. T. Sherman at Vicksburg. The stationer George Cole had been a teen drummer boy who provided the cadence for Sherman's "March to the Sea."

Charter Club member B. M. Hampton needed a place to recount colorful stories of war to appreciative groups around the bar. One of his favorites went like this:

> I shook hands with General Sherman *and* General Lee at the end of the War and I was the last man to see General MacPherson alive. We had been driving the Rebs back all night toward Atlanta. About sunup Gen'l. MacPherson rode up and stopped, sighting me where I was trying to make coffee. He got down and stood by the fire, then ordered a scout sent toward town to see if anybody was at home. Sixty Reb guns soon answered his question.
>
> The General jumped in haste to leave, and by golly, threw himself over the horse, landing next to me and the coffeepot. Our faces came close together. I put my hand right in his face and said, "Now don't be in a hurry, General. We will have some coffee in just a minute."
>
> Old Mac saw the joke was on him, and replied, "Not just any at

the present, thank you." He started for the rear, laughing, but the Rebs were coming up behind us and they shot him and his horse, and killed him. A great loss to us, a fine man and a great general.

Hampton would then pause to let it all sink in.

Veterans and Union Leaguers were not far enough away from the great war of rebellion to forget that openly avowed loyalty to the Union was the duty of every citizen—a responsibility that had to be inculcated and impressed on the rising generation.

Others who came into the Club early were, however, not so much interested in the patriotic dimension, though they didn't say as much. What they really wanted was a gentleman's club in the heart of the city that would conduct a first-class restaurant and whose membership would be exclusive. There was big demand for such a club. This would be a place for cold, calculating business deals over luncheon and warm camaraderie around the bar.

The Chicago Club had been started a decade earlier and was reserved for a small number of very wealthy leaders of business and society—those who had already made it. The Union League was to be a Club for those who were *going* to make it.

SOURCES

This chapter is richly informed by "Sketches of Club Life and History" by Frank Aldrich, serialized in the *Union League Club Bulletin* in 1925 to 1926. During that same period, the Club solicited the reminiscences of early members about both the Union League of America and the Club. I have drawn verbatim at times from letters and interviews conducted in the 1920s with E. R. Bliss, R. S. Critchell, Andrew McLeish, B. M. Hampton, J. S. Starrett, I. S. Blackwalader, and O. S. Cook. All these documents are located in the archives of the ULCC.

I also draw heavily from a fine article by Richard Schneirov, "Chicago's Great Upheaval of 1877" (*Chicago History*, Spring 1980).

Other sources utilized include:

Andrews, Wayne. *Battle for Chicago.* New York: Harcourt, Brace and Co., 1946.
Bliss, E. R. *Beginning of the Union League Club.* Chicago: E. R. Bliss, 1916.
Bushnell, George D. "Chicago's Leading Men's Clubs." *Chicago History,* Summer 1982.

Dedmon, Emmett, and Edward T. Blair. *A History of the Chicago Club.* Chicago: Chicago Club, 1960.

Dennis, Charles H. *Victor Lawson.* Chicago: University of Chicago Press, 1935.

Fehrenbacher, Don E. *Chicago Giant: A Biography of "Long John" Wentworth.* Madison, Wis.: The American History Research Center, 1957.

Chapter 3

LIFE IN THE EARLY CLUB

In 1880, attorney Ira W. Buell, an early Union League of America man, informed his client Bob Critchell, the insurance man, that a new "downtown" club might be started. He was going into it and would like to have Critchell join. From his description of the plan and the men who were to go in, the insurance man concluded he would be glad to put his name in—but only if the club would develop into a social club with a restaurant. That really wasn't friend Buell's interest. Like John Wentworth, he was more interested in politics. Yet, Buell quickly added, the club would certainly develop into whatever its members might determine.

Buell, Critchell, and a handful began meeting weekly in the Club Room at the Sherman House. Shortly, they rented rooms in the Honoré block, 204–6 South Dearborn. The strictly partisan "dyed-in-the-wool" Republican politicians among them, such as Wentworth, Phil Hoyne, Judge Bradwell, and other founding members, did not sympathize with the social and restaurant feature at all.

The big issue in the first years of the Club was whether it would be a political club or a social club. "Politics alone cannot sustain a club," declared Bob Critchell at one of the monthly, then quarterly, Club member meetings. Critchell also argued strongly to exclude Chicago visitors who were not members of the Club, something the political element was congenial to, especially in 1880 when the Republican convention was in town.

The second election of officers and directors turned on these issues. Each side had its own full slate of candidates. The Critchell ticket won and the new officers basically ignored the political and office-seeking element, at least when it came to operating the Club. This gave the Club a different tone from that envisioned by Wentworth, Judge Bradwell, and Phil Hoyne, but it ensured the success of the club.

To get the restaurant started, it became necessary for Critchell with a few other men to sign as guarantors for all the costs of outfitting the restaurant beyond the amount of cash on hand in the treasury, which was all the "political" gentlemen would vote. When the signers of this guarantee found that the bill amounted to twelve thousand dollars, Critchell and his "social" friends had pressing reasons to accelerate the building up of the Club membership.

The Club restaurant in the Honoré Building opened in 1881 to great applause from most members. The Scotch broth was such a hit that it has been served every day since in the clubhouse. The Club became so popular, Critchell bragged, "that a couple of clubs [unnamed] sought to join our club as entire bodies, but their overtures were rejected."

In the first year, Wentworth chaired the admissions committee. His nominees were elected unanimously by voice vote. After his humiliation at the 1880 Republican convention, however, Wentworth lost interest in the Club. In his few remaining years, Long John visited the dining room once a year and dined alone, a sad figure, his loneliness self-imposed.

In the first decade, many names were proposed and many were rejected, failing to receive the two-thirds secret vote of the membership. Even with a large number of rejections, some other men were voted in so much against the wishes of certain members that resignations of the latter often followed. As the numbers of proposed candidates increased, the Club instituted a "black ball" process. Candidates were grouped in fives. Each member had both a black and a white ball to put in a box. If a group of five received a black ball among the white balls, then those nominees were voted on separately rather than as part of a slate.

From 260 members by the end of 1880, the Club grew to more than 1,000 members in 1890, the largest membership of any club in the city. Club minutes applauded the membership committee for "patient courage and fidelity to a duty never inviting and frequently of a painful and disagreeable character."

The Club was sometimes characterized by naysayers, such as the Chicago lawyer (and poet) Edgar Lee Masters, as "a club for rich and oldish men." Many were neither old nor rich. They often looked old, however, in the fashion of the day, with beards, heavy sideburns, and waistcoats.

Shortly after joining, for example, Julius Starrett remembered being confronted by older members. "One thought I was too young to be a member, and the other that I was too young to be married. So I thought something ought to be done about it, and right away. So I let my beard grow to make me look older and have sworn by it ever since [1925]. There was no further discussion of my youth."

And, yes, the Club added to its rolls many men who were either prominent then or soon to become illustrious—a *Who's Who* of Chicago: Armour, Field, Ogden, Glessner, Pullman, Ryerson, Swift, Shedd, Buckingham, Harris, Smith, Smyth, Wrigley, McCormick, Mayer, Deere, Palmer.

But there is less in this list than meets the eye. It was the fashion of that day for men of prominence to be courted by and to join several clubs, even if they never crossed the threshold of the clubhouse. Many belonged to six, seven, and more social clubs. A number from the exclusive Chicago Club joined the Union League Club because of its "good government" political dimension, appreciated by the city's capitalist leaders, or because it was more fun, and maybe because the ladies were often included as guests.

These men were proposed for membership in the Union League and other clubs, often without having been consulted. And often they accepted the honor, joined, and paid their dues.

For example, the Commercial Club of Chicago was started in 1877 by the city's leading men, nearly all of whom belonged to the Chicago Club, which had been started in 1869. The Commercial Club met over luncheon or dinner to discuss and promote the civic and economic development of Chicago. In 1911, the Commercial Club adopted the visionary "Burnham Plan" for the urban design of a Chicago with great parks and ease of travel. According to the *Chicago Blue Book* for 1911, all 102 members of the Commercial Club were members of the Chicago Club and fifty-three were also members of the Union League Club.

The Union League Club recruited heavily among the young businessmen who were marked for success. In the first year, for example, Wentworth pushed for Byron Smith, who was only twenty-six and a Democrat. "This man will become the next John Jacob Astor," Wentworth boomed at a Club meeting when Smith's name was proposed. And to the present, Byron Smith family descendants are successful business and civic leaders in Chicago.

Not all marked for success, however, achieved that goal. Frank Aldrich was also in his twenties in 1880 when his father, a founding member, brought him in. Financial success, however, eluded Aldrich. In his later years, Aldrich wrote historical reminiscences of the Club for which he was compensated, a valuable increment to his modest income.

More important to the Club than the biggest names were members who took an active part as Byron Smith did in the early days, serving on committees and helping make a go of things. Others included Frank O. Lowden and Charles Gates Dawes. Lowden almost became president of the United States in 1920. Dawes missed his shot at the presidency in 1924 when

Coolidge filled Harding's unexpired term; Dawes settled for the vice presidency and the Nobel Peace Prize. William Rainey Harper, head of the new University of Chicago, and philanthropist Julius Rosenwald both served three-year terms on the six-member political action committee.

Lowden joined the Club in 1891 in his twenties. That same year he joined the Calumet Club at fashionable Eighteenth Street and Michigan Avenue, where he took a room, and also the Sunset Club. Lowden became very active, however, in the Union League Club. He chaired the political action committee for several years, spearheading patriotic initiatives. This didn't hurt his political ambitions, of course. By the end of the 1890s, Lowden's name was struck from Club rolls and added to those of the Chicago Club, where his father-in-law George Pullman was a leading member. As governor, however, Lowden continued to call on the Club for assistance, as is also noted later.

As in the present-day Club, the early Club had good representations of lawyers and traders. "It will be noticed a large proportion of the members in 1891 were lawyers," recalled early member C. H. Coffin. He was referring to a "Round Table" that was a popular gathering place for luncheon in the Club. "The discussions at the table were always free, full, and sometimes quite hot. I remember seeing one of the prominent members burst into tears at a bit too sharp sarcasm. [But] mostly this was taken in a good-natured way."

When the Board of Trade moved up to Jackson Street in 1885, "a lot of us Board of Trade men joined the Club," said Charles B. Van Kirk, who joined in that year. "Most of us lunched regularly at the Club."

The early membership also had stimulating concentrations of architects and newspaper publishers, editors, and writers. Major Jenney was elected to membership in 1882, followed by Daniel Burnham, Louis Sullivan, Dankmar Adler, William Holabird, John Wellborn Root, and William Mundie, most of whom worked in Jenney's office at some point.

In addition to Joseph Medill of the *Tribune* and William Penn Nixon of the *Inter-Ocean*, editors active in the Club included the great Victor Lawson of the *Daily News*, Herman Kohlsaat of the *Times-Herald*, and Melville Stone, who resurrected and built the Associated Press. Lawson also brought his popular Chicago journalist-writer Eugene Field into the Club and paid his initiation fee and dues.

Prankster Field enjoyed giving both extravagant and ofttimes eccentric dinner parties in the Club. In 1893, for example, Field honored his friend Edward Everett Hale, the prominent Boston civic reformer and clergyman, at a dinner that included the handsome, gray-bearded Marshall Field and a large company of noted businessmen and men of letters such as Chicago novelist Henry Blake Fuller.

The men were undoubtedly surprised to be served just baked potatoes, corned beef, and cornbread. According to dinner guest Charles Dennis, later editor of the *Daily News,* waiters poured from champagne bottles not fine bubbly but "a good quality of ice water." After the joke, all repaired to another room for a sumptuous repast.

Club life became an enjoyable mix of business, politics, and a glass of wine or two with lunch. In the 1880s, "no member would take a stranger to lunch at the Club," observed Nelson Thomasson, "without asking him to have some wine at the table." The social and political aspects of the Club were prominent but the aims of business life governed in the associations of men in the Club life. "'Every man for himself and the devil take the hindmost' was often a more potent motto among members than the lofty stated principles of the Club," according to H. W. Bacon in his reminiscences of early Club life.

But members also had fun. The annual election of officers and directors became an event in those early days. George P. Jones was a jolly, good-natured man, always laughing and telling jokes—the very life of the Club. Almost every year he mounted an independent slate to run against the regular ticket just for the fun of it. Both tickets had workers who buttonholed members at lunch, soliciting votes, just like an old-fashioned political contest. When results were announced, members had a big party in the lounge, the losers toasting the victors, all in great good spirit.

The daily newspapers carried news of the campaigns and reported the outcomes, which were talked about in the lounge for days. Members who never came at any other time came to lunch on election day to vote. On a table in the main clubroom, the albums contained photographs of members. Several members reviewed the album before election day so they would recognize those members who never came to the Club otherwise.

At the same time, a member could have as much privacy as he wished. W. E. Selleck recalled his satisfaction in having been a permanent roomer in the Club for many years. "One does not feel as he does in a public place," said Selleck, "because if he is approached by a stranger, he feels that the fact of the party having access to the Club is a sufficient passport for his being a gentleman."

A number of members made the Club their home in those days. As Selleck said, a certain of amount of companionship exists, but one could be strictly private if he were so disposed. "I was on the elevator," Selleck continued, "when a member said to me: 'It is a question who has lived here longer, you or I?'

"I asked him how long he had resided in the club. 'Four years.' I told him I had lived there twelve years at the time. The singular part of it is that

I didn't know the gentleman's name and didn't know that he had ever slept under the roof of the Club!"

In the Club's first decade, initiation fees ranged from $50 to $150, at the lower number in early years when the Club was encouraging younger members to join, higher as soon as the Club was established and popular so that a clubhouse could be built. Annual dues were $25, then $40, and $50 dollars later. A suit of clothes at the Parisian Suit Company downtown cost between $20 and $50.

The fees and dues were competitive with the other clubs that were springing up such as the Calumet Club at Eighteenth Street and Michigan Avenue on the fashionable south side; the Hamilton, another Republican-leaning group; the Iroquois, a club for Democrats; and the University Club, where only those relatively few with college degrees were eligible.

From the first, most members felt strongly that the Club needed its own clubhouse to accommodate a growing membership. Architect Jenney was commissioned to prepare architectural plans for a site at Dearborn and Monroe. When terms for the site could not be agreed upon, the Club took the present clubhouse site at Fourth (now Federal) Street and Jackson.

Jenney said his six-story proposal would accommodate 625 resident and 100 nonresident members. ("Resident members" live in Chicago or its suburbs. "Nonresident members" reside outside of the metropolitan area and find the Club convenient and comfortable for overnight stays.) The Club formed an auxiliary corporation to sell stock to members. Tussles commenced over the design and fittings. Younger members wanted extensive exercise facilities, even bowls (bowling). Jenney and older members politely quashed the latter and later jokingly complained that the younger generation spent more time exercising their elbows at the Club bar than they ever did in the exercise room.

The big issue was how to accommodate the ladies. There was no doubt they would be provided for handsomely, as they had been a part of the Club life since the Critchell team in late 1881 approved a resolution admitting ladies to the Club on Saturday when accompanied by a member. This was unusual among clubs in that day. As late as recent decades, for example, the Chicago Club never let a woman darken its doors.

Some think the early inclusion of women in the life of the Club derived from the tradition established earlier by the Union League clubs in New York and Philadelphia during the Civil War when their clubhouses were the scenes of much remarked-upon festive balls. The accommodation of women was also apparently urged by some of the younger members who pressed the case that times were changing.

One evening in 1884, Club president J. MacGregor Adams took home

Jenney's plans for the clubhouse. He spread them out on his library table, joined by his wife. She was shocked. As planned, the first floor was primarily devoted to a large clubroom, or lounge. Entering the front door, members would stop to examine the day's menu and write down their orders for luncheon or dinner. They then proceeded with their fellow members and guests into the clubroom to sit and converse. When the dining room, a floor above, notified the member that his meal was ready, his party walked up the grand marble staircase.

The staircase would present real problems for the ladies, declared Mrs. Adams. It would be unthinkable, certainly indecorous, for a lady to climb the staircase in full view of the men seated directly below in the clubroom. The chastened Club president took the plans back to Jenney, demanding change. Thus began the Club tradition of a separate entrance and staircase for women, which continued until 1972. Jenney was not happy. The following is from the September 1884 *Inland Architect*. While not attributed, the words are most likely those of Jenney:

> Though the interior plans have been practically finished, the ladies—who seem to have a voice in the matter—suggested many changes, and this, if considered, will interfere largely with making the building comfortable alike to the gentlemen members, unless better counsel prevails and the plans that suit the convenience of gentlemen are acceptable to the ladies as well.
>
> For instance, it seems out of place to destroy a beautiful entrance on Jackson Street because the ladies wish a special entrance and suite of apartments to themselves on Fourth Avenue.
>
> This, architecturally considered, is almost an impossibility considering the size of the lot and the needs of a properly planned clubhouse.

Architecturally possible or not, the changes were made, including a dining room set aside for the ladies. Gentlemen were not allowed in the ladies' dining room unless a guest of a lady. This dining room proved so popular that a larger dining room was soon designated for their use.

The *Chicago Tribune* provided this account of members' ladies and the new clubhouse:

> They were grateful for the hospitality with which they were received into the club, and expressed their gratitude openly. The Union League Club is the only club in the country which extends to the ladies the same privileges which it does for the members themselves. For the present there is virtually no difference. If a lady is accompanied by one of the members, the house is hers to do as she pleases. . . . The time may come when she will not even be required to burden herself with a male escort.

The wife of member Will Esmond penned this letter in 1888:

> While Will is attending a committee meeting of the union League Club,
> I am seated in the ladies' parlor. Martha Junior has been here with us for
> luncheon, but has now gone her way for some necessary shopping. Not
> having to shop myself, I'm glad to sit here and read and write.
>
> A distinctive feature of the club is the presence of ladies within
> its portals. Will tells me that a good many members—poor old grumpy
> bachelors, I dare say—opposed allowing the fair sex to have meals here,
> but they were overruled. It had been a profitable thing, since we help
> the commissary department make money. Many ladies use the club
> frequently. It's the only place downtown where we can sit about in
> privacy after lunching.
>
> The side entrance is reserved for us. As we enter, we are taken in
> charge by a man. There is a nice restroom, where we may use soap, tow-
> els, cologne, court plaster, hairpins, and hatpins. Meals are served in the
> ladies' ordinary. Or, if you have a private party, you may engage a private
> room. You can pay for your meal or have it charged to your husband's
> account. I take pride in never charging my meals to Will.
>
> Managed very well indeed, Will thinks, is the club, by a man
> named Glennie, who was with the Chicago Club for many years. Mr.
> Glennie came in a few minutes ago and, seeing me sitting here, asked
> if I would like to see the suite where the beautiful first lady, Mrs. Cleve-
> land, was entertained for a few minutes when she visited Chicago with
> the President. She was faint, on her way from the railway station, and
> Mayor Roche, in whose carriage she was driving, took her to this club,
> which was nearby. A cup of tea soon restored her.

In 1888, the records show that the Club had 3,315 female visitors during the
year and held several ladies' parties.

The next dramatic change for women in the clubhouse came when the
Club entertained the noted explorer and newsman Henry Morton Stanley
in 1891. Because Mrs. Stanley and several of her lady friends accompanied
Mr. Stanley, it was thought appropriate to have the wives of the officers,
directors, and members of the reception committee join them in the receiving line. Precedent having been established, it became the rule that women
be in the receiving line when Club functions involved the wives and ladies of
prominent guests.

Critchell had been right. Political interests alone could not sustain the Club.
But the passion for good government provided the Club a distinction and
justification attractive to many, especially in that period of socialist ferment
and scandalous corruption in government.

Political activists in the Club such as Judge Jim Bradwell were not to be dissuaded by an upstart like Critchell. "Don't forget," boomed Bradwell when the Critchell ticket took over the reins of Club leadership, "that the first three principles of our Club are about using political influence to promote loyalty to country, to preserve the purity of the ballot box, and to oppose corruption in office. This club will not abandon those precious patriotic principles."

And it didn't. Nor did Bradwell care to be bothered by details of what to put on the menu and whether to buy Queen Anne or Federalist furnishings. There was too much to be done in Chicago.

"Political action," along with membership, audit, and the library made up the only committees of the early Club. The political action committee met monthly and debated topics such as: "The Consolidation of the City of Chicago and Cook County," "Nonpartisan Control of State Institutions," "How Best to Dispense Charity," "What Form of Government Best for Chicago?" (no agreement on this one), and "The Smoke Nuisance in Chicago."

After "toasting" (debating) each topic, the committee voted whether and what action to take. Meetings often closed with the members standing to sing "My Country 'Tis of Thee" and "America the Beautiful."

When U. S. Grant died in 1885, the Club called a special meeting for a memorial service at which six former Union officers as well as members of the Club, including Phil Sheridan and Major Jenney, gave reportedly stirring speeches. Special memorial services for national heroes were held from time to time.

From the beginning, members with little enthusiasm for politics tried to rein in the political action committee. In 1880, one of the Critchell group moved to change the name of the committee from political action to the rather tepid "Committee on Questions of Public Interest."

That proposal lost, but in 1881 a Critchellite proposed that "no political action shall be had until all club members are notified of the proposed action, and it is adopted by two-thirds of members voting at a regular meeting of the whole club." Ira Buell, one of the founders of both the Union League of America and the Club, sought to defeat the motion, to no avail.

The social types worried primarily about the political types becoming mired in controversy, which could threaten the Club's prosperity.

The social-political divide in the Club proved not to be wide. Even the social members were for honest and efficient government. And many of the initiatives favored by the political action committee were actually carried out by committee members acting in their own behalf, or through other civic organizations the committee members helped create and spearhead, such as the Civic Federation and the Municipal Voters' League.

C. E. Culver, chairman of the board of managers, could report on his stewardship in 1883 that the restaurant had done $28,000 of business, liquor had brought in $7,600, and cigars $8,100. And, he added, "The type of proposed clubhouse for the members was less important than our work to promote the public good." Whether he meant it or not, an acceptable arrangement had been reached: The Club would be both social and political. The Club voted that 3 percent of dues would go for "political action." The Club flourished in part because of local politics, not in spite of it.

Or as early Club president Critchell recalled, "We became a gentleman's social club, political but not strictly partisan." By political, he meant the pursuit of civic reform, which we turn to in the next chapter.

SOURCES

This chapter was richly informed by Frank Aldrich's "Sketches of Club Life" and by Roger Henn's manuscript, "History of the Union League Club of Chicago" (1980). Also, the reminiscences of early members Thomasson, Bacon, Selleck, Hampton, Starrett, Van Kirk, Coffin, and Critchell.

Club member George D. Bushnell's "Chicago's Leading Men's Clubs" provides an informative look at early men's clubs.

References to Eugene Field come from Charles H. Dennis in *Men & Events*, January 1943.

In addition: Bruce Grant's *Fight for a City* (Chicago: Rand McNally & Co., 1955) and minutes of the Club.

The Chicago Blue Book of Selected Names for 1911.

Chapter 4

"IF CHRIST CAME TO CHICAGO!"

Political action and politics were serious fun in the early years. The politicians tried to see how much they could steal from the public purse filled largely by the capitalists. The reformers worked to see how much they could expose and punish. In the 1880s and 1890s, Chicago government was so corrupt that Mayor Carter Harrison characterized its aldermen as "saloon keepers, proprietors of gambling houses, with no outstanding characteristics beyond the unquenchable lust for money."

Local election fraud became a special target of the Club. In 1880, the first Club political initiative called for state legislation to require voter registration in cities of more than ten thousand in population and a prohibition on voting by the unregistered. Ten members of the Club were appointed as a delegation to Springfield to push for the bill, which failed, never even emerging from committee. The Club, however, persisted.

The local elections of 1883 were a travesty of democracy. The results were odoriferous of fraud. Numerous reports came in of decent voters beset by roughs and bullies who tried to intimidate and drive them from the polls.

The political action committee investigated. A team of Club volunteers decided to take an actual census of one precinct where the results looked particularly fishy. Through an insider, the team obtained the poll book for the second precinct of the Ninth Ward. The election tally counted 1,183 votes cast. To the astonishment of the Club team, but maybe not their complete surprise, the door-to-door canvass could find only 351 persons living in the precinct!

Thirty-six voted from vacant lots. Factories, foundries, stores, houses of ill repute, and especially saloons were all represented as having large numbers of voters. George Washington, Abraham Lincoln, Thomas Jefferson, and other distinguished Americans, as well as common citizens long dead, were among those who signed in as voters in the spring of 1883 in the second precinct of the Ninth Ward.

The Club committee took its evidence to the state's attorney. He indicted five election officials. In December 1883, before the trial, the political action committee offered a fourteen-page handwritten report to the membership on the fraud discovered. "True," declared the committee, "we have seen the greatest City of the continent given over to the control of the vicious classes, but we have seen too the best elements of the City rise in their might and place the roughs and slugs beneath their feet."

The judge threw the case out.

Chastened, the Club consoled itself on having "won at the bar of public opinion." Club president Elbridge Gerry Keith, a direct descendant of a founding father of the United States, declared the Club would provide the political action committee with the resources to continue the fight for good government.

The fight did continue. At the Club annual meeting in January 1886, the committee reported to 250 members over dinner that "changes in election laws in Springfield had been consummated and more than our fondest anticipations in that direction have been realized." The membership directed the political action committee to invite the Iroquois and Commercial clubs as well as the Citizens' Association to continue working with the Club to draft further changes in election law for the next session of the legislature.

A few Club members jumped directly into the political fray. In his "Sketches of Club Life," written as Club historian in the 1920s, Frank Aldrich recounted his unlikely but true ascendancy to the presidency of the Cook County board of commissioners.

Aldrich was a central figure in the Club almost from his first year of membership in 1880 at age twenty-six until his death in 1933. An engineer who dabbled in real estate and managed an inherited estate, Aldrich was commissioner of public works for the city during the World's Columbian Exposition of 1893.

He also served as a Republican member of Congress from 1893 until 1897 and then sought the ambassadorship to Belgium (unsuccessfully). Aldrich also chaired the civic committee that led to the creation of the Chicago Sanitary District, which reversed the flow of the Chicago River to relieve the city's critical sewage disposal problems.

At the Republican county convention of 1886, Aldrich and Murry Nelson were among five nominated for Cook County commissioners. Nelson protested that he couldn't accept and he wondered why Aldrich would be interested, given the gamy reputation of the county board. But

Nelson had been preaching for years in the Club lounge and over at the Citizens' Association that the board had to be cleaned up. He could not now decline the opportunity to put his preaching into practice. The two Club members were elected, along with two saloonkeepers and the owner of a cheap livery stable on the west side, according to Aldrich's account.

A crusty fellow, Nelson harrumphed to his colleague: "Aldrich, you and I are the only two men in this body who are in a position to make the fight. The rest are either crooks or imbeciles."

All the reform groups and the newspapers backed the two neophyte politicians. Of course, their top men were members of the Club and knew them well. Their most important ally, however, was state's attorney Julius Grinnell, a Democrat and a respected member of the Club. The three commenced a fight to root out the boodlers. When it was over, only four of the fifteen county commissioners came out untainted.

The "brains" of the conspiring gang of crooks in county government was William McGarigle, warden of the county hospital and a former chief of police. His gang controlled the chairmanships of the committees on the hospital, insane asylum, and poorhouse. Each committee controlled the spending for its institution. According to Aldrich, committee meetings were frequently held in gambling houses and other questionable resorts where McGarigle and his associates concocted schemes for the depletion of the treasury.

The committee chairs and superintendents of the institutions bulldozed merchants into paying "small commissions" to board members and wardens for the privilege of serving the county. Once drawn in, the merchants became vulnerable to blackmail and acceded to the demands made on them.

From the gang's standpoint, the committees on the judiciary, education, and finance were purely ornamental. Nelson and Aldrich were assigned to the finance committee. How dumb of the gang. Nelson became chairman and the two new commissioners scanned all the unpaid vouchers. Aldrich extracted the suspicious-looking bills—all the big ones were suspicious—and took them to the offices of the Citizens' Association or to attorney friends. They photographed the documents before returning them to the county vault.

This evidence, along with that being piled up by Grinnell, ultimately forced participants to blab on one another and it sunk the boodlers. A majority of the county board was forced to resign; most went off to prison. In their places, according to Aldrich, came a true reform board of sterling citizens, handpicked largely by Nelson and Aldrich.

In opéra bouffe fashion, however, McGarigle escaped the clutches of justice. Canute Matson, the good-natured sheriff, decided that he personally would make the transfer of McGarigle to prison, since he was the biggest fish caught.

McGarigle asked Matson for one last favor—that he be permitted to go home for a final farewell to his family. This seemed reasonable enough to the affable Matson, who drove him there himself. Matson became a bit uneasy when Mac, as he was called, didn't return to the parlor where the sheriff had been sitting quietly and unperturbed. He decided to look around. It was too late.

The bird had flown. Mrs. Mac was in tears and could only explain that her husband had gone to the bathroom and had failed to return. Mac had gone through the window to a waiting buggy. He was driven to the lakeshore, where a boatman took him to a schooner and he was on his way to Canada. McGarigle finally reached Banff, where he ran a hotel for several years.

McGarigle was never extradited, but by some hocus-pocus returned to Chicago a few years later, where some sort of "settlement" had been made in his behalf. By then the authorities had either forgotten about Mac or lost interest. As Murry Nelson grumbled many times, and prophetically, "The trouble with reform is that the reformers won't stay mad for more than six months!"

After the boodlers were exposed and removed from the county board, the board reorganized and elected Frank Aldrich president. After considerable pleading, Aldrich secured the services of John Benham as superintendent of public services. Benham had broad powers to purchase all supplies for the county. One of the earliest and most respected members of the Club, he did a marvelous job, recounted Aldrich.

The Club also set in motion and promoted popular subscription for the construction of a monument in memory of the seven policemen killed at the Haymarket on May 4, 1886, allegedly by anarchists. The monument still stands, though it was twice bombed during civil disorders in the 1960s and 1970s and then moved to the police academy.

The Club's continuing patriotic celebration of George Washington's birthday was a direct response to the Haymarket Riot. Club members saw a clear need for a celebration and enhancement of patriotism.

The first celebration, in 1887, turned out to be less that that, however. The Club secured the services of James Russell Lowell, that distinguished man of letters from the East and former ambassador to the Court of St. James. On his way to Chicago, however, Lowell was told that the Club was full of conservative stalwarts who favored James G. Blaine, the "Plumed Knight" of Maine, for president.

Lowell was a mugwump, or more liberal Republican. At the last minute, apparently so as not to offend his audience, Lowell gave a talk about Shakespeare rather than a political speech about Washington. It was a disaster.

At the next Club meeting, the president chuckled, "Undoubtedly such members are not literary who cannot see the connection between Shakespeare and Washington."

The Club recovered from that less than stellar inaugural and a few years later, under Frank Lowden's leadership, arranged for nonpartisan exercises in every Chicago school on our first president's birthday. At each student assembly, a member of the Club told the children about their patriotic duties as citizens—and encouraged their fathers to demand that the new election law be enforced so as to bring cleaner government to the city.

Of even more concern to the Club than the boodlers were the socialist, communist, even anarchist labor leaders such as Eugene V. Debs, August Spies, Albert Parsons, and Samuel Fielden. The more conservative skilled craft unions, with whom business could work, had been overshadowed by masses of unskilled laborers who were necessary for Chicago's meatpacking houses and iron-mongering factories, dock, freight yards, and the like. Each economic bust in the boom-and-bust cycles of the late nineteenth century brought these unskilled workers to the streets in protest, where they were encouraged by labor orators who often preached violence, even revolution.

The response to all the social strife was a surge of reformism among the city's leading citizens. A crusading liberal journalist from England focused their energies. William T. Stead arrived in Chicago at the conclusion of the World's Columbian Exposition to write about its effect on the city.

He toured the notorious Levee district with its elegant houses of ill repute, talked with politicians, church, civic, and labor leaders—and talked and talked. The joke went around that at his wedding, Stead's best man was a speaker's podium.

Stead organized a series of speeches at the Central Music Hall. Citizens of all stripes came by the thousands to listen to "civic revivalism." Stead called the city's leaders to task for the mess he saw around him. "If Christ came to Chicago," Stead thundered, "what would he change?"

Out of these revival meetings emerged the Civic Federation as well as welfare relief efforts. Club member and banker Lyman Gage became president of the Federation and the participation of the city's best was assured with the naming of the redoubtable Mrs. Potter Palmer as the first vice president. Jane Addams and several liberals were also on the first board as well as Club members Ralph Easley, Frank McVeagh, George Adams, and Edward Butler.

Joseph Medill's earlier strident calls to send the newcomers back on a boat to where they came from had been replaced by the more refined and progressive style of Gage. Gage sought reconciliation between labor and management and to uplift the newcomers, not shun them.

Like many bankers of the time, Gage had been born to his position and had a sense of noblesse oblige. He believed that moderate social responsibility by business was the truest form of conservatism in a rapidly changing world. Not so, thought many of the new industrialists such as the meatpackers Armour, Cudahy, Swift, Mayer, and Morris, all of whom were on the rolls as early Club members. These men had made it on their own and so should everyone else.

So, while Gage and Club activists such as John Hamline, William Kent, and Victor Lawson might have wished otherwise, the Club had to steer clear of the divisive issues of labor-management strife and controversial social reform.

Lawson had come to Chicago, joined the Congregational Church choir, married a couple of octaves above himself, and joined the Club (where his father-in-law was an officer). Most important, Lawson built a great American newspaper, the *Chicago Daily News*. He and his paper were always at the ramparts with Gage and the progressives even when it hurt his paper's business.

But the Club couldn't afford that luxury. The Club was a business and needed to keep membership up. The Club lost 150 of its 1,200 members during the hard times of 1893 to 1896. The Club finance committee chairman reminded members of that fact a few years later after an expansion of the first clubhouse. "To repeat, gentlemen: We have provided accommodations for 1700 members, and we need them to help pay $115,000 now borrowed from the bank."

Some Club members even became rather comfortable with the boodlers' way of getting political business done. In her first book about Hull House, Jane Addams recalled being bribed in the clubhouse. That is, a bribe was attempted. A good friend of Addams had invited her to lunch at the Club. Two of his friends wanted to talk with her about the factory inspection bill (known as the "sweat shop" legislation) she was advocating in Springfield. One of the luncheon group made promises of lavish philanthropy for her Hull House if only she would drop her factory inspection bill.

"My friend," recalled Addams, "immediately hastened to cover the awkward situation by scurrying away from ugly morality, which seems to be an obligation of social discourse."

Even the prominent Civic Federation, moving ahead with great purpose on the wings of William Stead's impassioned revivalism, stumbled against the realities of hard-nosed business. In 1894, workers walked out of the massive Pullman railroad car factory to the south of the city. They could not live on the reduced wages imposed by Pullman, the workers declared, and at the same time pay rents, which had not been reduced, in his factory town of Pullman. Labor leader Eugene Debs realized, however, that the impetuous Pullman workers couldn't win this strike. He implored Lyman Gage and the Civic Federation to persuade George Pullman to meet with the strike leaders.

Gage and vice president Mrs. Potter Palmer called on Pullman, their longtime associate, but to no avail. Pullman brushed them aside as if to say, "Don't meddle in my business!" Ultimately, fearing violence and a nation-wide rail stoppage, President Grover Cleveland sent in federal troops to ensure order. Soldiers set up camp in the heart of the city. After several months, Pullman won his strike. Gage and Mrs. Palmer were shaken by their impotence in the affair.

That same year of 1894, Frank Lowden became the chair of the political action committee. He also began courting Pullman's daughter Florence. They married not long after. Pullman, by the way, was tough on anyone who failed to meet his standards. From all his millions, he left his twin sons each only three thousand dollars a year because neither had, in his eyes, developed a sense of responsibility.

Constrained as it may have been by the realities of Club life, the political action committee was the civic conscience of the larger Club. Committee members were no shrinking violets. They continually exhorted the Club membership to become involved in making Chicago a better place, not only because it was the right thing to do but also because reforms could reduce social strife and unrest, improve the image of the rough-and-tumble city, and generate public appreciation for the business community and the Club.

Gage and Hamline recalled the horrors of earlier riots and uprisings in order to enlist the support of less socially conscious members. The Club sponsored tenement reform and improved sanitary conditions because, as a member put it, such actions are "fundamentally antagonistic to Socialism in all its forms."

Club members were Protestants and capitalists. They appeared to want a better life for the laboring classes and for them to become good, orderly citizens. For example, the political action committee held discussions for the full membership on how to encourage home ownership. The Club also pushed, successfully, for an increase in the local liquor license fee from one hundred to five hundred dollars to reduce the number of saloons.

The political action committee also took a lead role in advocating legislation to create mutual savings banks in Illinois. Eastern states had led the way on this. The laboring classes in Illinois saved paltry amounts, the committee observed. These banks, owned by the depositors themselves and not by capitalists, would be a great charity for the workers. The bank bill had languished in Springfield before the Club became interested in it. The political action committee proclaimed that it was subsequently enacted as a result of the Club's influence with the legislature.

The board of managers directed the committee to organize presentations at each quarterly dinner meeting of the Club, which was attended by from 180 to 250 members. After hearing from the experts, Club members discussed topics such as "The Immigration Problem in Chicago" and "The Oregon Idea of Popular Government" and held several sessions on juvenile delinquency, a topic in which the Club later developed a keen interest through creation of a Boys Club and summer camp.

The political action committee held a discussion one evening on the issues of foreign immigration. A number of gentlemen of foreign birth were invited to join the discussion. Their sentiments echoed those of the Club, according to committee minutes. That is, the guests also favored the suppression of that class of immigrants whose sole desire was to overthrow society. Club member and U.S. Representative George Adams had a proposal before Congress to suppress this group of aliens and expel them from the country. Naturally, the Club endorsed this.

The committee sparked a special meeting of the whole Club in 1908 to discuss the deplorable state of the county buildings for the care of the poor and the consumptive.

The committee report declared the facilities so overcrowded and in such need of repair as to menace the health and lives of the persons living therein. The Club responded by unanimously endorsing the sale of bonds by the county to erect new buildings.

Also at the political action committee's urging, the Club supported various bond issues for more parks, police, libraries, and public baths. Now and then the Club took positions on national issues, as in 1908 when it supported preservation of the Appalachian and New Hampshire's White Mountain timber reserves, which required elimination of existing federal law. According to the Club resolution, the law had "demonstrated conclusively that its effect has been to turn over the public timber to great corporations. It has done enormous harm; it is no longer needed, and it should be repealed."

The Club also played a key role in bringing civic groups together. For several years in the 1890s and early 1900s, the Club hosted for dinner twenty to thirty reform organizations along with fifty or more state legislators to discuss reform bills the Club wanted the legislature to pass.

Following the spring 1895 dinner, twenty-five Club members traveled to Springfield with representatives of other groups to lobby for civil service reform, a pet project of Club president John Hamline. Hamline addressed the entire House on behalf of merit selection of workers in Chicago. The following week, Hamline, Gage, and other members returned to Springfield again. A civil service bill was enacted that session and signed by the governor.

Like the crusading Stead, young writers were compelled to visit Chicago for its yeastiness, tumult, and texture. As if perched on the lip of the fishbowl of life, they pondered what it all meant. And they didn't like what they saw in the clubs. Robert Herrick from the East and Theodore Dreiser from rural Indiana saw the Union League Club, as well as the Calumet and Chicago clubs, as refuges for scoundrels and hypocrites—hollow, money-crazed men. To Herrick, who never took a liking to the city, Chicago presented stark choices: virtuous poverty or corrupt success.

Club members Charles Yerkes, the traction (trolley) magnate, and Philip Armour, the meat packer, provided the larger-than-life personalities for the novelists' work. Dreiser's trilogy, clearly about the driven and corrupt Yerkes, refers now and again to the Union League as the "favorite club" of the associates of Frank Cowperwood, his protagonist. Ironically, Dreiser displayed a grudging admiration for Cowperwood (Yerkes): Cowperwood had magnificent audacity; he saw business as an art form; he was alive! And so was Chicago. Cowperwood and men like him were Chicago, for better and worse.

In *The Pit*, his novel about capitalism, Frank Norris finds as well that the most creative men in the city moved in a world with few creative choices other than to "buy" or "sell." Frank Jadwin, who may have been patterned after any of several of the Club's trader members, is taken to the Union League Club almost immediately upon his arrival from the East. Supremely self-confident and sure of his own morality, Jadwin attempts to corner the market on wheat but ultimately fails. And though Norris finds cornering a market a wrong-headed goal, he sees in Jadwin a heroic figure beside whom most men pale.

There was no ambiguity in Edgar Lee Masters' view of the Club. The Chicago lawyer and poet offered this take on the Club in *The Tale of Chicago:*

> Though gambling was continually denounced by the press and inveighed
> against by theologians, for many years gentlemen of the city, federal
> judges, contributors to the Civic Federation and Municipal Voters
> League, reform state's attorneys pledged to rid the city of sin, corpor-
> ation lawyers taking occasion to flatter visiting federal judges with
> presents of whisky and by allowing them to win at poker, these and
> others of like disposition of mind associated themselves together in the
> rooms of the Union League Club, for the delight of mulcting a dull capi-
> talist once a week of thousands of dollars, thereby adding drains to his

purse, already generous toward movements to suppress gambling, political corruption in the wards, prostitution and villainies of Yerkes.

Around the corner from the Club on Sherman Court were bagnios, to which these hircine spirits stole through the darkness.

The next day across the street in the federal building many young and industrious lawyers who had diligently prepared meritorious cases found themselves suddenly worsted at the instance of a United States Senator, or corporation lawyer expounding the law to a federal judge; while the judge by no expression betrayed the fact that the night before he had been handsomely entertained at the Union League Club.

These powerful men soaked in hypocrisy, to whom the ward balls [extravagant and coarse parties thrown a few blocks south of the Club by First Ward bosses "Bathhouse" John Coughlin and Michael "Hinky Dink" Kenna] were unspeakable offenses, who were shocked by the song and joy of errant youth, and the unlicensed conduct of gay offenders in the Democratic populousness of the city, saw no inconsistency in their social attitudes.

Masters appears to have been, it might be noted, rather cynical about human nature in general, as recorded in his *Spoon River Anthology*. So the Club was not alone in his pantheon of unworthies. And if hypocrisy there might be in the Club, the hypocrisy was not in short supply either among those associated with Masters. The well-known liberal crusader Clarence Darrow, a partner of Masters for a period, represented the traction-line interests of master briber Charles Yerkes—even as Darrow headed a committee for the public ownership of the same traction lines and otherwise excoriated the capitalist class.

If Stead had come back to Chicago a decade or so after the world's fair closed in 1893, he would have found the city a bit more civil, refined, and progressive. Just a bit more, but that is generally how progress comes.

The political action committee of the Club, and its members acting for themselves or via other groups, played a part in achieving that progress. If you still doubt this, read on to the next chapter and the observations of muckraker Lincoln Steffens, who found the efforts of Club political activists to merit national acclaim.

SOURCES
This chapter relies heavily on the minutes of both the Club and its political action committee. Also, Frank Aldrich's "Sketches of Club Life and History," especially "The Debacle of 1886" in the *Union League Club Bulletin*, September 1926.

The chapter was also richly informed by Ray Ginger's *Altgeld's America* (New York: Funk & Wagnalls Co., 1958) and Emmett Dedmon's *Fabulous Chicago* (New York: Random House, 1953).

The unpublished Club histories by Roger Henn and George Bushnell richly discuss the early political action of the Club, as does Bruce Grant's *Fight for a City*. In addition, the reminiscences of Club members Robert S. Critchell and B. M. Hampton in the Club archives proved valuable.

The author is indebted to the fine dissertation of Sidney I. Roberts, "Businessmen in Revolt: Chicago 1874–1900" (Ph.D. dissertation, Northwestern University, 1960).

Also, Herman Kogan, "Myra Bradwell: Crusader at Law" (*Chicago History*, Winter 1974–75).

I also enjoyed either reading or rereading the following novels from the turn of the nineteenth into the twentieth century: *The Pit*, Frank Norris; *Memoirs of an American Citizen*, Robert Herrick; *Sister Carrie, The Titan*, and *The Financier*, Theodore Dreiser; and *The Jungle*, Upton Sinclair.

Other works drawn upon include:

Addams, Jane. *Twenty Years at Hull-House*. New York: Macmillan, 1910.

Baumann, Edward. "The Haymarket Bomber." *Chicago Tribune Sunday Magazine*, April 27, 1986.

Buenker, John D. "Chicago's Ethnics and the Politics of Accommodation." *Chicago History*, Fall 1974.

Citizens' Association of Chicago. *Annual Reports*, 1874 to 1925. ULCC archives, General Historical Information, Box 11.

Duis, Perry. *Chicago: Creating New Traditions*. Chicago: Chicago Historical Society, 1976.

Duncan-Clark, S. J. *The Progressive Movement*. Boston: Small, Maynard & Co., 1913.

Grosch, Anthony R. "Social Issues in Early Chicago Novels." *Chicago History*, Summer 1975.

Howard, Robert. *Mostly Good and Competent Men*. Springfield: *Illinois Issues* and Illinois State Historical Society, 1988.

Hutchinson, William. *Lowden of Illinois*. Chicago: University of Chicago Press, 1957.

Kogan, Bernard, ed. *The Chicago Haymarket Riot: Anarchy on Trial*. Boston: D.C. Heath & Co., 1959.

Masters, Edgar Lee. *The Tale of Chicago*. New York: G. P. Putnam's Sons, 1933.

Scriabine, Christine. "Upton Sinclair and the Writing of *The Jungle.*" *Chicago History,* Spring 1981.

Sutherland, Douglas. *Fifty Years on the Civic Front.* Chicago: Civic Federation, 1943.

Tarr, Joel A. "The Urban Politician as Entrepreneur." *Mid–America* 49, January 1967.

Chapter 5

THE TITAN VERSUS
THE SECOND-CLASS BUSINESSMAN

Charles Tyson Yerkes and George E. Cole were both members of the Club. There the similarity ended. For three years in the late 1890s, the two men locked horns in a battle for political control of Chicago. The larger-than-life Yerkes was the stuff of great novels. His life was chronicled with but a gossamer veil of fiction in Theodore Dreiser's trilogy, *The Financier, The Titan,* and *The Stoic.*

In the other corner stood George Cole, no taller than a fireplug, self-admitted to be a second-class businessman. Eastern muckraker Lincoln Steffens focused, nevertheless, on Cole, and the tussles between David and Goliath, between good and evil, as Chicagoans came to see it. In *Shame of the Cities,* Steffens set the scene:

> I trust reformers will pick up some pointers from—Chicago. Yes, Chicago. First in violence, deepest in dirt, unlovely, ill-smelling, irreverent, new; an overgrown gawk of a village, the "tough" among cities, a spectacle for the nation. . . . With the ingenuity and will to turn their sewer, the Chicago River, and make it run backwards and upwards out of the lake, the city cannot solve the smoke nuisance. They can balance high buildings on rafts floating in mud, but they can't quench the stench of the stockyards.

Enter Charles Yerkes, 1886. Reared in Philadelphia in comfort and refinement, Yerkes built and lost a fortune, spent time in prison for financial shenanigans, returned from the jail cell to leave his loyal wife and six children for a stunning young Philadelphia beauty. Shunned by that city's society, Yerkes headed west.

Yerkes brought to Chicago brains, deep experience in finance, no conscience, and a large appetite for the finer things of life, including one young beauty after another. Yerkes saw Chicago's need for urban rail transportation. He borrowed money against operating leases, bought out horse-drawn and underground cable, or traction, companies with the borrowed money.

Yerkes also created new traction companies and guaranteed huge dividends, which caused the value of his controlling interests to soar. Nobody could understand the razzle-dazzle of his financial pyramids, but they worked. In 1895, he built the Union Elevated ("el") tracks around downtown Chicago, creating the "Loop" that still defines the city center.

To finance an ever-expanding utility business, Yerkes had to sell bonds. The capacity to sell bonds was inseparable from equally long-term monopoly franchises. Chicago aldermen held him up for bribes to get what he needed from them. Yerkes played that game with a vengeance, the only game the boodlers in the council understood.

Yerkes simply bought most of the sixty-eight members of the city council. Through lavish gifts of racing horses, fine furnishings, stock, and plain old cash, Yerkes controlled the council. He established a market value on votes of different kinds; other business supplicants fell in line. The two-hundred-dollar-a-year job of alderman became worth twenty-five thousand dollars, often more, to the boodling lawmakers. The powerful alderman Johnny ("de Pow") Powers declared publicly: "You can't get elected to the city council unless Mr. Yerkes says so!"

By 1896 Yerkes controlled forty-eight separate traction lines and was worth $29 million, it was reported. His homes held one of the world's finest art collections, which included two Rembrandts, several Rubens, a Vandyke, and a Turner valued alone at $67,000. When he traveled east, the magnate stayed at his $1.5 million home on Fifth Avenue.

In his ascent, Yerkes alienated almost everyone. He refused to consolidate his many lines, which required passengers to pay separate fares at each transfer. The traction cars were filthy and crowded. When passengers petitioned investors for better service, he snubbed both, declaring, "It's the people who hang to the straps who pay your big dividends."

Yerkes even swindled Marshall Field and the merchant's fellow investors in an Evanston line. Field thought Yerkes would allow them to connect to his line into Chicago. Yerkes refused, leaving the suburban line several blocks short of a connection, almost valueless. A year later, Yerkes allowed Field and his associates to connect—for $1.5 million *and* half the stock in the Evanston line. Field let it be known, tersely, that "Mr. Yerkes is not a safe man."

Safe, no, but cunning and brilliant, even in his philanthropy. In 1892, rumors circulated that Yerkes was on the verge of failure. Nobody would lend him a cent. Yerkes went to Dr. William Rainey Harper, head of the new University of Chicago. He offered to contribute one million dollars to build the world's largest telescope—on three conditions. First, that the announcement of the gift be made immediately. Second, that payment would be made sometime later. Third, absolutely no one was to know that. After the announcement, Yerkes was overwhelmed with credit. The university's Yerkes Observatory at Williams Bay, Wisconsin, still observes the stars.

The franchises Yerkes had obtained from his pliant city council were limited by state law to twenty years. Not long enough, thought Yerkes, to entice investors and guarantee long-lasting profits. At the end of a franchise, a cable car company was required to tear up its tracks and cable. To rip up a mile of tracks cost about $150,000 a mile. Short-term contracts could have been ruinous.

Yerkes contributed heavily to state legislators in their 1894 campaigns. In 1895, he called in his markers and also sweetened the customary "jackpot" of bribe payoffs, which was put together by the big interests for supportive lawmakers at the end of the session.

Known as one of the "Eternal Monopolies Bills" passed that year, the Yerkes-originated Humphrey Act would have extended several of the traction magnate's key franchises for ninety-nine years—without providing any payment at all to the city of Chicago. All the bill needed was the signature of Democratic Governor John Peter Altgeld.

Club members detested Altgeld's liberal—members might have said radical—politics, but came grudgingly to admire his integrity. Elected in 1892, the Prussian-born Altgeld promptly pardoned the "Haymarket bombers" who had been convicted for their alleged roles in that infamous 1886 event. Altgeld's eighteen-thousand-word pardon statement bitterly criticized Judge Joseph E. Gary, who presided at the trial, and police inspector John Bonfield.

A month later, the Union League Club displayed its unwavering support for law and order in an unsettled society by unanimously electing Judge Gary to honorary membership in the Club, a distinction generally reserved for U.S. presidents and national figures.

Altgeld's promising political career collapsed in a firestorm of public outrage. Adding salt on his wounds, Altgeld's personal financial situation became desperate by 1895 in the middle of that decade's economic depression. The governor's capital was tied up in the Unity Block of commercial real estate in the Chicago. His rental income had fallen disastrously. He was hard-pressed to make his interest payments. Banks denied him further loans.

There are two stories about what happened between Yerkes and Altgeld. In one, later corroborated by persons who were there, an agent of Yerkes walked into the Unity Block carrying a valise. He talked privately with the governor's cousin, John Lanehart. In a bank vault was either five hundred thousand dollars or possibly a million. Both sums were astronomical. All Altgeld had to do was sign the legislation and the key to the vault that was in the valise would be his.

The other story had Yerkes meeting with Altgeld in the governor's office, where he offered him the money, knowing of the governor's financial straits. The governor told him he could not take the money. Yerkes replied: "I admire you, but there will be other governors." As he left, Yerkes added, "If you ever need a loan, please come see me."

Yerkes did indeed say publicly that he admired Altgeld, claiming that he cast his vote in 1896 for Altgeld for governor even as he threw the support of his political machine behind the winner, Republican John Tanner.

Charles Yerkes held man in contempt because almost every man he knew had a price. He cared not that his purchase of the city council gave Chicago the title of "Boodle Capital of the World." But the city's civic leaders were aghast that this reputation might undo all the marvelous good done for the city's image by the World's Columbian Exposition of 1893.

In 1895, the new and heady Civic Federation, led by the biggest names in Chicago, made a major effort to root out corrupt city councilmen at election time. Instead, the civic worthies were themselves routed, humiliated by the entrenched councilmen. Federation president Lyman Gage, the city's leading banker and one of its most prominent civic leaders, was exasperated, shaken. What in God's name could be done to erase the hideous blemish of corruption from the city's image?

Gage called a war council of all the leading clubs—Union League, Iroquois, Standard, Columbus, Commercial, Bankers, Merchants, Citizens' Association, Civic Federation, and others. He asked each to provide two members for a committee of one hundred.

Gage declared the city council "unparalleled in the sublimity of its infamy." Another leader talked of "that aldermanic malady known as fatty degeneration of the conscience." A third reported overhearing a conversation between two members of the council—carried on in German no less—about the price to be asked for an upcoming ordinance!

The hall was abuzz, but the meeting disintegrated, so a smaller committee of fifteen was directed to take action. Gage and the committee created a Municipal Voters' League for the purposes of electing honest men to the council, irrespective of party affiliation, and opposition to the granting of any more traction and gas franchises without full compensation to the city and ultimate reversion of ownership to the city.

But they couldn't find anyone to head up the new group. Understandable, given the Civic Federation's failure on the same front. One civic leader after another turned down the daunting task. Finally, colonel John Cooper recommended George Cole. "Who?" asked Gage. No one in the group had heard of him.

George Cole was third string, at best, on the civic leadership roster. He was a member of the Club, his only affiliation. He had a stationer's and office supply business. It made sense for him to belong to the largest club in the city.

Cooper told the committee that Cole had been bitten by the bug to do some good. The year before, Cole had taken on his local alderman, the prominent Martin Madden, and gave him a real scare. Cole was tough, had joined the Union army at fifteen, weighing less than a hundred pounds, and had drummed for Sherman through Georgia.

"Okay then, go get Cole," declared Gage.

Cole knew they wanted others for the post. "Look, I know I'm your fourth or fifth choice. But if you want me, I'll do it—on these conditions. First, you provide $10,000 up front for the election campaign, which is less than two months away. Second, I have the right to name my own executive committee, and third, I have a free hand to do things as I wish." Not having much choice, and liking his take-charge attitude, the committee agreed.

George went around the Club to the men he wanted and, where necessary, shamed them into agreeing to serve by appealing to their sense of civic responsibility. His executive committee was made up of Bill Colvin, a wealthy retired businessman; Frank Wells, prominent real estate man; R. R. Donnelley, the printer; Hoyt King, a lawyer with a flair for investigations; Edwin Burritt Smith, lawyer and publicist; and M. J. Carroll, an ex-typesetter, union leader, and editor of a labor journal. All were members of the Club with the exception, of course, of the labor leader.

Cole also created an advisory committee, most of whom were also members of the Club. The most colorful was young Club member and alderman William Kent. Wealthy, patrician, and passionately opposed to the boodlers, Kent provided great newspaper copy from the floor of the council chambers, where he decried Yerkes as the "buccaneer from a Pennsylvania penitentiary."

Cole was perfect for the job. Five feet tall, he wore a size eight hat, had a bulldog jaw accentuated by a goatee, and was stubborn and egotistical. He too made great copy. "I have short legs," he told the press, "but they're long enough to reach the floor." Popular columnist Finley Peter Dunne and other writers started stopping by his campaign office. "Old King Cole" and "Buzz-Saw" Cole became the perfect caricature for *Tribune* cartoonist John McCutcheon.

Boodlers and the public alike smiled on Cole and his crew—just another silk-stocking reformer; nothing more than a puff of cigar smoke that will waft away in the first breeze. Yet, as Steffens said about Chicago: "No matter who you are, where you come from, or what you set out to do, Chicago will give you a chance. The sporting spirit is the spirit of Chicago."

The battles between Cole and Yerkes for control of the city council became the talk of the town. The city had six intensely competitive dailies. The three-year, do-or-die contest was made in heaven for reporters and editorialists. Yerkes made the perfect devil—imperious, contemptuous of all, ostentatious, a voluptuary, high-handed, brilliant, crooked, envy-inspiring. A "Napoleon of fraud and chicanery," boomed Cole, probably paraphrasing the then-popular Sherlock Holmes's description of Professor Moriarity as the "Napoleon of crime."

Club member Walter Fisher characterized the council as "gray wolves," hungry predators tearing at the public purse, a term that sticks even today. Finley Peter Dunne and young William Kent became drinking buddies during these political wars. The two stopped by Cole's headquarters in the afternoon to see what was up, then toured the saloons, looking for copy and "intelligence." Dunne's famous saloonkeeper "Mith-ur Dooley" would wax on the next day about the scandalous "Yerkuss" and his merry band of boodlers. Kent would tuck away gossip overheard about the councilmen's latest hijinks.

Cole's sole focus was the issue of the fitness of the aldermen. His campaign tools were information, publicity, and the recruitment of candidates who could win where no one else could, even if the candidates were not good guys, so long as they would oppose Yerkes. George hired detectives to get "the goods" on the council. Back in the campaign headquarters, his own team researched their voting records.

In the 1896 aldermanic elections, Cole declared that fifty-seven of sixty-eight aldermen were thieves. No mincing of words here. Cole and his colleagues scoured the city's thirty-four wards for candidates to oppose the thieves, half of whom were up for reelection (there were two alderman per ward). Candidates were asked to take a pledge that, in effect, they opposed Yerkes and his ilk, would oppose his franchise bills, and favored civil service reform. On that pledge—and Cole's sense that the candidate could win—the League provided its backing.

The League published reports on all the aldermen. Of "Bathhouse" John Coughlin:

> Democratic candidate; lives at No. 165 Van Buren Street; the notorious "Bath-house John" born near Waukegan, Ill., about 1854; been a leader in the politics of his ward for many years; was elected to Council in 1894; voted for all questionable ordinances; conducts a bath-house at No. 145

East Madison Street; patronized chiefly by gamblers and racing men; owns a string of racing horses; runs the "Silver Dollar Saloon" at No. 169 East Madison Street; saloon is a resort for prostitutes, gamblers and thieves; is uneducated and coarse in conduct; the friend of toughs and thugs; a disgrace to his ward and city; is supported by "Hinky Dink" Kenna and "Johnnie" Morris.

Cole and his committee of Club members played by the rules of the alley, like the boodlers. If the detectives' information proved too private for publication, the candidate was sent for, the "dirt" spread out before him along with the advice to get off the ticket. Several did.

As the spring 1896 aldermanic campaign approached its final days, the Municipal Voters' League headquarters became a madhouse of politicians, reformers, reporters, messenger boys, and favor seekers. Wards were flooded with circulars and house-to-house canvassers from the forty thousand citizens who had signed cards favoring reform. There were torchlight parades and throw-the-rascals-out meetings in most wards.

The newspapers were crucial. All but one of Chicago's major newspapers cooperated fully with the league's campaign. They made Cole a celebrity, picturing him as a reaping machine cutting down the rascals, a lion tamer, and a human buzz saw. Because of the press, Cole quickly captured the public's imagination. His biggest newspaper backers were club members Victor Lawson of the *Daily News* and Herman Kohlsaat of the *Herald*. Lawson also acted as an unofficial advisor and assigned several reporters to work for the League while still on his payroll.

The corrupt councilmen became interested, if not too concerned, about this little colonel and his reformers. Reporter Justin Smith tells this story:

> Mr. Cole and his secretary were alone at headquarters. It was the close of day. No one was expected when in walked a long man and a short man. Every murder in those days involved a long man and a short man. This is mentioned to emphasize the solemnity of the occasion. The secretary knew the long man. Cole knew neither. Cole was behind the counter of the old banking room. On the raised floor inside he could lean on the counter. The tall man towered over it. The short man's eyes just about reached its level. The tall man said:
>
> "Mr. Cole, I am John J. Coughlin." [Bathhouse John].
> "Glad to meet you, Mr. Coughlin."
> "This is my friend, Michael Kenna." [Hinky Dink.]
> "How do you do, Mr. Kenna."
> "Now Mr. Cole, I have come to see you as man to man, to say you have done me a very great injustice in your report."

Mr. Cole is handed a printed copy of the record. [The one noted above.]

"Yes, Mr. Coughlin, if we have made any mistake we will be glad to correct it. Our records show you voted for all these questionable ordinances."

"That is not the point, Mr. Cole. In this record you say I was born in Waukegan. Now, Mr. Cole, I was born right here in Chicago, and I am proud of it."

The correction was made next day in the newspapers as requested.

In just fifty-eight days between its creation and the March primaries, Cole and the MVL endorsed candidates in thirty of thirty-four wards and saw twenty-five through to election. It was the first great victory against the gray wolves. Combined with a few good-government aldermen who weren't up for election, the MVL had built a veto-proof minority (that is, the gray wolves now lacked the extraordinary majority of votes needed to override a veto by the mayor). In the 1897 contests for the other thirty-four aldermanic seats, the MVL picked up more seats. Yerkes was on the ropes.

In 1897, Yerkes shifted the fight back to the Illinois legislature and a new, more pliant governor. Cole and yet another committee of one hundred, most of whom were Union Leaguers, followed the robber baron and his utilities buddies, several of whom were also Union Leaguers, down to the capital to do battle.

This time Yerkes asked for fifty-year extensions and new franchises from a state regulatory commission, not from city councils. He testified coolly that he was appealing for state action on this "Humphrey bill" (named after its legislative sponsor) because he was unable to obtain honest treatment from the mercenary and corrupt city council of Chicago!

Ironically, according to Forrest McDonald (biographer of Samuel Insull, Yerkes' successor as utilities magnate of Chicago), the Humphrey bill was model legislation, "one of the most progressive pieces of legislation ever considered by the state of Illinois." The bills would have granted fifty-year licenses and created a state regulatory commission and would have required companies to pay escalating fees to the cities served.

Wisconsin created its pioneer utility commission in 1907, patterned after the Humphrey bill. Had this legislation been enacted in Illinois, says McDonald, "the history books would say that the Progressive movement was launched by Illinois in 1897 rather than by Wisconsin" a few years later.

The reformers would have none of it. If Yerkes was behind the proposal, it was bad.

Yerkes operated a nonstop reception suite for lawmakers at a nearby hotel throughout the spring legislative session. He directed his lobbying from the floor of the House. The committee of one hundred worked equally hard and felt they had the bill beaten in the Senate; they publicly doubted the bill would make it to third reading. The Chicago press lauded their worthy efforts.

Then, to their disbelief, the upper chamber advanced and passed the bill in two days. Word got around that two hundred thousand dollars had been put in escrow to be distributed later among the senators, with three hundred thousand set aside for use later in the House.

The Chicago press was aghast. Yerkes was vilified as the incarnation of evil. The *Daily News* and *Tribune* acted as if they were in the midst of a major crisis in the course of human affairs. If Yerkes could buy anything he wanted, what mattered democracy?

Stirred by the papers and the civic organizations, mass meetings were held in most wards. The cry was "the noose for state lawmakers who voted with Yerkes." The committee called a mass meeting for Easter Sunday afternoon. Nearly every Protestant minister urged his congregation to attend. Thirty-five hundred alarmed citizens filled Central Music Hall to standing room only. The leaders declaimed that every lawmaker who voted for the Yerkes bills was to be targeted for defeat.

Under this pressure, the House rejected the Yerkes bill.

A week later, Yerkes tried again, this time with a bill that would grant municipalities power to issue fifty-year franchises and extend those already granted for the same period. Herald trumpets, or so one might have imagined, called the reformers back onto the field of battle.

The traction magnate converted a chair under the rotunda of the Capitol into a command post where he issued orders to his political lieutenants, Republican Bill Lorimer and Chicago Democratic boss Roger Sullivan. Money was cast about the Capitol with reckless abandon. Bill Kent reported that new members of the legislature were offered two thousand dollars for their votes; veteran members commanded more.

A reporter for the *Chicago Evening Journal* was inadvertently offered money for his "vote." Sitting in the seat of a member of the House before the day's session got under way, the journalist was mistaken for that member by a nearsighted old state senator.

"The lawmaker sat down beside me," the reporter told Kent, "and opened with the explicit statement that he would pay twenty-five hundred for my vote on the traction bill. He quickly discovered his mistake, and there was much scurrying in the ranks of the grafters."

Again the reformers thought they had beaten the bill. Again they were wrong. This time logrolling complemented the boodling. A representative from dairy country in Boone County saw his butterine bill (which prohibited yellow food-coloring in butter substitutes)—at a standstill until then—

passed into law. Supporters of bills to regulate cheap bumboats (which ped-dled wares) on the Illinois River got what they wanted, and so on. All this seemed fair to these downstaters. After all, this Yerkes bill didn't affect them. It just put the franchise issue back with the Chicago city council. The bill passed and Governor John Tanner signed it into law.

The Cole forces doubled their efforts. The 1898 aldermanic elections approached. Theater became their new weapon. On the council floor, Kent and alderman John M. Harlan, a member of the Union League and Chicago clubs, repeatedly threatened the boodlers with tar-and-feathers and lamppost lynchings. The packed council galleries became the hottest tickets in town.

Were the reformers really serious in their threats, wondered the anx-ious gray wolves? The tall but slight Kent was constantly accompanied by "Doc" Green, a former safe blower and ex-member of the Chicago under-world. At crucial council meetings, the front seats in the galleries were occu-pied by bruisers such as Bernard Rogers and Jack Corey, who sympathized with the League. If a speaker indicated he favored a Yerkes measure, Corey would lower his rope with a noose at the end and allow it to dangle in plain view. The MVL precipitated at least one violent reaction from the gray wolves. Council members' desks and chairs became kindling wood in the melee.

Out in the wards, Cole and his crew fought Yerkes' money with pam-phleteering, exposing the corruption of the Yerkes gang. The major political parties counseled with Cole before making their nominations, then sought league support. The voters began to accept the league's recommendations as fiat. They loved their fireplug of a fighter George Cole. The ranks of reform-ers in the council grew following the spring 1898 aldermanic elections.

That same year, Yerkes launched his last campaign for "eternal monopolies." He even bought the *Inter-Ocean*, a major Chicago daily, and hired a hotshot former editor of the *New York Sun* to take on the "trust press," as he called the dailies that opposed him. Every issue of his paper blasted his enemies and extolled the benefits of long-term leases.

The *Inter-Ocean* was particularly venomous toward Yerkes' most out-spoken critic, Victor Lawson and his *Daily News*. The paper called Lawson a "friend of socialists," the recipient of "hush money," a "moral bankrupt," and "a debaucher of youth." This last allegation was provoked by the fact that newsboys were being taught boxing in Lawson's gymnasium! (The Lawson YMCA on the near north side is, by the way, still operating.)

Lawson retorted crisply to the personal attacks: "The public knows that Mr. Yerkes has been in jail, and I have not. Why say more?" Lawson poured even more newspaper resources into helping Cole and the League.

Everyone knew a franchise extension bill would be introduced in the council. Yerkes' first leases began to run out in 1903. Late in 1898, a Yerkes henchman in the council quietly introduced an extension bill. He asked that it be assigned to the streets and alleys committees—there was one each for the north, west, and south sides—all controlled by Yerkes' men. The bill called for fifty-year extensions and compensation to the city ranging up to 3 percent of the traction companies' gross incomes.

Even if the bill made some sense now, the reformers couldn't let it pass. They had to drive Yerkes out of town. The newspapers went wild with attacks on Yerkes, the council, one another, Cole, and Mayor Harrison. This was a fight to the death, so to speak. Cole and his colleagues were rallying on street corners across the city. Schoolchildren stoned an effigy of a man wearing a sign, "I am a Boodler."

Men on the street wore tiny nooses in their buttonholes. Rumors circulated that the mayor threatened to call out the militia to prevent bloodshed. A delegation visited alderman Kenna and threatened to lynch him. Bathhouse John admitted as how "things are getting pretty warm."

Carter Harrison, Jr., who was to serve five terms as mayor, was no great friend of reformers. But he was savvy enough to know that Yerkes and his bills, good or not, were now bad politics.

Sensing defeat of his first measure, Yerkes prepared a substitute that called for thirty-five-year extensions and compensation up to 5 percent to the city. Yerkes offered a fortune of $150,000 to First Ward aldermen Bathhouse John and Hinky Dink, his longtime backers, for their votes and help in this battle.

Mayor Harrison also went to Coughlin and Kenna, appealing for their help in beating Yerkes. Bathhouse told the mayor, "Mr. Maar, I was talkin' a while back with Senator Billy Mason and he told me, 'Keep clear of th' big stuff, John, it's dangerous. You and Mike stick to th' small stuff; there's little risk and in the long run it pays a damned sight more.' Mr. Maar, we're with you. And we'll do what we can to swing some of the other boys over."

With parliamentary savvy, Kent and Harlan moved that all bills dealing with traction matters be assigned, not to the traction committees, but to the previously meaningless committee on city hall, which reformers controlled. Pandemonium reigned. Harrison was finally able to call the roll on the motion, which passed 32–31, with Bathhouse and Hinky Dink voting yea. All Yerkes' bills were henceforth buried in committee, never to rise again.

Charles Tyson Yerkes sold most of his railway properties the following year for ten million dollars to his old friends and financial backers in Philadelphia, and his elevated-line stocks and bonds to another group that included Marshall Field. Later these investors complained bitterly that he had duped them, selling them watered stock. En route to London, where he would head the syndicate that built that great city's subway system, Yerkes was heard to say, "The secret to success in my business is to buy old junk, fix it up a little, and unload it on the other fellows."

Before leaving town, Yerkes made a major campaign contribution to the unsuccessful 1899 campaign for mayor of John Peter Altgeld, though Altgeld never knew the source, according to Waldo Ralph Browne, an Altgeld biographer.

George Cole suffered for his efforts. In his interviews and research for *Shame of the Cities,* Lincoln Steffens found that all but one of the great Chicago business leaders opposed the Municipal Voters' League. They found "government by purchase" more certain and reliable. They took their business away from the "second-class businessman." To these and all opponents, Cole replied: "I have a wife and a boy. I want their respect. The rest can all go to hell."

Nor did the libel suits against Cole, many of them initiated by Yerkes, deter him, even though a single judgment could have ruined him.

George Cole continued battling corruption in government until the 1920s. After his success in cleaning up the city council, Cole took the reins of a new Legislative Voters' League. And once again, nearly all his executive team were Club members.

George applied the same hard-nosed publicity and campaign tactics as before to ridding the state legislature of many bad actors from Chicago. In their place he helped elect trial lawyer Clarence Darrow, wealthy patent lawyer Francis Parker, and Joseph Medill Patterson of the *Tribune* family, among others.

On another front, Cole abolished the wasteful sinecures known as Chicago's township governments. Cole had the goods, he said, on officials in Lake Township who were taking regular paychecks for no work. The job description for one fellow was simply "to watch things." He apparently didn't show up even to do that. George and his team worked hand in glove with state's attorney, later governor, Charles Deneen on prosecutions.

Cole was approached by Republican politician Fred M. Blount.

"Mr. Cole," Blount said, "I think I know you well enough to know that your main object is not to send a lot of cheapskates to [the state prison at] Joliet. Now, what are you after?" Blount, you see, had friends higher up who would be embarrassed by any prosecution of the ghost payrollers.

"Frankly," said Cole, "my main object is to wipe out township governments, and I propose to keep this fight up as long as I have any ammunition to fight with—or until you people in Springfield grant our petition and do away with township governments."

"I tell you what I'll do. If you agree not to try these cases, I will promise to see that your bill is passed during this session of the legislature." Cole promised to do what he could to see that this man's friends were not tried before the end of the legislative session. The bill passed and the men were never tried.

Did the Union League Club—as a club—drive Yerkes out of the city and many corrupt councilmen out of office? No. That would have torn the Club apart. Did the spirit of the Club's original patriotic and civic reason for being, which brought many men into membership, help propel George Cole, Bill Kent, Victor Lawson, Walter Fisher, and their Club colleagues to their successful reform efforts? Absolutely.

SOURCES

Historian Sidney I. Roberts is the best student of Chicago businessmen in reform politics and I acknowledge a heavy debt to him for contributions to this chapter. See his "Businessmen in Revolt: Chicago 1874–1900" (Ph.D. dissertation, Northwestern University, 1960), "The Municipal Voters' League and Chicago's Boodlers" (*Journal of the Illinois State Historical Society,* Summer 1960), and "Portrait of a Robber Baron: Charles T. Yerkes" (*Business History Review,* Autumn 1961).

Insull, the biography of Samuel Insull by Forrest McDonald (Chicago: University of Chicago Press, 1962), provides a solid academic history of the Yerkes legislation.

Also of great value: Hoyt King, *Citizen Cole of Chicago* (Chicago: Horder's, 1931); King was a reform colleague and confidant of Cole. J. Frank Aldrich, "Reminiscences" (a *Union League Club Bulletin* that ran monthly throughout 1926).

Other sources drawn upon include Andrews' *Battle for Chicago,* Dedmon's *Fabulous Chicago,* Ginger's *Altgeld's America,* Howard's *Mostly Good and Competent Men,* and:

Barnard, Harry. *Eagle Forgotten.* Secaucus, N.J.: Lyle Stuart, Inc., 1973.
Browne, Waldo Ralph. *Altgeld of Illinois.* New York: B. W. Huebsch, Inc., 1924.
Duis, Perry. "Whose City? Part Two." *Chicago History,* Summer 1983.
Harrison, Carter H. *Stormy Years.* Indianapolis: Bobbs-Merrill, 1935.
Miller, Joan S. "The Politics of Municipal Reform in Chicago during the Progressive Era." M.A. thesis, Roosevelt University, Chicago, 1966.
Schneirov, Richard. *Labor and Urban Politics.* Urbana: University of Illinois Press, 1998.

Simpson, Dick. *Rogues, Rebels, and Rubber Stamps*. Boulder, Colo.: Westview Press, 2001.

Steffens, Lincoln. *Shame of the Cities*. New York: Hill & Wang, 1904.

———. *The Autobiography of Lincoln Steffens*. New York: Harcourt, Brace & Co., 1931.

Tarr, Joel Arthur. "William Kent to Lincoln Steffens." *Mid-America*, January 1965.

———. *A Study in Boss Politics*. Urbana: University of Illinois Press, 1971.

Chapter 6

"THE WEST END OF THE NEXT WORLD"

Inebriated with the dizzying growth of the city and its seemingly unbounded wealth, the leading men of Chicago in the late 1880s believed they could do anything. Chicago doubled in population in the decade, crossing the million mark by 1890. The city had become the second largest manufacturing and the largest trading center in the nation. The buildings, reaching ten and more stories, were the tallest in the world. Club member Charles N. Fay enticed conductor Theodore Thomas to Chicago to start a symphony, describing the city on the lake as "the west end of the next world." (Four of the five incorporators of Fay's Orchestral Association and thirty-two of its fifty-one guarantors were members of the Club. But they were also members of other clubs, primarily the Chicago Club. Coincidentally, the Club was subscriber number 78 to the Chicago Telephone Company, where Fay was the general manager. The Club's phone number was thus 78, which eventually became HArrison 78, and at present 427-7800 [HA7-7800].)

Travelers tumbled from six major railroad stations into the melee of the central business district. Two hundred fifty trains brought thirty thousand passengers daily into the Union Station alone. Steamers and schooners crossed the Great Lakes with passengers and freight, tying up at wharves in the Chicago River. Canal boats from the Illinois-Michigan Canal arrived at Bridgeport, southwest of the central city.

In 1886, the Illinois Central Railroad attempted to build a pier to carry its trains from Fourteenth Street into the lake. John Wentworth would have none of it. He led a mass meeting to assert Chicago's right to control the lakefront over the national government's approval of the project. "I hold," declared John, "it is the duty of the mayor [no longer Wentworth] to arrest these works!" The railroad gave up its efforts.

Visitors had their choice of several fine, even opulent hostelries. Potter Palmer's Palmer House, rebuilt immediately after the 1871 Fire, had seven hundred rooms, refectory (dining hall), greenhouse, a barber shop floor inlaid with silver dollars, an elaborate billiard room, and a popular mirrored bar. More comfortable to local leaders was the Grand Pacific operated by John Drake. Drake made everyone feel at home and his annual game dinners were famous the world around. He served tongue of buffalo, loin of bear—either brown, black, or cinnamon, *au choix*—antelope steaks, roast beaver, prairie chicken, grouse, anything that roamed the continent.

By 1887, Marshall Field had become the best known among many prospering dry goods merchants. Beyond the store, Field was the leading wholesaler to stores in cities, villages, mining communities, even Indian trading posts, throughout the Midwest, South, and West. Because of the fame of his name, upon arrival in the city, travelers headed first to his store. Marshall had omnibuses at the train stations ready to negotiate his customers through the crowded streets to his emporium, where he had arranged a separate department of goods on each floor.

On their way from the train stations, visitors gawked upward at the ten-to-twelve-story "skyscrapers" that filled the central city. Of particular interest was the Home Insurance Building designed by William LeBaron Jenney and completed in 1885, the first structure with an iron skeleton to help support the weight of the building. Many of the new and exciting buildings in the city were being designed by Club members: John Wellborn Root, Dankmar Adler, Louis Sullivan, Daniel Burnham, William Holabird, and William Mundie.

Ferd Peck and Harlow Higinbotham were, like Aldrich, part of the warp and woof of both the Club and the city. Peck was a charter member in 1880 at age thirty-two, climbed the chairs to become president in 1893, and lived in the clubhouse in his later years. Higinbotham was first vice president of the Club in 1887 and a staunch supporter of the Club's civic progressivism. The press of business at Marshall Field and Company, where Higinbotham was one of Field's partners, owning 10 percent of the stock, probably caused him to demur on taking the presidency the following year.

Ferd Peck's family arrived in Chicago in 1833. As a boy, Peck often walked from the family home at the corner of Clark and Jackson, now in the heart of the Loop, through the sand to the beach at Lake Michigan to go swimming. Fortunately for Peck and his brothers, their father amassed a great deal of land near their house.

Peck had a deep sense of noblesse oblige and devoted all his energies to the cultural development of the city. He was tall, slender, and restless, brimming with nervous energy. He loved the geniality of fine dining, drinks, and parties, and enjoyed entertaining his large troop of friends on one of his two yachts at his summer residence at Lake Oconomowoc, Wisconsin. In Chicago, the yachtsman was called "Commodore" and favored a white silk top hat.

Ferd Peck didn't have a mean bone in his body and had a soft spot in his heart for the workingman. Educated in the law in Chicago, Peck expanded his horizons by sailing to Europe frequently, where he absorbed grand opera in Italy, Paris, Bayreuth.

Peck returned with visions of bringing opera to his unsophisticated city. In 1884, he organized and led the Chicago Grand Opera Festival Association; nine of his eleven directors were members of the Club. He engaged Club associates Dankmar Adler and Louis Sullivan to enclose the north end of the cavernous Interstate Exposition Building as an auditorium. Two weeks of grand opera were staged with more than eight thousand persons attending each performance, good seats priced as low as one dollar. Peck achieved his objective of making opera available not just to the wealthy but also to those of more modest means.

Son of a rabbi and cantor, Dankmar Adler came to Chicago in 1861, served in the light artillery during the Civil War, returned to continue his studies and then work in architecture. For the opera festival, Adler built a massive sounding board that arched outward from the stage. This device ensured that the softest voices would carry to the rear of the house, so spectators in the most remote seats could hear as well as those in the front.

Still, Peck wanted a grand and permanent home for opera, symphony, plays, and lectures to be enjoyed by all the city's residents. At the conclusion of the first season of opera in the makeshift auditorium, Peck told the appreciative audience that he "hoped people would look upon this as a stepping-stone to a great permanent hall where similar enterprises would have a home." He observed that magnificent music at prices within the reach of all would have a tendency to diminish crime and socialism in the city by educating the masses to higher things.

Peck's honest convictions about the role of culture in lifting the masses played well to the city's capitalists. In May 1886, just weeks after the tragic riots at the Haymarket, he outlined his vision for a permanent Auditorium Building to the Commercial Club as well as to Club members.

By July of that year, Peck created the Chicago Grand Auditorium Association. He pledged $100,000, Marshall Field added $30,000, and soon 150 investors, most of whom were members of the Chicago, Commercial, and Union League clubs, had increased the capital stock to $1.5 million.

There were to be no box seats for investors because Peck thought such distinctions symbolized the differences in social classes that were already too sharply etched in Chicago. Ultimately, Peck had to relent to his fellow investors on this point, but only 40 boxes were allotted versus 250 at the Metropolitan Opera House of New York. And Peck took great pleasure in a more than symbolic victory by noting: "We are democratic in America, and the masses demand the best seats. The boxes, you see, are on the sides and do not furnish the best possible view."

Now began the great collaboration among the entrepreneur and visionary Peck and the pathbreaking genius of the team of Dankmar Adler, forty-two at the time, and his young associate Louis Sullivan, thirty. Peck and Adler traveled together to Europe to tour the great opera houses and theaters.

Peck kept insisting that their new building not be erected solely for the people who are able to pay extravagant prices for amusement but for the masses as well, that they may enjoy the higher order of entertainments at a price within their means. This was fine with the liberally inclined Adler. Sullivan was simply delighted to have a great commission by which he could apply his decorative and ornamental talents to the interior. His older partner focused on the challenge of creating exquisite acoustics, which would reach equally all four-thousand-plus seats in the huge hall, eight thousand when the stage was opened for conventions.

Peck sold the project to investors as a business investment. This would be not only the largest opera hall in the world, he declared, but also an equally grand commercial venture. And it was. Peck included 4 stores, 136 offices, and a 400-room hotel in the Auditorium Building. The hotel was so oversubscribed that the Congress Hotel, across Congress Street to the south, was added a few years later with an underground passageway to connect the guests.

Peck was on the site every day during construction, always in his dark suits and white silk hat. At the end of the day, he and the architects would likely retreat to their club four blocks away to regale those in the bar with a blow-by-blow description of the day's progress.

When the bricklayers went on a protracted strike in 1887, Peck and Adler sympathized, but only briefly. The architect was concerned about four other major commissions also brought to a halt and nine on the drawing boards. They circumvented the strikers by using stone on much of the facade that was originally to be of brick and continued the work with strikebreakers.

The Auditorium Theatre became a building in a class by itself. The legendary acoustics created by Adler still astound those who tour the building. Today, a tour guide whispers from one side of the cavernous balcony. The sound slides along the curved ceiling and reaches the hearer at the other side, a seeming football field away, undiminished. Incredible.

The acoustics were not luck. Adler did eleven theaters; all had great sound. Only one other remains; in Carnegie Hall there is a plate: ACOUSTICS BY DANKMAR ADLER.

In addition, the Auditorium was the first to be fully lighted by electricity and it had air conditioning, which Adler had tried earlier at the McVicker's Theater in Chicago.

The dedication of the Auditorium was a major event. President and Mrs. Benjamin Harrison, Vice President Levi P. Morton, and officials from throughout the nation and world came to dedicate Ferd Peck's cultural palace. Peck hosted the president and his entourage for luncheon and a reception beforehand, at the Club, naturally. The menu: blue points, schloss Vollrader, crème de terrapin, sherry solero, fillet of white fish, Roman punch—which carried a real punch—chicken wings, champagne, larded quail, Château Pichon, cheese and crackers, fruit, cake, and coffee.

President Harrison had been criticized back East for coming out to help dedicate, of all things, a commercial enterprise. The president remarked the critics had never seen the city's great buildings. He let that simple comment speak volumes. Chicagoans applauded heartily.

According to Emmett Dedmon, the big public debate leading up to the dedication was not about the construction of the building but the construction of the finery the leading ladies of the city would wear that evening. Only the most formal wear would be appropriate, of course, and to many ladies this meant the décolleté gown, which was still considered daring in Chicago, not fit, said many, for public display.

Ever eager to pounce on a story of real significance, the *Tribune* surveyed the social arbiters of taste in the city. Mrs. William B. Howard expressed the opinion of most ladies of fashion: "The luster of the evening is undoubtedly increased by the appearance of women in low-necked dresses." Mrs. Marshall Field was more circumspect, saying she never wore a low-necked gown, believing a slender woman's appearance is vastly improved by the Bernhardt style of dress (named after the French actress Sarah Bernhardt).

"Of course," she continued to the enterprising reporter, "it is all right for women who have handsome necklaces to cut the dress low enough to display them." Mrs. Field added quickly that she never wore jewelry of that kind.

Several critics declared low-cut gowns a health hazard, as wearers increased their chances of catching cold from the exposure. They were rebutted, of course, by testimonials from ladies who had worn low-cut bodices for years—without the hint of a cold resulting.

A crowd of twenty thousand gathered outside the Auditorium for the grand opening to catch sight of, among other things—how should we say it—grand displays of necklaces. Club member Wirt Dexter called the gathering of onlookers "a well-dressed mob, and with wit enough to become exasperating." The gawkers called out pointed comments to the city's finest as they descended from their hansom cabs. A noisy but not unfriendly crowd, Dexter thought, like the city itself.

The evening was a smashing success. After a long evening of tributes—especially to Peck, Adler, and Sullivan—the Apollo Chorus, augmented to eight hundred voices, graced those gathered, fittingly, with the "Hallelujah Chorus" from Handel's *Messiah*.

Harlow Niles Higinbotham lived much of his life in the shadow of his senior partner, Marshall Field. Except, that is, when the city needed him. Then he stepped forward to make signal contributions to the greatness of the city that neither Field nor all his money could ever have accomplished. Higinbotham represented the best of what the Club aspired to—entrepreneurial spirit, civic duty, and the sharing of successes with the city.

Higinbotham grew up near Joliet before the Civil War. Tall, rawboned, and always kindly, he became as solid of character as the boulders that stood guard on the Illinois River near his father's sawmill. Years later, after he had become respected the world around, Higinbotham did some reminiscing in a talk at the Club. His observations spoke indirectly about the shaping of Midwestern character in his generation:

> Our fathers were pioneers on the prairies of Illinois. There we early learned the lessons of Nature, and recognized and loved the message that the recurring seasons had for us. The flowers of the field and the forest were our companions, and we knew when and where to look for them; we knew the habit and habitat of each, and they were an open book to us.
>
> We knew the birds, and were not long in discovering that by their flight and their notes we could tell the season, and almost the hour of the day. When we heard in the field the love-note of the pinnated grouse, or in the woods heard the drumming of his ruffed cousin on the logs, we knew that it was time to plough and plant.
>
> An approaching storm was announced with certainty by the coming of the quail from his seclusion in the thicket to a position where he could make his message heard. The crowing of the cricket, and the call of the katydid, each had a meaning and message that we understood. These constituted the catechism from which we learned to believe in deity, and the larger and diviner life for man.

After the War, Higinbotham came to Chicago to use his bookkeeping skills in the office of the merchants Field and Leiter. During the Fire of 1871, he organized men and horses to carry goods out of one end of their store while the other side was an inferno. The day after the fire, Higinbotham convinced the distraught Leiter that they must reopen immediately. Higinbotham went east that same week to collect on claims from shaky insurers and to reorganize the flow of goods from the East to their wholesale and retail company.

Even though the company lost two million dollars in goods to the conflagration, the company turned a profit of three hundred thousand dollars that same year. Recognizing a sharp man, Field and Leiter made young Higinbotham a partner. They entrusted him with the responsibilities for finance and the extension of credit to customers around the country, credit being the lifeblood of the merchant customers of this burgeoning wholesaler.

New York merchants, wanting to break into the lucrative western market, offered to double the salary of this "credit genius" Higinbotham, as he came to be known in business circles. He would simply smile and shake his head. When Field bought out Leiter, Higinbotham received a 10 percent partner's share in the new business, as did several other key longtime associates, with Field retaining 46 percent. The shares made fortunes for all of them.

The World's Columbian Exposition of 1893 was, to the minds of many objective observers, the greatest world's fair ever. And it was largely a Club affair.

Ten years before the fair, Chicago leaders talked about becoming the host city to celebrate the four hundredth anniversary of Columbus' arrival in the New World. It wasn't, however, until a series of meetings in 1889 at the Club that the idea fired the members' imaginations. A citizens' committee was established by Mayor DeWitt C. Cregier; it set up offices in the Club.

Congress was to award one city the honor. St. Louis, Washington, and Minneapolis were among the applicants, but most assumed New York would be chosen.

Furious buttonholing of congressmen in the corridors of the nation's Capitol by teams of Chicago leaders secured the prize for Chicago. Smitten New Yorkers derided the decision, calling it a certain embarrassment, and disaster, at best. Fortunately, Chicago had just produced the magnificent Auditorium Building, which reassured members of Congress that important works could be created in this rough midwestern city.

Even the city's own confident leadership became a bit daunted, however, by the magnitude of the challenge of mounting an exposition to rival that held in oh-so-sophisticated Paris—the center of the world—a few years earlier.

Architect and Club member John Wellborn Root was given the task of designing a plan for the fair. When he died unexpectedly in 1891, Root's partner Daniel Burnham, another Club member, took over and displayed marvelous administrative and creative skills. He brought in other architects from the Club, plus the best from the East.

The task: transform a square mile of swamp at Jackson Park on the city's far south side into an otherworldly exposition for the latest technologies and the best of culture from forty-six nations and every state in the nation. And accommodate more than twenty million visitors over a six-month period.

By August 1892, it looked as if the grand project would fail. Soaring costs, delays, squabbles, and the Herculean task that had forty thousand workers on the site took their toll. Lyman Gage had resigned earlier as president of the fair board. His successor William Baker resigned after a short time. Despondency reigned.

The fair board turned to Harlow Higinbotham, who had been on the directorate throughout. Marshall Field directed Harlow not to take the job. Field felt failure with Harlow at the helm would embarrass their own company. Harlow went through the numbers closely, determined he could see the fair through to completion and even pay the investors a dividend. He ran the numbers by Field who, persuaded by hardheaded business talk, finally consented.

For more than two years Higinbotham spent twelve to sixteen hours a day leading the fair. Ferd Peck was his first vice president and chair of the finance committee. One of their first chores was a meeting at the Club to sell an additional five million dollars in bonds to offset reduced and niggardly support from the federal government, which nevertheless meddled via a national exposition commission.

Frank Aldrich was director of public works for Chicago throughout this period. He observed all close-up and declared friend Higinbotham magnificent. Higinbotham displayed diplomacy in keeping the national commissioners reassured and at bay. He became a good friend and colleague to the scores of architects, each demanding this or that for his particular commission on the grounds. Of course, his closeness with Burnham and all the local architects from the Club helped and gave him standing with their visiting associates.

Most important, Higinbotham clamped down on expenses. Contractors saw the fair as a soft touch for exorbitant profits. They got a rude awakening when Higinbotham took over. Local electric companies had, for example, colluded to present bids averaging $18 per incandescent lamp for the six months of the fair. But by playing other companies against the locals, Higinbotham gradually reduced the bid to $5.95 per lamp and finally gave the contract to another company at a still lower figure. Ferd Peck reported later that the entire sum paid for electric lighting was $399,000, as against $1,675,720 originally demanded. Such savings, multiplied by other examples, provided the difference between collapse and financial success.

The financial problems, though, paled beside those prompted by the self-inflated egos of fair functionaries. The Chicago poet Harriet Monroe, who created the respected journal *Poetry*, gained immense respect for Higinbotham because of a fray he resolved in her favor. Her poem "Columbian Ode" had been unanimously requested of her by the committee on ceremonies and accepted by the committee for the dedication of buildings. But a small group in the latter committee suddenly ceased to favor the poem and set up a concerted effort to have it taken out of the dedication ceremonies. The committee became hopelessly and bitterly deadlocked, so the matter was referred to the council of administration for settlement, which Higinbotham also chaired.

Monroe was called to present her side of the question. She recalled this session:

> I had never met Mr. Higinbotham. He appeared a simple, quiet man in the prime of life, of slight figure, finely shaped head, regular features rather delicate in contour, and dark wavy hair and beard streaked with a few threads of gray. Near him were two other members of the Council of Administration.
>
> I was struck be how simply and easily a wide range of complicated details were disposed of—details of a roofing contract, the power plants, the sewerage system; applications from would be concessionaires, plans for transporting and seating the vast throng of over a hundred thousand persons invited to the Dedication Ceremonies, all under the vaulted roof of the Manufacturers' Building.
>
> And one of these details in dispute was my poem! The opponents spoke first. They were satisfied neither with the poet, who should have been of distinction like the aged Whittier, nor the poem, which was too long and devoted many lines for a tribute to a deceased relative of the poet, a tribute I declined to omit.
>
> I met those objections as best I could. The brief tribute in question was to the fair's first architect and to his memory on the great day of dedication. Mr. Higinbotham asked me to read the questioned tribute, following which he said that a poem for this dedication which did not refer to John Root would be gravely defective. He decreed that as much of the poem be read as there was time for in the program.
>
> From that day I observed Mr. Higinbotham at every opportunity. He carried himself with simple dignity of bearing and speech, in contrast to the bombast and self-congratulation so popular in that day.

Aldrich saw Higinbotham months later, however, when even his positive demeanor was tried mightily. The financial panic of 1893 broke out in May, almost immediately after the fair opened. The Chemical National Bank had a branch on the fairgrounds and held the deposits of many fair exhibitors from other nations. The bank failed. Higinbotham, George Pullman, Martin Ryerson, and others had to guarantee depositors against losses, which forced them to dip into their own pockets.

To stanch runs on banks in the city center, Higinbotham and other prominent leaders stood in lines with panicked depositors to put money in, not take it out. Aldrich recalled Higinbotham patiently standing in a queue holding the baby of the lady in front of him while she fumbled in her purse. All the while he had to be frantic about the impact of the panic upon the fair's receipts.

When Aldrich next saw Higinbotham in July 1893 his face was white, drawn, stern. The toll was showing on even this rock of a man. Attendance had been light during the first three months of the fair. But then in August the crowds started pouring in. Higinbotham relaxed a bit.

And pour in they should. This wasn't just the White City, as it was called for the alabaster walls of its awesome buildings. No, it was another, magical world. Chicagoan Frank Baum clearly based the Emerald City in *The Wizard of Oz* on his memory of the fair.

There were great fairs before and after the Chicago fair of 1893. But, according to Bolotin and Laing, "when it comes to pure scope, grandeur, and far-reaching legacies, the World's Columbian Exposition of 1893 outshines them all. Twenty-seven million visitors. Buildings that each stretched a third of a mile." The first amusement section at a fair. Replicas of a full-size battleship and Columbus' three caravels on their own special lake.

Towering above the grounds was George Ferris' wheel, which lifted thirty-six streetcar-size carriages, each holding forty people, 264 feet into the air. Seventeen major buildings provided covered floor space of two hundred acres. The building exteriors were of staff on lath. Staff is a mixture of plaster, cement, and fiber. It will last for several years but is not permanent.

The only building left from the fair is the Fine Arts Building, which had been made permanent with a stone exterior and served as the Museum of Science and Industry, just in time for the Century of Progress World's Fair in 1933. This building was one of the smaller edifices at the fair, its 184,000 square feet dwarfed by the 1-million-plus square feet of the Manufacturers Building, which its boosters claimed could seat three hundred thousand people, though that number was never tested.

Beauty and grace dominated all. Most buildings were in the classical beaux-arts tradition of order and proportion—just what civic leaders were striving to create in Chicago itself. The grounds were graced by broad promenades lined by lagoons, canals, and by the colonnades of the major structures.

Never before had so many experts congregated at a single location. Six thousand addresses were presented to seven hundred thousand people as part of the World's Congress Auxiliary. The World's First Parliament of Religions was held at the fair. Higinbotham declared this gathering the proudest work of the exposition. Another Club member, (Reform) Rabbi Emil Hirsch, chaired the opening session. Such harmony and understanding reigned that many participants, giddy with good will, declared the millennium at hand.

Under Mrs. Potter Palmer's irrepressible leadership, a Women's Building foreshadowed the accomplishments and potential of women in the century to follow. The first U.S. coin bearing a portrait of a woman was minted for the fair. The Isabella quarter, issued to mark the aid given by the queen of Spain to Columbus, remains the only commemorative coin ever struck by the United States. Dvorak's *New World Symphony* was written for the fair. What a fair. One reporter declared the fair to be the greatest event in American history since the Civil War!

This was a true world's fair but it was also Chicago's fair. Visitors were as fascinated by the skyscrapers as by the sights at the White City. The Club was the social hub for the fair's luminaries, for Ferd Peck was not only a major officer of the exposition, he was also president of the Club in 1893. Higinbotham was in and out every day, hosting one after another group of visitors. Several members of the U.S. commission on the fair made the Club their home for the duration.

All summer of 1893 the champagne flowed at the Club. One member created "champagne ice," which became the rage. To make this "drink," plug a watermelon, scoop out the center, pour in bottles of the bubbly, re-plug it and let it stand in the icebox.

And when it was all over, the fair was a financial as well as critical success. Critics derided the "Barnumization" of the fair.

It was commercial, more so than the Paris exposition of 1889. But this was a fair for everyone and everyone's pocketbook. The carnival Midway was a great success and innovation with its belly dancers and hucksters. Now that more Americans were traveling across our marvelous land, the exposition trinkets and mementos they purchased became both minor heirlooms in family attics and the difference between profit and loss for the fair.

And Higinbotham was determined to turn a profit. Twenty-seven million people went through the gates and nearly all of them paid. Expenses were thirty million dollars and receipts from all sources thirty-three million dollars. Stockholders were amazed and relieved to receive their principal, plus a ten-cent dividend on each share of stock issued.

In 1897, President William McKinley offered Higinbotham the ambassadorship to France, wanting a man with his skills at diplomacy for that challenging post. Higinbotham said, no, thanks, I have much I want to do here at home.

The following year he became president of the Field Museum of Natural History, which housed collections of scientific interest that had been brought to the fair. But what Higinbotham probably had in mind with his "no, thanks" was his devotion to the Chicago Home for the Incurables, which he helped establish in the early 1880s. From the day of his retirement from Field's in 1902, Higinbotham visited the home daily and remained devoted to its inmates until his untimely death in a freak accident in New York City in 1919.

The stories in the Club about Higinbotham's kindliness were legion. One recounted that he traveled to Atlanta, Georgia, to intercede with the governor to spare the life of Leo Frank, whose conviction he felt unjust. His efforts, and that of others, were successful, though Frank was lynched later.

Another member told of accompanying Higinbotham to the Cook County hospital to visit a poor woman who had been transferred there from the home for incurables. "Is this really Mr. Higinbotham?" she asked. Bursting into tears, she drew from beneath her pillow his picture, cut from a newspaper, which she had carried for many years.

In contrast, Ferd Peck's later years were the stuff of tragicomedy, at least so far as Peck and the Club are concerned. Peck was living at the Club in 1919 when Prohibition arrived. He always hated to live by the rules, especially one that attempted to curtail his enjoyment of spirits in the company of friends. Peck continued, of course, to invite his friends to the Club and to his room for drinks. A couple of years into Prohibition, a new Club president and his board of directors decided to enforce the constitutional prohibition seriously. They even went through members' private lockers, emptying them of liquor bottles, which caused no little consternation among members.

Peck was outraged by the new Club policy. One day in the fall of 1922, he brought all his liquor bottles down to the lobby and lined them up on the floor. He then invited everyone who entered the Club to join him for a drink. According to George Haight, on another occasion Peck invited a women's band, which had stopped in front of the Club during a parade, into the women's lounge for drinks. This was all too much for the board of managers, who expelled this giant of American cultural development and former Club president.

He moved to the Chicago Athletic Association, where he lived until his death two years later. To celebrate the opening of the new clubhouse in 1926, the Club produced a history of its first fifty years. At the bottom of each page, on the left side in muted green ink, is a line drawing of one of the larger-than-life Club leaders such as John Wentworth, Joseph Medill, and Harlow Higinbotham. Ferdinand Wythe Peck is among that pantheon so memorialized. Fitting.

SOURCES

Writing about the Chicago World's Fair of 1893 appears to be a cottage industry. Among books I drew upon extensively are Stanley Applebaum, *The Chicago World's Fair of 1893;* Norman Bolotin and Christine Laing, *The World's Columbian Exposition;* C. Dean, *The World's Fair City,* and Reid Badger, *The Great American Fair.*

The Auditorium Building has been analyzed in exquisite detail by Joseph M. Siry, "Chicago's Auditorium Building" (*Journal of the Society of Architectural Historians* 57:2 , June 1998). Helen Horowitz in *Culture and the City* also provides valuable context for the development of this building.

Emmett Dedmon, *Fabulous Chicago;* Ray Ginger, *Altgeld's America;* Robert Howard, *Illinois;* and Bessie Louise Pierce, *History of Chicago,* vol. 3, all provide rich observations about Chicago in the 1880s and 1890s.

Harriet Monroe edited a partial autobiography of Harlow Niles Higinbotham and added her appreciative comments about his life: *Harlow Niles Higinbotham.*

The author's tour of the Auditorium Theatre was led by Bart Swindall, then tour coordinator and archivist for the Auditorium, in the fall of 2001.

Other sources drawn upon include:

Berger, Miles L. *They Built Chicago.* Chicago: Bonus Books, 1992.
Field Museum News. Fiftieth Anniversary Number, 14:9–10, September 1943.
Higinbotham, Harlow. "Letters". In Caroline McIlvaine Papers, Newberry Library, Chicago.
Hirsch, David Einhorn. *Rabbi Emil G. Hirsch.* Chicago: Whitehall, 1968.
Hirsch, Emil. "Dankmar Adler." Eulogy at Temple K.A.M., Chicago, April 13, 1900. In Dankmar Adler Papers, Newberry Library, Chicago.
Saltzstein, Joan W. "Dankmar Adler, the Man, the Architect, the Author." *Wisconsin Architect,* July-August 1967.
Wendt, Lloyd, and Herman Kogan. *Give the Lady What She Wants!* Chicago: Rand McNally & Co., 1952.

And the unpublished histories of the Union League Club of Chicago by George Bushnell, George Haight, and Roger Henn, all located in the ULCC archives.

Chapter 7

THE BUYING OF A U.S. SENATE SEAT—AS REVEALED AT THE UNION LEAGUE CLUB

The Club almost tore itself apart over the prominent roles the Club and its leading members played in the expulsion of William E. Lorimer from the U.S. Senate in 1912. The scandal behind the expulsion provided renewed momentum for the adoption a year later of the Seventeenth Amendment to the Constitution and the popular election of senators.

The downfall of Chicago Republican boss William Lorimer started in the first clubhouse in a conversation between members Edward G. Hines, the lumberman and president of the National Lumberman's Association at the time, and Clarence Funk, general manager of the McCormick International Harvester Company.

First, a little background.

Many in the Club detested Lorimer. He liked to be known as the "Blond Boss" of Chicago. In the 1880s, Lorimer wrested control of the city's Republican Party from Joseph Medill and Herman Kohlsaat, both members of the Club, respectively the publishers of the *Tribune* and the *Record-Herald,* the staunchest of Republican newspapers.

Lorimer was a classic boodler and he and his lieutenants made deals to gain the support of Catholics and immigrant groups. To the civic-minded who wanted order, efficiency, and honest government, Billy Lorimer represented Tammany-style politics at its worst. And he called himself a Republican! As Chicago lawyer, poet, and observer Edgar Lee Masters put it, "Lorimer did not belong to the best set." He did, however, get into the Hamilton Club, the other major Republican club in town. It must be said that Lorimer didn't have any bad habits, was soft spoken, and resembled a kindly, plump Sunday school superintendent.

As a member of the U.S. House, to his credit, he worked hard for a deep waterway link between the Great Lakes and the Gulf of Mexico. Members of the Club agreed this was needed economic development for the great transportation hub being built in Chicago.

In 1909 the Illinois legislature was to elect a U.S. senator. Albert Hopkins, the Republican incumbent, had been put in the Senate six years earlier by Lorimer. In the interim, however, Hopkins double-crossed Lorimer by supporting reformer Charles Deneen for reelection as governor. Lorimer was no fan of reformers. Hopkins had won the nonbinding preferential primary over U.S. Representative George Foss, a Club member who had the support of Republican newspapers.

From January to late May, the legislature was deadlocked. Deneen, who had been narrowly reelected, pushed for Hopkins, but an odd combination of Lorimerites and progressives refused to support him. The Democrats stayed on the sideline, enjoying the intraparty fracas among the Republicans, who had majorities in both chambers.

After ninety ballots and no senator, the Legislature became exhausted and grouchy. Lawmakers began voting for newspaper reporters, people in the galleries, clerks, and pages.

Lorimer proposed his enemy Governor Deneen for senator. With Deneen out of the state, Lorimer would be in charge. Deneen owed much of his political success to the major Chicago newspapers—the *Tribune,* then being run by Joe Medill's grandson, Joseph Medill McCormick; Victor Lawson and his powerful *Daily News,* the biggest paper in the city, and Kohlsaat's paper. Word in the Clubhouse was that they had told Deneen not even to think about going for the Senate. And he didn't.

Lorimer began to think he could put together the votes for himself, even over the strident opposition of the reformers in his party, but he would need lots of Democrat votes to do it.

In Washington, President William Howard Taft and high-tariff Republican senators such as Nelson Aldrich of Rhode Island, who ran the Senate, and Boies Penrose of Pennsylvania were anxious to see either Hopkins, a high-tariff man, or a like-minded replacement elected.

In April, Aldrich had introduced a tariff bill that contained hundreds of upward revisions in rates; this had set off a furious struggle between low-tariff Republican Progressive reformers and the Old Guard.

Ed Hines of Chicago was also out in Washington. A successful lumberman at home, Hines was the top lobbyist in Washington for the national association he headed. Hines wanted higher rates on imported wood, especially that from Canada. Hines liked Lorimer and knew he was a high-tariff man.

Hines loved being a player, rubbing shoulders with senators and presidents, making things happen. Whether Hines convinced Aldrich and Penrose of the importance of getting behind Lorimer isn't known, but in May Hines started sending telegrams to Lorimer intimating support for his candidacy from President Taft and the two senators. "Highest authorities want you elected before legislature adjourns," read one of the telegrams from Hines that Lorimer showed around Springfield.

On the ninety-fifth ballot, Lorimer allowed his name to be placed in nomination for the first time and was elected with 55 Republican and 53 Democratic votes. He needed 102 for election. The pieces had been put together neatly by Lorimer, who had worked the lawmakers hard in preceding days—and by his friends.

Keep two things in mind: Votes were for sale in the Illinois legislature. Second, the leading Chicago newspapers were partisan advocates whose reporters often doubled as lobbyists to push their papers' causes.

At the time of Lorimer's election, the Springfield saloons frequented by legislators were abuzz with rumors of a huge "jackpot" being put together for the end of the spring session of 1909. These end-of-session collections of money were common knowledge around the bar at the Club and elsewhere that businessmen gathered. The jackpots had been put together for many legislative sessions reportedly by major interests such as Pullman, the meat packers, grain elevators, railroads, liquor, and others.

The legislative leaders apparently divided the jackpot among members who had supported the interests with their votes and actions. Since this was thought to be the way business was done, there was understandable speculation that votes had been bought to ensure Lorimer's election. But no reporter could pin down the vote buying.

The newspapers also competed ferociously for readers. Some papers used lurid headlines—not the *Tribune* or the *Daily News*—to attract readers. JERKED TO JESUS, proclaimed one paper a few years earlier on the public hanging of four woeful miscreants.

The papers would also pay big money for sensational stories as rewards or bounties for information the paper couldn't extract otherwise.

A year after Lorimer's election, for example, the *Tribune* paid $3,250 for the revelations of Democratic state representative Charles White, who confessed in print that he had been paid $1,000 to vote for William Lorimer for the Senate. The story took up the first two pages of the Sunday *Tribune* and continued for days. Papers all over the country started covering the juicy story. From that day, the Lorimer scandal became a big story in American politics, which ran for two years.

White told of how Democratic House leader Lee O'Neil Browne and his Chicago lieutenant, representative Robert "Bathroom Bob" Wilson, doled out $1,000 to White and others for a vote for Lorimer, with the promise of $1,000 more in the end-of-session "jackpot." Bathroom Bob was famous, one might say, for passing out boodle to fellow members from the bathroom of his hotel room.

Two thousand dollars was a lot of money in 1909. A new Model T, which Henry Ford brought out the year before, cost $805.

Before the investigations were over, eleven legislators admitted receiving money for their votes for Lorimer but since they claimed they would have voted for Lorimer anyway—after not having done so for ninety-four ballots!—the bribe takers were not prosecuted. Democratic leader Browne was tried twice before friendly hometown juries and acquitted.

Tribune editor James Keeley wrote petitions demanding that the Senate investigate Lorimer and had them submitted by prominent civic groups. With the nation's press screaming for action, the Senate reluctantly took a halfhearted look into the charges.

In 1910, brazen corruption was not limited to Illinois and Chicago. The American public and reformist newspaper community had had enough of boodle and pelf and progressive, throw-the-crooks-out movements were in the ascendancy across the country. This also threatened the system of electing senators by state legislatures, a process the incumbent Old Guard was quite comfortable with. Only the Senate itself stood in the way of direct election by the voters. Time and again, the Senate beat back resolutions to amend the Constitution.

The Lorimer scandal was an embarrassment the Senate didn't need.

Since the Senate wouldn't provide any staff for its investigation, the *Tribune* paid for lawyers to present the case against Lorimer. The name Ed Hines kept popping up to the *Tribune's* investigators as the mastermind behind the election of his old friend and political associate. Hines was not, however, called before the Senate by the *Tribune* lawyers. It was rumored the *Tribune's* law firm feared some of its major clients might be implicated. By the time the Senate took a vote on Lorimer in March of 1911, there was a general sense that bribery had been committed but Lorimer could not be linked to it.

During the investigation, Hines had been tireless in his efforts for Lorimer's vindication. As Progressive senator Bob LaFollette of Wisconsin told a friend, Hines "waylaid senators at every turn, and was brazen and impudent in his work." Hines even offered to reduce his bitter opposition to trade reciprocity with Canada, a hot issue in the Senate, in return for votes to retain his friend.

The U.S. Senate voted 46 to 40 to retain Lorimer.

The *Tribune* and the national press were furious with the Senate action. The "evil Chicago newspaper trust," as Lorimer continually called the three Republican publishers, wasn't going to let the issue die.

Herman Kohlsaat, Club president in 1896, now felt he simply had to betray a confidence. Kohlsaat was also known as a man who couldn't keep his mouth shut.

Clarence Funk had told Kohlsaat of a conversation he had with Ed Hines at the Club bar in late May or early June of 1909 right after Lorimer's election. "Ed came up to me, told me how he had 'put Lorimer over in Springfield, but that it had cost him $100,000 to do it.'" Hines then said the share for McCormick company to replenish the fund was about ten thousand dollars.

Funk, a member of the board of the Chicago Theological Seminary, told Hines that he and his company didn't do business that way and let it drop. Naturally, Funk wanted the conversation kept in strictest confidence because if it ever came out, as he said later, it would just be one man's word against another's.

Kohlsaat promised to keep the confidence and then promptly told Victor Lawson, without divulging Funk's name. Lawson mentioned the hundred-thousand-dollar fund in an editorial and to senator Elihu Root of New York. Root asked that the person upon whom Hines imposed his solicitation testify.

Kohlsaat told Root that it would absolutely ruin his friend Funk to take the stand. After all, he was approached as an officer of his company and could not come out in the open without the consent of the directors, some of whom were friendly to Lorimer.

Well, it came out, a little later.

After the U.S. Senate failed to oust Lorimer, the Illinois Senate, controlled by reformer Deneen, began its own investigation into the bribery of state legislators in the Lorimer case. They were most interested in where the money came from to bribe the confessed bribe takers. Kohlsaat told the Funk-Hines conversation story to the state panel.

Kohlsaat didn't divulge Funk's name but the feisty state Senate panel declared it would hold Kohlsaat in contempt if he failed to do so. To save friend Kohlsaat from such a fate, Funk agreed to testify to his conversation.

Sensational stuff—two leading Chicago businessmen talking bribery inside one of the nation's elite business clubs. The newspapers loved it.

The *Tribune* had a field day with the Funk story, running editorials such as WHAT LUMBER CO. BUILT LORIMER'S SENATE CHAIR? and WAS IT SAWDUST? WHO FURNISHED THE DUST TO BRIBE THE LEGISLATORS TO ELECT WILLIAM LORIMER?

Hines denied the facts of the conversation, then fired back that it was Funk who had solicited him for money for Lorimer!

The Club went into an uproar. Funk was, like most Club members, among those who liked to think of themselves as *gentlemen.* Solid to the core, men of the highest principles. In contrast, Hines was loud and boastful and anything but a reformer—and a Catholic as well.

Hines was of the old school of politics, the school that the political action committee kept trying to root out.

The Club's good name was of course being linked to the scandal across the country and it was embarrassing.

In May of 1911, right after Funk and Hines testified in Springfield, the Club board of managers discussed the revelations by Funk, all of which is in the Club minutes. They directed the Club president, the lawyer William Sidley, to "communicate with Mr. Edward Hines and present certain facts relating to his eligibility for membership in the Union League Club, and give him an opportunity to take such action with reference to his resignation as he might see fit."

A week later, Sidley reported back that he had met with Hines, who "denied all charges made against him and declined to take advantage of the opportunity offered him to resign his membership in the Club."

This prompted a petition to the board signed by leading Club members such as Frank Loesch, Lessing Rosenthal, and others stating that the conduct of Edward Hines, disclosed by the state Senate investigation, was "hostile to the avowed objects and high purposes of this Club," urging the Club to take such actions as may be appropriate, meaning expulsion.

The petition restated verbatim the purposes of the Club as provided in the first three articles of the Club charter, which are worth noting:

> 1ST: To encourage and promote by moral, social and political influence, unconditioned loyalty to the Federal Government, and to defend and protect the integrity and perpetuity of this Nation.

> 2ND: To inculcate a higher appreciation of the value and sacred obligations of American citizenship; and to aid in the enforcement of all laws enacted to preserve the purity of the ballot box.

> 3RD: [and this was underscored in the petition, but not in the original charter] To resist and oppose corruption and promote economy in office, and to secure honesty and efficiency in the administration of national, state and municipal affairs.

The lengthy petition restated the Funk version of the Funk-Hines conversation. The Club petitioners also included the revelation reported by the state

Senate of alleged efforts by Hines to deny evidence to a Cook County grand jury that was looking into the Lorimer election.

According to the Illinois Senate report, Hines had sent his brother-in-law and business associate Charles Wiehe, also a member of the Club, on a "midnight ride" across the city to the Grand Pacific Hotel "for the purpose of inducing two persons to leave the jurisdiction of said grand jury [that night!], so that they might not be called to testify." The Senate committee concluded that such testimony would have implicated Hines in the legislative corruption.

Ed Hines calmly and simply asked that the charges against him in the petition to the Club be deferred until a second U.S. Senate investigation, just then under way, was completed. He had to be in Washington most of the time to help defend his friend Lorimer.

In May of 1911, the Illinois Senate approved its special committee's investigative report by a 39–10 vote, which found that the "election of Lorimer would not have occurred had it not been for bribery and corruption." Funk's testimony was critical to its conclusions.

In the U.S. Senate, the outspoken Bob LaFollette drew upon the Illinois Senate testimony to induce his body to reopen the Lorimer case, notwithstanding the Senate's earlier exoneration of the Illinois senator.

LaFollette and reformers in both parties had been dealt a stronger hand for the 1911 session of Congress. In the 1910 elections, they had gained several members for their reformist causes, in no small part because of the Lorimer scandal, which had become a national cause célèbre in the press.

With Democrats and Progressive Republicans now comprising a majority of the Senate, the proposal for direct election of senators was adopted by the Senate in June 1911. This was the day before the Lorimer investigative committee headed by senator William Dillingham of Vermont, a Lorimer supporter, began its deliberations.

The Dillingham committee met from June 20, 1911, until late February 1912. The committee heard 186 witnesses, ranging from senators Aldrich and Penrose to the cigar clerk at the Union League Club. The published record of the hearings comprises nine thousand pages and fills eight volumes.

The focus of the investigation was on the Funk charges against Hines and the "jackpot" corruption conditions in Springfield. The committee held hearings in Chicago as well as in Washington.

The Lorimer forces put unbelievable pressure on Funk. The day before he left for Washington to testify there for the first time, Funk was served an alienation-of-affections suit by a Loop hotel clerk who claimed Funk had been dallying with his wife.

The charges were splashed all over the newspapers, of course. They were thrown out of court and months later the couple confessed that they had lied about the whole affair, neither of them ever having met Funk. They had been promised "all the money they would ever need" to sign onto the suit. Their lawyer was disbarred.

Funk told Club members his life was hell for two years. He was watched at all times, presumably by detectives trying to get the goods on him somehow, and his life was threatened in telephone calls and by strange visitors to his office.

Hines testified before the U.S. Senate that he had indeed worked hard for Lorimer's election, but primarily at the bidding of President Taft and senators Aldrich and Penrose. The senators desperately needed protectionist votes for Aldrich's proposed tariff increases, which were in trouble in 1909. Hines vehemently denied using money to influence votes.

For his part, Funk recounted the conversation he had with Hines at the Club. He also told of a subsequent visit by Hines to his office. During that visit, Hines reiterated that Funk's company should feel an obligation to help replenish the fund used to "put Lorimer over."

In testimony in Chicago, Funk characterized Hines as a "man quite inclined to boast of his achievements, quite disposed to be familiar on short acquaintance, and quite anxious to have people think he was a large factor in large matters."

Lorimer took the stand before Dillingham's committee for the first time in the scandal. While emphatically denying any involvement in bribery, he did distinguish between the practical, get-things-done style of politics he pursued in contrast to "the way men talk who reach the clouds." Lorimer was surely talking about reformers such as those who dominated the Club's political action efforts. Lorimer saw them as holier-than-thou moralists who were above politics, while at the same time they enjoyed the riches from the good things he got done for Chicago in Washington.

In response to tough questioning from Senator John Kern of California, a Lorimer antagonist, the Illinois senator admitted without apology that "my friends have a great deal of influence with me, and men that help me in the world have a great deal of influence with me, and they can very frequently get me to do things that if I were just left to myself I would not do.

"I do not think that I am owned body and soul by the men that influence me just because I sometimes do things that, if I were left to myself, I would not do. I am just a human being."

Lorimer also castigated Funk as a liar, declaring "his tongue seemed to be hung in the middle and it ran at both ends at the same time."

At the same time as the Senate hearings on Lorimer, the Club was reviewing Ed Hines' suitability for membership. This was also covered widely in the

Chicago press, though less so across the nation. The papers all referred to it as the Club's "trial" of Ed Hines. William Sidley, the Club president, hoped the matter could be dealt with quietly, among gentlemen. It was not to be.

The Club board of managers, or directors, comprised fourteen members. The bylaws provided—and still do—for expulsion of a member on the vote of two-thirds of the board.

The Dillingham committee was holding hearings in May when the petition with its charges was filed with the Club president. Through his attorney, Hines asked that the Club's hearings on the charges be deferred until the U.S. Senate proceedings were over. The board agreed to defer hearings on the charges without specifying when hearings should take up.

Lessing Rosenthal, one of the petitioners, asked that the charges be published but the board voted against publishing them.

The Dillingham committee was still sitting in November, six months later. By then, many Club members were demanding action against Hines, threatening to resign from the Club otherwise. Reluctantly, Sidley and the board proceeded. The hearings, from November through February, would often start at 4 P.M. and not end until midnight, with an hour off for dinner in the Club dining room. One session went for twenty-eight hours straight with a little time off for all concerned to get some rest in Club sleeping rooms.

Hines insisted on being represented by counsel. The board first objected, then relented, requiring however that his counsel be a Club member. As a result Marquis Eaton replaced Charles Allen as Hines' counsel. Since the focus of the hearings was on the Funk-Hines conversations, Clarence Funk felt compelled to have counsel as well. Frank Scott and later Frank Loesch represented Funk. This "trial" became as formal as a case before the U.S. Supreme Court. The transcript of the proceedings runs 969 typed pages.

Business in the Club bar increased while the sessions were going on in the boardroom, with members trying to pick up intelligence on the closed proceedings. The Club general manager reported that bar business almost doubled in 1911 and 1912 over preceding years.

Sidley, head of a leading Chicago law firm that still bears his family name, kept a firm hand on the proceedings. The lawyers split hairs over the dates and timing of the conversations and of representations by numerous men as to what did and didn't take place. But it all boiled down to one man's word against another's, so in the Club the deck was stacked against Ed Hines. Hines should have been smart enough to know that from the start.

The reformers "knew" that Hines was lying—because Funk would never do so—and that Hines had put together the money to bribe legislators. They just couldn't prove it, nor could the U.S. Senate.

The big issue for the Club became whether the board should delay a vote on the Hines charges until after the Senate acted on Lorimer. The Dillingham committee was still at work when the Club board of managers took its final testimony on February 23. One of the original petitioners, Frank Loesch, called on the board to await the Senate action, but the board decided to proceed.

The board didn't want it to appear that Club actions might be affected by the Senate, and possibly the Club "trial" could have some impact on the Senate.

Before the board's secret vote, Hines was given one last chance to resign, which he emphatically rejected. The board voted 11–2, with one member absent on a pressing matter, to expel Edward Hines because of conduct "hostile to the objects and injurious to the character of the Club."

The following morning, local newspapers all carried front-page stories on the expulsion. For the benefit of the newspapers, one Club director repeated parts of the remarks he had given his colleagues just before the vote:

> The Club will be split wide open unless he is ousted. The Club is not merely a place to eat and loaf, but stands for something in good government. It was organized at a time when patriotism was high and men thought something of their country's welfare.
>
> The men who are inspired by the same sentiments will not stand by and permit this matter to be dropped. They will walk out in a body, and I will go with them.

By a 5–3 vote, the Dillingham committee reported to the Senate in late March of 1912 that new evidence they had gathered did *not* justify reversing the Senate's earlier action in retaining Senator Lorimer. The majority contended there was no proof of either a Lorimer "jackpot" or of Hines' involvement in any corrupt election effort. Dillingham attacked Funk's story as insidious because it was circulated without a legal test and had incited the public against Lorimer. In contrast, the minority report of the committee found Hines to be an accessory to the corruption that resulted in Lorimer's election.

Throughout June and July the full Senate debated the issue of William Lorimer. In oppressive Washington heat and humidity, Dillingham alone spoke for four days. He and other Lorimer supporters attacked the character assassins and blackmailers of Chicago journalism with their "disposition of the snob."

Senator Kern attacked not Lorimer but the "great interests" of the country who decided they needed Lorimer's vote in the Senate. Hines was their representative, he went on, who bought the votes of Democrats that put Lorimer over.

There had been talk earlier, about 1910, of a fund put together by Senator Aldrich, banker J. P. Morgan, and many of the major corporations for the purpose of electing high-tariff lawmakers to stem the rising tide of low-tariff Progressives. U.S. Representative Medill McCormick of Chicago told banker George Reynolds he understood that $128,000 had gone from Washington to Springfield to elect Lorimer. It is possible, though never proved, that these men provided the fund Hines used for Lorimer, which he later tried to replenish. (Already a member of the University and Chicago clubs, McCormick joined the Union League Club of Chicago in 1919, the same year he became a U.S. senator.)

Kern also attacked the "corrupt field" of Chicago and Illinois politics in which Lorimer was embedded, with the likes of "Hinky Dink" Kenna, Cyril Janus, and Manny Abrahams. These are not "the real people" of America, Kerns contended. The fault lay not so much with Lorimer, with "his good heart, his humane impulses and domestic happiness," but with *the system* and its reprehensible methods to thwart the popular will. That system, Kern declared, had to "receive condemnation at the hands of the American Senate."

For fourteen hours over three days, Lorimer defended himself on the floor of the Senate. Lies purchased directly and indirectly by the *Tribune* had brought him to this final stand, he declared.

But the Blond Boss Billy Lorimer knew it was his last stand. Amidst the sounds of sobs from the gallery and the floor, it was reported, William Lorimer finally sat down and the Senate voted 55–28 to expel him from its chambers.

Lorimer returned home to a hero's welcome. His lieutenants, "Poor Fred" Lundin and "Big Bill" Thompson, gathered 2,500 cheering supporters at Orchestra Hall. In his introduction, Thompson described Lorimer as a martyr, a "living example that a trust press controls this city and nation, and that a man who will not bend his knee to its dictates can be driven from political or public life."

Lorimer was indeed driven from political life. A bank he had created to take in "political" accounts failed as well. He tried to regain his congressional seat but was overwhelmed by a candidate backed by his one-time associate "Poor Fred" Lundin.

Ed Hines never gave up efforts to clear his name.

A month after he was expelled from the Club, the *Western Catholic* newspaper devoted its front page and a special section of sixteen full-size newspaper pages to a defense of fellow Catholic Hines and to an attack on the anti-Catholic newspaper trust. Other newspapers reported that one million copies of this special edition were sent out by this newspaper for members of that faith who lived all over the Midwest.

The church newspaper carried a formal photo of Hines with his family and asked its readers to "go to the able and reverend Metropolitan of the province, the Archbishop of Chicago, and ask him what kind of man is this Edward Hines. The answer will convince you that he is a model Christian, an honest businessman—a friend to be loved and admired."

The *Western Catholic* suggested strongly that Hines was caught up in an anti-Catholic conspiracy. The paper also attacked Clarence Funk as a simple operative of the McCormick family and the *Tribune*. Cyrus McCormick created International Harvester, where Funk ran the business. McCormick was a great-uncle of Medill McCormick and of younger brother Robert R. McCormick, who was just then becoming a major figure at the *Tribune*.

Hines hired Frederick Upham Adams to write, very quickly, two books that sought to exonerate him. The first was a booklet titled *The Plot That Failed,* which devoted twenty-four pages to an "exposé" of how James Keeley, editor of the *Tribune,* had hired William Burns, head of a detective agency, to "manufacture evidence intended to convict an honest man of the crime of perjury" against Ed Hines. The booklet is undated but it is in the Club archives.

Adams appears to have also authored a hardbound book, dated June 17, 1912, *Edward Hines to the Union League Club,* a two-hundred-page brief in support of his formal request for a new trial on the issue of his membership in the Club. In the book, which, by the way, does not carry Adams' name as author, Hines attacks Funk for his wrongs to the Club. The book casts Funk as the liar, but the Club denied Hines' request for a new trial.

Remarkably, the story doesn't end there.

Several years later, in 1918, the Club received from prominent Club sponsors an application for membership from William S. Bennet. There is a thick correspondence on this application in the archives.

Bennet had an impressive pedigree. Before coming to Chicago, he had practiced law in New York City, served as a judge there, and been elected four times to the U.S. House.

He was also Edward Hines' attorney.

Bennet's first application was rejected because of this connection. He applied again, pointing out he didn't represent Hines directly but rather worked for the "Edward Hines Associated Lumber Interests," a distinction that escaped the membership committee.

One of the sponsors, all of whom must be Club members, was U.S. Representative and later U.S. Senator William B. McKinley of Champaign, Illinois.

Several of Bennet's sponsors and references, including the Sears, Roebuck merchant Julius Rosenwald, expressed embarrassment at not knowing about Bennet's associations. In Bennet's behalf, respected Club member Frank Loesch protested that Bennet's application was not, as others intimated, an "entering wedge" for Hines to somehow get back into the Club.

Since one of Bennet's sponsors would not withdraw the application, the Club membership committee wrestled with the matter for several years. Clarence Funk didn't mince words in his letter regarding Bennet's application.

First saying that he did not know Bennet and assumed him to be a man of high character and integrity, Funk continued: "It seems to me, however, this application raises a much more serious question, viz: should Edward Hines, by the use of his well known methods and by the manipulation of every friend whom he can reach and influence in any way, be allowed to force into our membership a man absolutely under his control. . . . I think the Board needs no enlightenment as to what this means." The letter continues in the same vein at some length.

In December 1925, the admissions committee recommended that approval be withheld on this second application. "There can hardly be any question," wrote the committee chairman in his memorandum to the board of managers, "that [Bennet's] election to membership would create considerable dissatisfaction among a number of important and prominent members of the club, to say nothing of the suspicion that would be aroused that he was acting solely as Edward Hines' tool."

Bennet was never admitted to the Club.

Clarence Funk died in January 1930, eighteen years after the scandal. Newspapers across the country carried his obituary, with headlines such as PRINCIPAL IN EXPULSION OF LORIMER DEAD and LORIMER'S EXPOSER DIES IN CHICAGO AFTER OPERATION.

As the newspapers reported, Funk never fully recovered from the strain of the two years of investigations, spying, and attempts at his defamation regarding the Lorimer case. Funk had been in virtual retirement from public life since that time other than to head a successful million-dollar building campaign for the Chicago Theological Seminary.

The *Chicago Post* obituary recalled that the investigation into Lorimer's election would have ended in early 1911 with the Senate's exoneration but, "Then in the Union League Club one day, it was charged, Edward Hines told Funk that he had helped 'put Lorimer over.'"

The *Tribune* obit stated simply that "the Senate expelled Lorimer, principally on Funk's testimony."

SOURCES

The author acknowledges a debt to Professor Joel A. Tarr for his fine biography of William Lorimer, *A Study in Boss Politics.* This work provided an excellent, detailed template for the Lorimer story.

Information about the Funk-Hines controversy came primarily from the well-organized, extensive archives of the ULCC. In addition to the minutes of the Club, the materials include a thick accordion folder entitled "The Edward Hines Case," rich with newspaper clippings such as those from the *Western Catholic,* cited in the chapter. "The Record of the Trial of Edward Hines" is located in the Gallagher Law Library at the University of Washington–Seattle.

The archives also holds the two works written or ghostwritten by Frederick Upham Adams for Edward Hines, cited in the text, plus another by Adams, *The Story of Edward Hines,* n.d.

In addition to searching Chicago newspapers of the period as well as the *New York Times,* I drew upon Howard's *Mostly Good and Competent Men* and the following for specific, very brief passages in the chapter:

Collins, Charles. "The Funk Case." *Chicago Tribune Sunday Magazine,* May 2, 1954.

Dennis, Charles H. *Victor Lawson.* Chicago: University of Chicago Press, 1935.

Tarr, Joel Arthur. "The Expulsion of Chicago's 'Blond Boss' from the United States Senate." *Chicago History,* Fall 1972.

Waldrop, Frank C. *McCormick of Chicago.* Englewood Cliffs, N.J.: Prentice-Hall, 1966.

Chapter 8

THE ROARING TWENTIES

All hell broke loose in Chicago in 1919. Just barely, the Club foresaw the problem. In June, the political action committee created a new subcommittee on the racial question. During the World War, African Americans were recruited by the thousands from the South to fill labor shortages in the stockyards, mills, and factories. More than a hundred thousand African Americans crowded into a small area on the south side. Called Bronzeville, the community numbered only half as many before the war. Something had to give. It did.

On July 27, just as subcommittee chairman Harry Eugene Kelly and his group initiated their study of the "Racial Question," a black boy was stoned by whites at the Twenty-ninth Street beach. Hanging on to a railroad tie, the boy had floated across an imaginary line in the water that separated the swimming areas for whites and blacks. Afraid to come ashore on the beach for whites, the black teenager let go of the tie, took a few strokes, sank, and drowned. Both black and white bathers plunged in to try to save the youngster, but they could not locate him.

A white policeman refused to arrest a white man accused by African Americans of throwing stones. At this crucial point, the policeman arrested a black man on a white man's complaint. Blacks mobbed the white officer. Whites retaliated and for six days bloody street fights raged through both black and white neighborhoods on the south side. Thirty-eight people were killed, more than five hundred injured, and thousands were left homeless as a result of fires. Of those killed, twenty-three were black men and fifteen were white men, though twice as many African Americans were injured.

Governor Frank Lowden appointed a Chicago commission on race relations and named former Club president (1903) Edgar A. Bancroft to head it. Future Club president Harry Kelly was named a key member of the group. Bancroft's report, *The Negro in Chicago,* opened many eyes in the white world for whom the African American community had been largely invisible. The commission criticized police, prosecutors, and the courts for discriminatory handling of cases involving blacks. Bancroft took city officials to task for neglect of garbage and rubbish disposal in black neighborhoods. He even suggested razing all housing unfit for human occupancy. The report went on the shelf.

The following year, Lowden sought the presidency. Frank Lowden had honed his political skills in the 1890s as a member and chair of the Club's political action committee. As governor from 1917 to 1921, he gained national recognition for his work in reorganizing the state's government. In Illinois, however, the silk-stocking Lowden could never work with Chicago Republican mayor "Big Bill" Thompson, who came out of the boodling Billy Lorimer school of politics. The cultural and class conflicts between the Lowden approach and the Thompson style were lineal descendants of the battles the Club had been fighting with politicians since its inception.

Thompson withheld his nineteen delegates from Lowden at the Republican National Convention in Chicago in 1920. Lacking the full support of his own state delegation weakened Lowden's stature as a political leader in the eyes of many at the convention. For nine ballots the convention was deadlocked among Lowden, General Leonard Wood, and Senator Hiram Johnson of California. Unable to break the impasse, the convention turned to Warren G. Harding of Ohio. Had Lowden been supported by Thompson's delegates, Lowden might well have been the nominee in a landslide year for Republicans.

The Illinois National Guard had basically ceased to exist following World War I. With the state's history of violent labor and now racial strife, an Illinois militia could be useful at times. Governor Lowden requested that thirteen members of the Club serve on a commission to reorganize and rehabilitate the Guard. The public affairs committee created a new subcommittee—the National Guard Recruiting Committee. Members of the recruiting committee were given a list of banks and business houses whose executives were members of the Club with instructions to interview them personally and obtain their active assistance in recruiting men from their offices.

To show real enthusiasm for the task, the Club decided to form its own company, made up of members, their sons, and Club employees. In 1920 the Union League company was sworn in as Company E of the First Infantry Regiment.

Membership in the company acquired social status among some in the city. But members of the unit took their soldiering seriously and were asked to organize and train other companies.

During the war, the Club had created a war committee which promulgated patriotic support for the soldiers overseas and distributed support-the-war pamphlets. Committee members put on talks for the large German population in the city, explaining why German Americans should be supporting this war against their fatherland. After the war, this committee and the political action committee were consolidated into the present public affairs committee. The consolidated committee had nineteen subcommittees and eight hundred members signed up for one or more panels.

The subcommittee on better citizenship spent the year focused on creation of the Club's first Boys Club.

Street urchins from the poor Irish, Polish, and other neighborhoods of recent immigrants were a big problem for the city. Based on boys clubs founded in the East, the Club set up a separate operating unit directed solely by members to fund and operate boys clubs.

The Club was enthusiastic about the project. Members were asked to contribute two dollars a month to support the new club for boys. Soon it became two clubs plus a summer camp in Wisconsin. The goal was to help two boys for every one of the Club's two-thousand-plus members.

By the 1920s, Chicago had matured as a civic and social community. At a public affairs committee meeting in 1921, the Club received a request for support of the Legislative Voters' League. This was one of the antiboodler groups started three decades earlier in the George Cole era. Now, the committee lamented, there were too many organizations doing this sort of work, without adequate results. So the public affairs group passed a motion urging that the Legislative Voters' League be discontinued.

The Club did not want its own public affairs function to become seen as similarly inadequate or irrelevant. In 1924, the Club hired its first full-time professional director of public affairs to support the work of the public affairs committee and its subcommittees. Edward Martin was a young man from the East trained in public administration. After joining the Club staff, he earned a doctorate in government at the University of Chicago and began writing tomes about reforming the judiciary. Martin was scholarly, professorial, and a real gentleman. Members said Dr. Martin added some class to the Club.

One of his first efforts was a joint project between the Club and the University of Chicago to survey all the civic agencies that served Chicago. Martin and his fellow scholars found eight hundred citywide and neighborhood groups and one million members involved in civic and community matters. Much of the growth had been generated by service clubs such as the

Rotary, Kiwanis, Lions, and women's clubs. Martin's job was to make sure Club efforts stood out from the pack and provided leadership.

Martin used the clubhouse for gatherings of scholars, civic leaders, public officials, and respected experts to discuss and possibly agree on how to change things. Martin and the subcommittees pushed for the adoption of voting machines, reform of the judiciary, city-manager government, and fair property taxation. Martin was good at what he did and revered in the Club. In the wild and wooly 1920s, however, government reform was useless if the guys in charge were rotten.

Murder was commonplace in Chicago from the end of World War I to the end of Prohibition in 1933. Murder of bad guys by other bad guys could be tolerated by members of the Club. Flouting the rule of law, sullying Chicago's reputation, and murder of good guys could not be. When it became clear that city officials were part of the problem, Club leaders ultimately resorted to old-fashioned vigilantism to help bring down Al Capone and his gang.

Adoption of the Prohibition amendment in 1919 fueled the illegal beer, booze, gambling, and prostitution that provided gangsters such as "Big Jim" Colosimo, Johnny Torrio, Dion O'Banion, and "Scarface Al" Capone with the wealth to buy—just as legitimate businessman and Club member Charles Yerkes earlier bought the city council—the support and protection of judges, cops, aldermen, even the mayor.

Beer cost three dollars a barrel to brew and sold for fifty-five dollars a barrel to the county's twenty thousand saloons, joints, speakeasies, and ice-cream parlors. Capone employed two thousand and had half of Chicago's six thousand policemen on his payroll as well.

Chicago had been carved into medieval baronies by gang warlords with their foot soldiers and mercenaries. A *Chicago Tribune* map of Chicago etched gang territories as salient as government boundaries and Catholic parish neighborhoods.

Denied beer and booze in their taverns (and later in the clubhouse as well, to the consternation of many members), Chicagoans appreciated the spirits and sporting life found in the speakeasies. Gangsters became celebrities. Patrons of the arts pointed out the somewhat refined Johnny Torrio, a student of classical music, at the symphony. Autograph seekers besieged Capone at Comiskey Park. Gang wars became street theater. No venue was sacred, not even Holy Name Cathedral, the backdrop for more than one drive-by gangland slaying.

Six strong men closely identified with the Club, three as presidents, one as a first vice president, played central roles in battling organized crime and in sending Al Capone to Alcatraz.

Charles Gates Dawes came to Chicago in 1895 to spearhead the Illinois presidential campaign of Governor William McKinley of Ohio. Financially successful at twenty-nine, Dawes was elected to the Club that year and took quarters in the clubhouse. For the campaign, he recruited William Edens, a young railroad union man and Republican activist from Galesburg, Illinois, to assist him (Edens Expressway is named after him and his son William later became a president of the Club). They operated their campaign for delegates largely from the Club.

Dawes took advantage of initiative wherever he found it. One evening at the Club, according to Paul Leach in *That Man Dawes,* Dawes gave his hat to the checkroom boy, Francis Kilkenny, who in return handed Dawes a large envelope.

"What the dickens is this?" Dawes asked.

"Clippings about Major McKinley, sir," replied the bright-eyed youngster in a heavy Irish brogue.

"Hmm. Where did you get them?"

"I picked them out of the newspapers that had been thrown away and saved them for you, sir."

Dawes hesitated, smiled, and then said: "What is your name?"

"Francis J. Kilkenny, sir."

"Come upstairs and have dinner with me."

"I am in uniform, sir, and employees are not permitted to eat in the dining room with members."

Dawes waved his hand. "Pshaw. See the manager. Get out of uniform."

Kilkenny did, and at dinner Dawes hired him as his confidential assistant. When McKinley was elected a year later, Dawes became his comptroller of the currency and Kilkenny went to Washington with him.

According to Chicago journalist and author Richard Ciccone, Dawes returned home from Washington in 1902 certain that he would be elected U.S. senator by the state legislature, but he ran afoul of the William Lorimer machine. In 1924, after creating the "Dawes Plan" for the refinancing of German war debt after World War I, for which he received the Nobel Peace Prize (in 1925), Dawes would have been a strong candidate for president. Harding died in office, however, and Calvin Coolidge ascended. Coolidge made Dawes his vice president. In February 1926, Vice President Dawes testified to the U.S. Senate: organized crime and Al Capone had become a cancer eating at the vitals of the Chicago government and of democracy. The solons were sympathetic but there was no role, they said, for the federal government in the affairs of the nation's local governments.

But, Dawes said, Capone owned the government of Chicago.

Dawes' exasperation was based in large part upon the frustration of efforts by men like Club public affairs committee chairman Harry Eugene Kelly to force the criminal justice system in Chicago to fight crime.

Kelly was tough. He had the cold, piercing eyes of a gunslinger. Kelly went to school in Iowa, taught literature at the University of Iowa, and earned a law degree there. He became the U.S. attorney for Colorado when cowboys rode the range and shot up the towns on Saturday night. He came to Chicago in 1915 and became a successful railroad attorney.

He took on the politicians in 1924. The chief judge of the criminal courts of Cook County was a law school buddy of Kelly. Judge Michael L. McKinley authorized a special grand jury investigation into misappropriations and general graft during the first term of Mayor "Big Bill" Thompson from 1919 to 1923; the grand jury's work was to be headed by Illinois attorney general Edward Brundage rather than Cook County state's attorney Robert Crowe. The Cook County board became highly nervous and refused to fund the inquiry.

Outraged, Kelly tried an end run around the county board and Crowe, a partner in the corrupt Thompson-Crowe Republican faction that ran Chicago for much of the decade.

Kelly declared the Union League Club would fund the grand jury. He raised fifty thousand dollars from Club members. McKinley declared the money could be used by the Illinois attorney general to pay the expenses of what became known as the "Union League Club grand jury" or "the runaway grand jury." Bob Crowe had a fit, seeing that Brundage was after some of his boys. After a year of work, the grand jury indicted half a dozen Crowe political associates.

The state supreme court declared, however, that the panel had been unconstitutional since the beginning and quashed the indictments. The indicted suspects came after individual members of the grand jury with charges of slander, seeking five hundred thousand dollars in damages from the jury members. The Club hired one of its own members to defend the grand jury members, successfully.

Kelly was frustrated but not finished.

Two months after Dawes had pleaded with the Senate in early 1926 to become involved in fighting Al Capone, Capone's men gunned down young Cook County assistant state's attorney Bill McSwiggin.

The cry went up from the newspapers and the public, WHO KILLED MCSWIGGIN? This attack was an attack upon the state, the assassination of an energetic young prosecutor of bad guys.

The cops yawned.

Harry Kelly, now president of the Club, went directly to the press. "A special grand jury, independent of state's attorney Crowe and of the county board, must be appointed. I have nothing against Mr. Crowe personally, but obviously he is unfit to go into the 'beer racket' because it is mixed up all down the line with politics—and Mr. Crowe is a capable politician."

Crowe created a series of grand juries that couldn't find coal in a coal mine, and nary a thing about who killed McSwiggin. Capone was treated with kid gloves throughout. He was even brought into custody—under conditions dictated by Capone himself, so he could plead his innocence to the press.

"I've been accused of every death except the casualty list of the World War," declared Capone. "Ten days before McSwiggin was bumped off, I met him as usual. I was no foe of McSwiggin. I knew him in a business way. I paid him—and I paid him plenty. I had some of my men with him. If we wanted to bump him, that was the spot. We didn't kill him. We didn't want to kill him, then or later."

Three days later Capone was released.

McSwiggin's murder was never solved, by the criminal justice system, that is. McSwiggin's father was at the time a veteran sergeant in the Chicago police force. He conducted his own investigation into his son's murder. Later the father named Capone and five accomplices as the murderers.

If nothing else, Chicago learned that both the gangs and prominent officials inside government, maybe even bright, shining young prosecutors, were all in the same rotten, stinking barrel.

Direct action by citizens themselves was the only course left, many came to conclude. Two more presidents of the Union League Club took up the torch in the crusade against Capone and the gangs.

The Chicago Association of Commerce created the Chicago Crime Commission in 1919. Julius Rosenwald was one of the largest contributors and a member of the board of directors. Small in stature, Rosenwald was a giant of a man; in person he was warm and generous. As a young man in the 1890s, Julius purchased a 25 percent share in the young Sears Roebuck Company where he was working. He built the company into a catalog and retailing colossus.

Before his death, Rosenwald contributed scores of millions of dollars for schools for African Americans in the South and for numerous social and cultural enterprises in Chicago. He was one of many Club members who had been active in preparing the report on *The Negro in Chicago* which followed the 1919 race riots.

Rosenwald joined the Club in 1910 and served on the political action committee. He may also have appreciated the Club because he was Jewish and many downtown clubs would not admit Jews. (The Standard Club, where most leading German Jews were members, was not to move into the Loop from its rather inconvenient south side location until 1926.

Rosenwald saw in the crime commission an advocate for swifter and surer justice. But the crime commission didn't live up to its promise, in the early years anyway. And the commission excluded from its sights the growing menace of organized crime. In 1928, Rosenwald decided it was time for action. He threatened to withdraw his support from the crime commission, unless, that is, Frank Loesch was elected president of the commission to wage a vigorous campaign against organized crime. Rosenwald and Loesch had earlier been associates on the Club's political action committee.

President of the Club in 1916, Loesch had been a silk-stocking railroad attorney whose firm handled, in addition, mostly trusts and estates. Loesch lived at the Drake Hotel, taught Sunday school across the street at Fourth Presbyterian Church, and was active in the city's high society. He was a member of the Casino Club, which is ever so old-family and old-money that even members of the Chicago Club might have trouble getting in.

Frank was seventy-six years old at the time of his appointment in 1928 to head the crime commission. He became known affectionately as "the Spirit of '76."

Frank Loesch took charge rigorously and in the process made fighting crime almost a club activity. A 1930 edition of the commission's journal, *Criminal Justice*, lists its officers and board members. Ten of the eleven members of the executive committee of the commission were Club members. Staff director Henry Barrett Chamberlin had become a Club member in 1926. This made sense, as many of the group's committee meetings and dinners were held at the Club.

Right away, state attorney general Oscar Carlstrom appointed Loesch to investigate election fraud. In addition, Loesch investigated the cesspool of patronage and pilferage that the Chicago sanitary district had become in preceding years during what the press called the "Whoopee Era" at the district. Frank got indictments against a dozen sanitary district officials, including chief engineer Edward Kelly, later to become mayor of Chicago. Many of the Whoopee Era defendants were convicted or pleaded guilty, yet Kelly came out unscathed. Loesch had served notice that he and the commission meant business.

More important, in Washington in 1928, Vice President Dawes persuaded President Coolidge to create a special intelligence unit of the Bureau of Internal Revenue to begin an investigation of the income tax affairs of Al Capone. (In 1927 the U.S. Supreme Court had ruled in *U.S. v. Sullivan* that illegal income was taxable.) Dawes had also been seeing to it that honest, aggressive federal prosecutors such as George E. Q. Johnson and Dwight Green were sent that same year to the U.S. attorney's office for the northern district of Illinois, headquartered in Chicago.

Frank Loesch pleaded with Dawes to return home to take on Capone. Dawes was more than interested. His brother Rufus was heading up the planning for a second world's fair for Chicago. Instead, President Herbert Hoover appointed Charles Dawes ambassador to Great Britain, where he served from 1929 to 1932.

By the end of the 1920s, things were getting wild in Chicago even by the city's standards. The St. Valentine's Day massacre in 1929 captivated national attention. Capone's men, some dressed as police officers, allegedly mowed down seven of "Bugs" Moran's hoodlums on North Clark Street.

Capone could also see that the end of Prohibition was only a matter of time. To develop a new line of business, he had been muscling into labor unions. According to Chicago Crime Commission information, Capone had taken over or had indirect control over two-thirds of the unions in Chicago, making life miserable for businessmen.

Since 1921, the construction industry had been operating under a favorable ruling from Judge Kenesaw Mountain Landis, which allowed companies to hire nonunion workers under certain circumstances. Capone wanted to impress unions that he could force construction companies to knuckle under to an all-union shop.

The H. B. Barnard Construction Company was one of Chicago's biggest; one year in the late 1920s the company accounted for 10 percent of all building permits issued by the city, according to his son William. Harrison B. Barnard (always H. B. to his friends and employees) had worked full time as a carpenter while attending the University of Chicago. H. B. appeared dour and distant to many, yet he was jovial among his peers at the Club over the chess and backgammon tables. Seven days a week, H. B. wore a three-piece suit, detachable collar, and watch fob. On Sunday afternoons, he might doff his suit jacket on the front porch of the family home near the University of Chicago.

Barnard was a member of the Club building committee when the present clubhouse was constructed. When the building was complete, he succeeded Harry Kelly as president in 1927. His photo in the Club pantheon of presidents shows a down-turned mouth and cold, steel-grey eyes.

Barnard and company did much of the construction at the rapidly expanding University of Chicago. H. B. served on the board of trustees. In 1908 and 1909 Barnard Construction built the Robie House, design by architect Frank Lloyd Wright. (The Robie House represents the apotheosis of Wright's famous Prairie Style; it is now owned by the University of

Chicago.) Barnard and Wright didn't get on. Wright wouldn't sign off on the building certificate; H. B. kicked him off the site.

Phil Meagher supervised construction for H. B.; the two were close. In February 1930, Meagher was shot as he supervised construction of the Lying-In Hospital at the University of Chicago. The mob had slipped a laborer onto the job two weeks earlier; he fingered Meagher to the driver of the car whose occupants sprayed Meagher with bullets.

Like H. B., Meagher was tough as nails. He survived two bullets to the body and one through the brim of his fedora, which he wore ever after as a good-luck charm.

Capone picked on the wrong construction company.

Livid, Barnard couldn't believe that legitimate business had become targets for Capone and his drive-by shootings. H. B. sat down with state's attorney John Swanson, also a member of the Club. Swanson had been elected on a good-government slate in November 1928 with the help of Frank Loesch.

In his memoirs of the period, judge John H. Lyle recounted the mayhem of the primary election of that year:

"The spring primary campaign had been one of murder, fraud, kidnappings, and sluggings. There had been bomb explosions at the homes of U.S. Sen. Charles Deneen, Judge John A. Swanson, candidate for state's attorney, and two members of Mayor Thompson's cabinet. . . . Bombs in gangland terminology, were pineapples. The newspapers called it the 'Pineapple Primary.'"

A columnist wrote: "The rockets' red glare, the bombs bursting in air; gave proof to the world, that Chicago's still there."

To help make Swanson's election possible, Loesch swallowed his pride in that first year as head of the crime commission. He went to Capone to plead for quiet elections in the fall of 1928.

Though he was pleading, his friend Lyle wrote, Loesch was blunt: "Now, look here, Capone. We want an honest election. Will you help by keeping your damned cutthroats and hoodlums from interfering with the voting?"

"Sure," said "Scarface" in princely assent. "I'll give you a square deal. . . . I'll have the cops send out squad cars the night before election. They'll throw the punks into the cooler and keep 'em there until the voting's over."

Capone kept his word. "It turned out to be the squarest and most successful election in forty years," Loesch declared later. Swanson and several other anti-Thompson candidates were beneficiaries.

Swanson told H. B. that his own investigators were all known to the gangsters; they had to sign their names and addresses to the payroll every month to receive their paychecks. Swanson suggested instead a "secret service" of private investigators. "Supply them with money to run with the wolf pack," Swanson told H. B., "and buy information from the jackals. With information, we can get convictions. Without it, we're dead in the water."

The Chicago Crime Commission seemed the logical place to take the idea. Barnard didn't think so. He felt the commission's board, made up of many Club members, lacked the stomach for direct action. Instead, Barnard went to Robert Isham Randolph, president of the Chicago Association of Commerce, to demand action. Barnard was a leading member of the association.

According to his son William, Barnard helped put together a luncheon for Randolph with Frank Loesch, Julius Rosenwald, Ed Gore (all active members of the Club), utility magnate Samuel Insull, George Paddock, and possibly others.

Chicago was becoming a laughingstock around the world, the men realized. And the Chicago Century of Progress World's Fair of 1933 was just around the corner. "The World's Fair will be a failure," Judge John H. Lyle, a reformer, had declared publicly, "unless Capone is exterminated."

Reluctantly and with some trepidation, the men agreed to take the law into their own hands. They raised a million dollars to finance their own strike force, much of it from Insull. Young Bob Randolph would be their public voice. Randolph was perfect. He loved the public stage—and to be called "Colonel" from his days as an engineer in World War I. In profile, Randolph looked a bit like Errol Flynn without the sparkling smile.

The press ate up this new private vigilante initiative. Randolph wouldn't disclose the names of his associates other than to say there were six of them. To the press, they became "The Secret Six." There were probably more than six but the names have never been made public.

The Secret Six hired ex-Texas Rangers, Canadian Mounties, soldiers of fortune, former gun molls. They set up the Garage Cafe, their own speakeasy, in Cicero, deep in Capone territory. The joint sold booze and beer and sucked information from low-level bootleggers.

The crime-fighting cabal also gave seventy-five thousand dollars, no questions asked, to Elmer Irey, chief of the enforcement branch of the U.S. Treasury. Irey used part of that money to insert a skilled federal agent into the Lexington Hotel on the south side, Capone's headquarters. The agent soon became a member of Capone's traveling entourage. The Secret Six's men raided Capone hideouts and shot it up with the gangsters. All the time, they were feeding information to state's attorney Swanson and the Treasury Department.

At the same time, Frank Loesch and Henry Chamberlin at the crime commission came up with a great public relations gimmick. In 1930, they issued a list of the twenty-eight top gangsters in Chicago and their lurid histories in crime. The newspapers ran their photos and criminal pedigrees. Loesch and his staff director Chamberlin, a former newsman, called them "Public Enemies." The name stuck. Capone was tagged Public Enemy Number 1. The Chicago police department detective bureau had no records whatever on eighteen of the public enemies, including three men who had been tried for three murders each.

Loesch, Chamberlin, and Lyle came up with the idea of prosecuting Capone and his henchmen on vagrancy charges, since they did not appear to be supporting themselves by lawful means. The drive lost steam, however, when prosecutors could not find one Chicago policeman who could or would testify to Capone's "vagrancy."

Desperate by 1930, because raids by the Secret Six and Eliot Ness's "Untouchables" were killing gang booze profits, Capone called Randolph to a meeting at his headquarters in the Lexington Hotel.

According to Dennis Hoffman, the meeting went as follows: Jake Guzik was known in the underworld as "The Little Fellow." He was the right hand man of "The Big Fellow," Capone. "This is the Little Fellow," Guzik told Bob Randolph over the phone. "I have the Big Fellow in a hotel near the Loop where you can talk to him without being seen. Will you go?"

Randolph agreed, slipped a .45 pistol in his pocket, and met Guzik. At the Lexington, after passing through numerous doors and past more numerous thugs, giving up his pistol in the process, Randolph met Capone. The two shook hands.

> "Hell, Colonel, I'd know you anywhere—you look just like your pictures."
> "Hell, Al, I'd never have recognized you—you are much bigger than you appear in photographs."
> "Colonel, what are you trying to do to me?"
> "Put you out of business, Al."
> "Why do you want to do that?"
> "We want to clean up Chicago, put a stop to these killings and gang rule here."
> "Colonel, I don't understand you. You knock over my breweries, bust up my booze rackets, raid my gambling houses, and tap my telephone wires, but you're not a reformer, not a dry. Just what are you after?"
> Before Randolph could respond, Capone made an offer.
> "I'll tell you what I'll do: If the Secret Six will lay off my beer, booze, and gambling rackets, I'll police this town for you—I'll clean it up so there won't be a stickup or murder in Cook County. I'll give you my hand on it."

Randolph refused the offer but did take another glass of Capone's beer. He put on his coat and hat. Capone returned Randolph's pistol.

"So even respectable people carry these things?" Capone asked, laughing. Then Capone shook Randolph's hand and said, "No hard feelings?"

"No hard feelings," Randolph responded. Guzik took Randolph back to his car.

Based on evidence gathered by the Treasury in collaboration with Secret Six investigators and informants, Capone was convicted of tax evasion in 1931 and sentenced to eleven years in prison. He was in Alcatraz by the time the Chicago Century of Progress world's fair opened in 1933. Opened in the depth of the Depression, the world's fair was so successful it was held over for a second year.

"The Secret Six licked the rackets," Capone told the *Detroit Free Press.* "They've licked me. They've made it so there's no money in the game anymore."

The Secret Six did play an important role, but probably not that ascribed to it by either Capone or Randolph, who was in the news continually.

Capone was brought down by unusually close cooperation and exchange of information among federal agents from the U.S. attorney's office, Treasury, the Ness Prohibition task force, and the free-spending, free-wheeling Secret Six and its operatives. For example, Treasury lent one of its top agents to the Secret Six; Alexander Jamie was a brother-in-law of Ness.

Eliot Ness didn't put Capone away. The single indictment generated by Ness, leveled against Capone for breaking Prohibition laws, was never prosecuted. Yet the colorful Ness team, with its ten-ton truck—complete with steel bumper and scaling ladders—did knock out nineteen Capone distilleries and cut into Capone profits sharply.

For its part, the Secret Six brought to the table big money that could be allocated at a moment's notice, no questions asked. For example, the Secret Six gave the Treasury Department ten thousand dollars to take Capone bookkeeper and key witness Jacob Ries out of harm's way on a ninety-day ocean voyage in the Atlantic until time for the trial.

The Secret Six also paid a low-ranking member of the Capone gang one thousand dollars for information that mobster Frank Nitti was hiding in a bungalow in suburban Berwyn. Federal agents surrounded Nitti, who was later convicted of income tax evasion; Guzik and Capone followed.

Public attention was also critical and Ness and "the Colonel" were their own best press agents. Ness, the Untouchables, Randolph, and the mysterious Secret Six became the ever-present good guys, the cavalry coming to the rescue to save a city grown weary of gangster mayhem.

Information put Capone away. The team of federal and private agents provided it.

H. B. Barnard carried a snub-nosed .38 pistol with him the rest of his life and every night put it on the table next to his bed. For years, he was accompanied by police bodyguards. He received several pieces of mail with messages made of letters cut out of magazines declaring, "We'll get you!"

Barnard assured his wife, "They wouldn't shoot me. I'm too much in the limelight." He didn't believe it. He never disclosed that he was a member of the Secret Six. Four decades after his death, Barnard's son William was paging through a scrapbook. He saw a news article about the Secret Six and Capone. H. B. had made a notation alongside the clipping: "I was one of the Secret Six, H.B.B."

Frank Loesch continued as president of the Chicago Crime Commission until 1937, retiring when he was eighty-five. He died in 1944. His obituary in the *Chicago American* noted, "Frank Loesch demonstrated two things: first, that decency can prevail, with courageous leadership, over even the most powerful alliance of crime and crookedness: and second, that a man's years are no fit gauge of his capacity for usefulness."

SOURCES

Historian Dennis Hoffman is author of the most authoritative account of the "Secret Six," *Business vs. Organized Crime* (Chicago: Chicago Crime Commission, 1989). Hoffman expanded this monograph into *Scarface Al and the Crime Crusaders* (Carbondale: Southern Illinois University Press, 1993). The author expresses his debt to the Hoffman works.

Equally important have been interviews (summer of 2001), personal papers, and extensive newspaper clippings provided by William and Burton Barnard, sons of H. B. Barnard, and William Barnard's son James. This information is, I believe, original with this book. William Barnard is a member of the Club.

I draw upon the memoirs of Judge John H. Lyle, *The Dry and Lawless Years* (Englewood Cliffs, N.J.: Prentice Hall, Inc., 1960).

The early reminiscences about Charles Dawes were taken from Bruce Grant, *Fight for a City,* and Paul R. Leach, *That Man Dawes* (Chicago: Reilly and Lee, 1930).

In addition to newspaper accounts from the period, the author drew upon the following:

Allsop, Kenneth. *The Bootleggers*. New Rochelle, N.Y.: Arlington House, 1961.

Ciccone, F. Richard. *Chicago and the American Century*. Chicago: Contemporary Books, 1999.

Demaris, Ovid. *Captive City*. New York: Lyle Stuart Inc., 1969.

Kobler, John. *Capone*. New York: G. P. Putnam's Sons, 1971.

Landesco, John. *Organized Crime in Chicago*. Chicago: University of Chicago Press, 1929.

Sullivan, Edward D. *Rattling the Cup on Chicago Crime*. New York: Vanguard Press, 1929.

Other, more general sources include Dedmon's *Fabulous Chicago* and Howard's *Mostly Good and Competent Men,* and:

Asbury, Herbert. *Gem of the Prairie*. Garden City, N.Y.: Garden City Publishing Co., Inc., 1940.

Bachmann, Lawrence P. "Julius Rosenwald." *American Jewish Historical Quarterly,* September 1976.

Chicago Civic Agencies. Chicago: University of Chicago Press for the Public Affairs Council of the Union League of Chicago, 1927.

Howard, Robert P. *Illinois: A History of the Prairie State*. Grand Rapids, Mich.: William B. Eerdmans Publishing Co., 1972.

Werner, M. R. *Julius Rosenwald*. New York: Harper & Brothers, 1939.

Darkness

Chapter 9

A GENTLEMAN'S AGREEMENT

In the early nineteenth century, Jews were not so victimized nor so exploited as were Irish Catholics, according to Leonard Dinnerstein, author of *Antisemitism in America* (1994). Successful, generally German, Jews (who often assimilated into their communities) were among, and continued to be among, the elites of many cities. Beginning in 1880, however, and continuing until 1920, a great number of Jews (as well as others) emigrated from Russia and Eastern Europe to America. From 300,000 Jews in the United States in 1880, the number grew to 3.5 million in 1920, according to Jacob Rader Marcus. In sharp contrast to the German Jews, Jews from Eastern Europe were generally poorer and less educated.

Anti-Semitism began to spread, however, by the 1890s. In Cleveland, Dinnerstein notes, Jews could no longer join the city's exclusive Union Club. Jesse Seligman, a founder of the Union League of New York, resigned in 1893 when his son was blackballed because Jews were no longer admitted.

This was not quite so, at least not in the nineteenth century, at the Union League Club of Chicago.

Dankmar Adler, son of a rabbi, was an early member of the Club as well as an officer at the Standard Club, a club for German Jews, which in the nineteenth century was located outside the central business district on the south side of Chicago. David, Isaac, and Levi Mayer were early members of both clubs.

There were apparently so many Jews in the early Club that it became an issue, at least to Julius Starrett, who joined the Club in 1883. The following is taken verbatim from Starrett's reminiscences of early Club life, written much later, in 1925:

I remember the complaint that was made against the influx of Hebrews into membership of the Club. At first, when there were only a few, they were generally sociable with the Americans, but afterwards, when they had attracted more of their race in considerable numbers, they flocked to themselves in some part of the lounge, and this was noticeable and displeasing to the other members. As the members would not tolerate a click [*sic*] in the government of the Club, so they did not like to see a racial click in a social way in the lounge, and there was considerable feeling about it expressed by the Americans.

Finally, this feeling ran so high that the Board of Managers resolved to refuse admission to the next Hebrew applicant for membership, solely on the ground of his race, however unexceptionable he might be in other respects. It was not long before E. Mandel, the State Street merchant, applied for membership, a fine gentleman in every respect. But he was refused admission because he was a Hebrew. Then most of the Hebrews withdrew from the Club and went up to Michigan Avenue and 24th Street and established the Standard Club with a purely Hebrew membership.

Thus was a rather annoying and delicate matter in the life of the Club disposed of to the satisfaction of everybody.

Starrett's recollections are flawed on at least two matters. The Standard Club was established in 1869, a decade before the Union League Club. The Standard Club did, however, move in 1889 to a new clubhouse at the address cited by Starrett. So it is assumed, maybe incorrectly, that his reference to E. Mandel precedes that year. However, in 1890 Emil G. Hirsch, the highly regarded rabbi of Sinai Temple, was elected to membership in the Union League Club and he became active on the political action committee.

Thus any value in Starrett's reminiscence is limited to the observation that in the 1880s the matter of Jewish membership was an issue, at least among some members of the Club. The issue of German versus Eastern European background is hinted at in the scrawled notes of admission committee members on the application in 1904 of another Hirsch. Hirsch's application was received February 8, 1904, and his name posted in the clubhouse February 26. "G.R.S. [one of the sponsors] says *German*" is scribbled near the top of the simple one-page application form, with the underscoring in the original.

The application lingered until November 13, 1905, almost two years later. There are two notations on the application that mention "withdrawal." One of which, "withdrawal asked," is also dated "Nov.13-05." On that same day Hirsh's application is stamped "elected, Nov. 13, 1905."

Withdrawal of application by the sponsors of a candidate is to this day the diplomatic way of handling an application that is likely to be rejected. Nothing is clear, other than that an inquiry was made of the lead sponsor on the application as to Hirsch's ethnic background. He was elected to membership, but that would be moot if his application had been withdrawn on the same day. The applicant's name never appears in any subsequent annual Club directory, where all member names are listed.

There are many reasons clubs reject members—for example, unsavory business or social practices, hidden in the past that come to light during an informal review of an applicant's background. That is why most city clubs post the names of candidates for membership in the club or in the club newsletter for all members to see. A member may, after all, know something the admissions committee does not.

The Club was certainly not closed to German Jews in the early 1900s. After the apparently awkward handling of the application just noted, prominent Chicagoan Lessing Rosenthal was elected to Club membership in 1907. Rosenthal was also an officer in the Standard Club. The legendary merchant Julius Rosenwald was elected to Club membership in 1910. Rosenwald became an active member of the Club's political action committee. According to his biographer, Rosenwald refused to cross the thresholds of several other prominent downtown clubs because they excluded Jews as members.

Anti-Semitism in America increased further in the period from about 1918 until peaking at the end of World War II. In response to an influx of seventeen million immigrants between 1890 and 1914, most from southern and eastern Europe, the National Origins Acts of 1921 and 1924 allocated quotas of immigrants according to "superior" and "inferior" races, favoring Nordics over Alpines and Mediterraneans, including Jews.

The Bolshevik Revolution of 1917 led to a "Red Scare" in the United States that cast suspicion on many foreigners, including Jews. Manufacturing icon Henry Ford conducted an anti-Semitic diatribe in the 1920s in his local *Dearborn Independent* newspaper. He featured a reprint of the scurrilous, fabricated "Protocols of the Elders of Zion," which reported on a fictitious conference that plotted to destroy Christian civilization and rule the world. Other commentators picked up the drumbeat of anti-Semitism that began to throb across the country.

The Standard Club moved in 1926 from the south side to a new clubhouse in the south Loop. This present clubhouse is less than a block away from the Union League facility, separated only by the Monadnock Building. The Union League also constructed its present clubhouse at the same time, on the same location as its predecessor clubhouse, at 65 West Jackson. The

Standard Club laid its cornerstone September 23, 1925; the Union League, less than a month later on October 12. Both clubs opened their new facilities the following year.

Each club sold bonds to finance its construction projects. Members were called upon to buy these bonds.

Isaac Mayer was a member of the Club from 1891 until the club year 1967, when he died. Shortly before his death, Mayer was interviewed by Roger Henn, who reported the following: Jews who belonged to both the Union League and Standard clubs generally gave their first allegiance to the latter. With the Standard Club's new clubhouse, members of that club now had a facility in the heart of the city for dining and social events. As a result, these members often invested in the Standard Club bonds and not those of the Union League. This apparently left a bad taste with some Union League members and from that point Jews were made to feel less welcome at the Club.

While that might have been the case, a review of the club members in 1922 who had possibly Jewish names—such as Fischer, Mayer, Reichmann, Rosenwald, Rosenthal—finds that these members were still on the Club rolls in the 1929 Club directory. There is no way of determining from Club records who was Jewish, as questions of religion and family background were not then asked on the application for membership.

The Depression came on the heels of the new clubhouses. In the minds of Christian radio evangelists Gerald L. K. Smith and Father Charles E. Coughlin, Jews represented the Devil incarnate, largely responsible for American woes. Each week, Smith and Coughlin reached millions of listeners across the country with virulent hate messages that attacked Jews for their alleged roles in the birth of both the world monetary system and communism and for the Jewish denial of the Messiah.

According to Frederic Cople Jaher, even the *Christian Century*, a magazine of liberal Protestantism, with the largest number of subscribers among Protestant weeklies, "relentlessly assailed the Jews."

In 1949, Gregory Peck starred as a New York City writer who assumed the role of a Jew in the movie *A Gentleman's Agreement*. The Peck character became appalled at the pervasive anti-Semitism he encountered. The movie received the Oscar for best picture in 1949. It was considered courageous at the time for bringing to American audiences the significant anti-Semitism found in business, social, and club life.

A "gentleman's agreement" apparently existed among many members in the Union League Club of Chicago, primarily from the 1930s to the early

1960s, it would appear, based on a limited number of notations and letters found in membership files in the Club archives.

The original application for membership in the Union League Club in 1880 was a three-by-six-inch card on which the applicant put his name and address. In addition, there were two lines for signatures under the words: "We recommend this applicant." And a place for the date. That was it.

Over the years, the Club requested additional personal information. By the 1920s, the application sought information as to profession, business, date and place of birth, military record, clubs and societies, and finally, church membership and name of church.

By the 1940s, requested family detail expanded to include father's name, mother's maiden name, and wife's maiden name, as well as the place of birth of each.

The height of detail was reached in 1964 when all of the following information was requested:

> father's name, nationality, religion, place of birth
>
> mother's maiden name, nationality, religion, place of birth
>
> wife's maiden name, nationality, religion, place of birth
>
> wife's father's name, nationality, religion, place of birth
>
> wife's mother's maiden name, nationality, religion, place of birth

In 1936, the issue of "foreign" and Jewish background appears in notations on at least one application. The applicant in question is the president of a prominent oriental rug company in Chicago. A letter in the applicant's file from a sponsor reassures an admissions committee member that the applicant's "folks in Armenia were both Congregationalists," and that his wife's father was a Congregational minister in Armenia and later in Massachusetts. "That should be positive evidence," the letter goes on, "that there is no racial question such as has been raised in his family."

There is, however, another letter in the file from a Club member: "Suggest you boys be cautious here. This man is an Armenian Jew and is so known by many members, and his election might cause internal unpleasantness. In our zeal for new members we must not let down bars."

Admissions committee members were clearly concerned about "a cloud over this man," as one notation puts it on the application folder. Another handwritten comment reports that a Club member "has done an investigation on nationality and finds he is *not* Jewish—is making another check" (emphasis in original).

Another adds this note: "References are excellent. File would justify approval. Outside information suggests caution. Is applicant an Armenian Jew. Would his membership and presence in the Club embarrass the members. When in doubt I would favor the [unintelligible word]."

The candidate *was* elected to membership in the Club and remained in the Club until his death in 1948.

A 1944 application from a man born in Prague in what was then Austria-Hungary also raised deep concerns among the admissions committee. As the folder is reviewed by one admissions committee, then another, these notations appear. "How about nationality? Father [crossed out, but legible] changed name. Probably not Jewish or wouldn't [following is blackened out, but appears to read] want in here."

"Changed his name to Americanize it—not Jewish." "NATIONALITY!" (emphasis in original).

The sponsor of the candidate sought a reference from the man's Ivy League university dean, who reported that the candidate had served admirably as president of the Chicago alumni club of the distinguished university.

The committee asked a nonmember to check out the candidate. He reported that: "One of his close social acquaintances reports that the question of nationality had never occurred to him in all of his years of association with Mr. ——— and that he was positive he was a gentile. Inquiry was also made of the president of the [suburban Chicago] Country Club, of which Mr. ——— has been a member for the past two years. Their Admissions Committee is very strict on the question of nationality and after a thorough investigation they admitted him to membership. He has conducted himself in a most satisfactory manner."

Nevertheless, the admissions committee voted three to approve, one to defer, and four to withdraw the nomination, which the sponsor did by letter in early 1945.

Several applications in the 1940s and 1950s appear to gain approval when comments are noted by references or committee members that the applicant is "not Jewish."

Or, "Tell those who marked 'defer' that we are assured this man not Jewish."

The most dispiriting correspondence in this regard found in the files of Club archives comes from 1957. A prominent, conservative downstate publisher, known to the author by acquaintance, wrote the Club secretary as follows:

> One of our local doctors and physicians, Dr. ——— has asked me if he could file application for [nonresident] membership in the Union League Club. I told him I would find out.

His wife is Jewish and a very lovely person. The doctor is not Jewish and I think perhaps it best that I ask you to find out from the committee if they would allow a person to join whose wife is Jewish.

It so happens that the doctor and his wife are very well thought of, fine citizens of our community and he happens to be my personal family doctor and I am trying to avoid an embarrassing situation in case our club has certain rules. I assure you that no one would ever be embarrassed for having either one of them in their company. In case you have rules to the contrary, would it be possible to send me a letter saying the quota of non-resident membership has been filled temporarily? I do not know whether this would solve the problem because they would ask me to let them know when there would be an opening.

I will appreciate anything that you might do. I personally would not hesitate one minute to recommend Dr. ———— for membership and I consider his wife also a very lovely, fine person. I will appreciate your letting me know of the above.

Ten days later the Club secretary responded tersely to the inquiry:

Your letter of May 3rd was presented to the Admissions Committee of the Club at their meeting last Friday afternoon.

The committee discussed this matter at length and most regretfully reached a decision that an application from Dr. ———— would probably not be approved if it were submitted.

These few illustrations represent the only ones found in archival files that discuss the issues of nationality and religion. Most files lack notations of any kind; indeed, such permanent personal notations are generally discouraged. There don't, however, have to be many such for a "gentleman's agreement" to become known and understood throughout an urban community, even one as large as Chicago.

Indeed, a person interviewed for this book who was in the Club daily in the 1950s recalled that when a Jew might express interest in membership in the Club, he was told, "Oh, you don't want to belong here. You'd prefer the Standard Club, which is next door. The food is better there anyway."

The "gentleman's agreement" apparently dissolved in the 1960s and the questions of religion and nationality of parents were dropped in the mid-1970s. An infusion of new and younger members in 1952 probably contributed to the change in Club attitude.

Vernon Loucks was Club president that year. Times were tough. The Club was losing membership and money. Something drastic had to be done. Loucks announced that the five-hundred-dollar initiation fee would be waived for the month of October. Members were encouraged to bring in young men from their business, law, and banking offices. More than a thousand new members joined, most of them under forty. This increased the size of the Club by more than a third and was to change the nature of the organization.

"When I came in in 1952," a man who later became Club president recalled, chuckling, "there were two types of members—those who couldn't piss and those who couldn't stop." Soon, however, the place was loosening up a bit under the influence of the influx of younger members.

"When I came to the Club in 1959," recalls Roger Henn, public affairs director for two decades, "the place was stiff and formal. But change was in the air. I got a number of the younger members involved in the public affairs committee, which is the best route to officership in the Club."

"Charlie Weaver came in after me as president," notes Henry Pitts, Club president in 1962. "Charlie upset the group that controlled the admissions committee. He got rid of most of the old guard."

In the 1960s, Jews began to feel more comfortable in the confines of the Club. A few became members. By 1997, *The Forward,* the nation's leading newspaper for Jews, ran a major feature story titled UNION LEAGUE GROWS JEWISH ROOTS: ONCE RESTRICTED CLUB NOW SERVES MATZOH BALL SOUP.

The article begins by noting that *Business Week* rated the Club as the best private city club in the city and one of the ten best in the country and adds immediately: "The Union League Club's wood paneled walls—where a few years ago a Jew would have been a rare sight—have become a center of Yiddishkeit in downtown Chicago. The club recently sponsored a mission to Israel, and last year hosted a 'Third Seder,' attended by Jewish and non-Jewish members alike."

Hugh Schwartzberg belonged to the former Covenant Club of Chicago, which was created by Eastern European Jews with a clubhouse at 10 North Dearborn. Schwartzberg joined the club in 1988 and has been a director of the Union League, chair of the public affairs committee, and president of the Civic and Arts Foundation. Seymour Persky, a member of the Standard Club, has also been a director of the Club as have a number of other Jews. In 1997 the Israeli consulate held its Chicago golden anniversary celebration of the country's founding at the Union League Club.

Instead of "growing Jewish roots," the Club had returned to its roots of openness to Jews.

SOURCES

The comprehensive archives of the Club provided the primary source material for this chapter. This was complemented by a number of interviews with

Club members and staff. These included: Everett Barlow, club historian; Henry L. Pitts, Roger Henn, Hugh Schwartzberg, and Marsha Pender.

Other sources include:

Birmingham, Stephen. *The Rest of Us: The Rise of American Eastern European Jews.* Boston: Little, Brown & Co., 1984.

Dinnerstein, Leonard. *Antisemitism in America.* New York: Oxford University Press, 1994.

Jaher, Frederic Cople. *A Scapegoat in the New Wilderness.* Cambridge, Mass.: Harvard University Press, 1994.

Marcus, Jacob Rader. "Background for the History of American Jewry." In *The American Jew,* edited by Oscar I. Janowsky. Philadelphia: The Jewish Publication Society of America, 1964.

"Union League Grows Jewish Roots." *The Forward,* September 5, 1997 (located in ULCC archives).

Chapter 10

OLD CROW AND JIM CROW

Taylor Hay was well built, dark, and handsome; possibly some American Indian blood, say people in the Club who knew him. He had a full face, bushy, dark eyebrows, and a commanding presence. Descended from President Zachary Taylor, his great-grandfather was E. H. Taylor, who started the Kentucky distilleries that produced Old Taylor and Old Crow bourbon whiskies.

Hay was proud to be a Kentucky colonel and an unreconstructed southerner.

His branch of the family lost its wealth during Prohibition. As a young man Hay sought his fortune in Baja California, working as assistant manager of a lush resort owned by Baron Long. In 1937, he was lured to Chicago to become assistant manager of the Drake Hotel. Upon arrival, he found the job to be less than he expected. That same year a member of the Union League Club observed him at work and brought him over to the Club to become its manager.

Hay ran the Club well, certainly to the liking of about thirty mostly older single men who had permanent rooms at the Club. According to Roger Henn, "Hay ran the Club like a plantation. He knew every employee; every employee reported directly to him." Hay lived in the Club, returning some weekends to Kentucky and his family home.

Together, Hay and his friends dominated the Club throughout the 1940s and 1950s. Together, they changed longstanding policy in 1940: as of that year, African Americans were no longer to darken the front door of the Union League Club of Chicago.

The dramatic change in policy, invoked quietly, startled F. A. Hathaway, general secretary of the Young Men's Christian Association of

Chicago. On December 27, 1940, he wrote to his YMCA board member, and Club member, George B. McKibbin:

> I was greatly surprised to get your report with respect to the policy of the Union League Club in refusing to accept reservations for service in the private dining rooms where [when] Negroes are included. As you know, it has been the policy of the YMCA for many years to hold various meetings at the Union League club in which Negroes have been included. On January 18, 1934 and January 17, 1935, we held the Annual Meetings of the YMCA of Chicago in the Union League Club *in the Main Dining Room,* and at each meeting there were from thirty-five to forty Negro men and women present. The question was never raised [emphasis in original].
>
> About six weeks ago Mr. Jeffrey R. Short invited the chairmen of all local boards of the YMCA to a dinner in the Steel Room which included the Negro chairman of our Wabash Avenue Department. No questions were raised. It is because of these past experiences that I assumed the former policies of the Union League Club with respect to this matter had not been changed, and it was only at the suggestion of an outsider that I called the catering department to check the matter.

George McKibbin followed this letter with one of his own to the president of the Club to protest the change in policy and express his deep embarrassment: "As a member of the club I desire to enter my protest against such a rule and respectfully request that the Board of Directors take such action as may be necessary to permit the Y.M.C.A., and similar organizations, to hold such a meeting in the Club in the future."

McKibbin went on to list fourteen members of the YMCA board who were also members of the Club, including several surnames that might be known to Chicago readers today, including William P. Sidley, John Nuveen, T. E. Donnelley, M. Hadden MacLean, C. T. B. Goodspeed, and Stanley G. Harris.

The rule stood.

The next expression of concern found in the Club archives about the rule barring blacks from the Club is dated February 15, 1949. A memorandum was sent to the board of directors by six Club members who served as chairmen of committees of the Club. First on the list was James E. Kidwell, chairman of the race relations forum. Extracts from the memo follow:

> This memorandum is submitted to the Board of Directors in support of the following suggestion: That the rule against the admission of colored guests in the Clubhouse be modified to the extent that it would be possi-

ble for civic committees of the Club, with the approval of the President of the Club and the Chairman of the Public Affairs Committee, to invite Negro leaders as occasion arises to visit the private dining rooms of the Clubhouse for the purpose of conferring with them concerning public affairs.

At the present time, three Club committees desire to confer with Negro members of public agencies on specific matters, but are not permitted to invite them to attend meetings in the Clubhouse. . . .

We would remind the Board that for many years Negroes were permitted to attend meetings in private dining rooms. We suggest this is *not* a restoration of that general practice, but merely an authorization for the Club's own committees . . . to confer from time to time, in further-ance of the Club's civic and patriotic objectives as stated in its charter objects [emphasis in original].

The rule stood.

Dr. Percy L. Julian was named Chicagoan of the Year in 1950 by the *Chicago Sun-Times* and the Junior Chamber of Commerce. A world-famed chemist, Julian developed synthetic drugs for the treatment of arthritis, rheumatic fever, and glaucoma, and a fire-fighting foam that saved thousands of lives during World War II, among many other scientific accomplishments.

So it was understandable that New York scientist and businessman Joseph Barker would invite Julian to join thirty-five scientists to hear the discoverer of vitamin B-1 report on his recent investigations in Asia on the use of American-made vitamins to reinforce rice-based diets. The luncheon meeting was to be held in July 1951 at the Union League Club.

However, when Taylor Hay saw Julian's name among place cards at the luncheon table, he called host Barker to tell him Julian would not be per-mitted to enter the building.

Barker called Julian to "apologize deeply" for not being able to have him at the luncheon.

Percy Julian was not one to take this sitting down, for understandable reasons. According to the *Chicago Tribune,* in November of the preceding year Julian's home in Oak Park, a suburb that abuts Chicago on the west, was entered by arsonists who splashed its interior with gasoline and tried to set it afire. On June 12, 1951, a bomb exploded in the Julians' yard. Julian and his family had been the first blacks to move into that comfortable suburb.

Julian lashed out at the Club to reporters:

It appears to me that organizations like the Union League Club are as directly responsible as any other agency for such un-American incidents as the bombing of my home in Oak Park and the Cicero riot [July 10–12, 1951].

When individuals supposedly in high places behave as the Union League club has behaved, ordinary citizens of lesser intelligence follow suit.

While they may not be able to deny a Negro American civilized treatment by forcing the revocation of an invitation, they can resort to the bomb and mob violence. (*Chicago Tribune,* July 19, 1951.)

The *Chicago Sun-Times* and other publications, including *Time* magazine, contrasted the Club policy with the roots of the Union League.

The Encyclopedia Americana says the Union League Club is an offshoot of the Union League of America, an organization of whites and Negroes set up during the Civil War.

In the North, the movement began to die out after 1865 and the surviving leagues became social clubs.

In the South for many years after the Civil War, the league was a political machine controlling the votes of Negroes.

In recent years, the Union League clubs have been accused of being strongholds of wealthy conservatism and reaction and of influencing Republican Party politics. (*Chicago Sun-Times,* July 19, 1951).

Two months later a Club spokesman issued a statement, reported in Chicago newspapers, that "Negroes will not be barred from club functions in the future when they are invited by club members."

"The members agreed," said the unnamed spokesman, "that barring Julian from the luncheon . . . was a mistake."

But few if any members did bring blacks into the Club. Race still mattered mightily to Taylor Hay and his group of Club residents on the sixteenth floor, as the James Parsons controversy a decade later illustrated.

"I never expected to be appointed federal judge," Parsons told Club historian Everett Barlow some years after the incident. "I dropped a dish when I heard it on the radio."

In 1961, President John F. Kennedy nominated James Parsons to become a district court judge for the northern district of Illinois. He was the first African American to be appointed to a federal district court. The district court for the northern district of Illinois had met in the federal building across the street from the Club for decades. For almost as many decades, the Club had extended "privileges" to the federal judges. This meant they could use the Club facilities as if they were members, paying their own charges but neither an initiation fee nor dues. The judges met weekly as a group in the Club and took luncheon frequently as individuals or in small groups.

Until James Parsons became a judge, that is.

The Club Board immediately revoked the judicial privilege.

This generated much, often agitated, comment in Loop legal circles. A flurry of board meetings ensued and several months later the privilege was reinstated. But a strong statement had been made about how the Club leadership really felt about having blacks in the Club, even black federal judges.

Nineteen sixty-nine was a big year for the Club. *Men & Events*, the Club magazine, trumpeted the nominations by President Richard M. Nixon of longtime Club members David M. Kennedy and Maurice Stans to be secretaries of the Treasury and Commerce departments, respectively. In Illinois, Club member Richard B. Ogilvie had been inaugurated governor of Illinois and Ogilvie had appointed Club member and Better Government Association executive director George Mahin to head the state's important Department of Revenue.

Men & Events was also filled with the vibrant social life of the Club. The popular Saturday afternoon travelogue series included Cleveland Grant, who presented "Garden of Africa," and Lisa Chickering and Jeanne Porterfield on "Europe's Miniature Countries." Dick Jurgens and orchestra played for a buffet dinner dance and Woody Herman and his "New Herd" gave a concert in the main ballroom.

Each month the magazine provided brief biographies and photos of some of the new members elected, noting they were president of this, executive vice president of that, and partner at such-and-such law firm.

Nowhere in the twelve issues of 1969 did the Club publication mention the issue that threatened to tear the Club apart and consumed the energies and emotions of men on both sides of the matter.

Fred Ford is the type who would never push an issue nor ever back down from one. He is tall, quiet, self-confident, successful. In the 1940s, he was the first African American elected president of the student senate at the University of Illinois at Urbana; he also served as president of Kappa Alpha Psi, a black fraternity. He became one of the first black certified public accountants in the nation. When he was graduated from the university's accounting program, he went on for a master's degree. Unable to get a teaching fellowship while in graduate school, probably because of race, Ford got by with "meal jobs" and work in the summer.

Ford entered accounting in Chicago for Mary Washington, the first woman of color in the United States to earn an accounting degree. After a few years, he joined Draper & Kramer, a mortgage banking, property management, and development company in Chicago where he still works.

Ford was executive vice president of Draper & Kramer in 1968. He was active on many boards including the Chicago YMCA, where he served with Milton F. Darr, Jr., president of LaSalle National Bank, and E. Stanley Enlund, president of First Federal Savings.

"Fred was astute, sharp, capable," recalled Darr, who became president of the Union League Club in 1968, to serve by tradition for one year until June of 1969. "Stan and I thought Fred would make a good member of the Club. We didn't think about the race issue."

This last comment is a bit disingenuous, given all that had gone before. Darr joined the Club in 1955 and Taylor Hay was still the Club manager in 1968. Indeed, Fred Ford had cautioned them: "Don't you know what you're getting in for?" Ford neither pushed nor backed down. He agreed to sponsorship for membership by Stan Enlund and John McEnerny, chairs respectively of the important house and public affairs committees. Enlund was a highly visible member of the Chicago business and civic community.

Darr was a good club politician. He knew his board would back him. "We had a cohesive board," Darr recalled. First, however, he and the sponsors had to see Ford through an admissions process that would draw the entire club into a bitter debate.

Proposals for membership, sponsored by no fewer than two Club members, went into an application folder. References from six additional persons were to be added to the folder.

Members of the admissions committee reviewed the folders. Five signatures were required to authorize a personal interview with the candidate by the full committee. Committee members had these options: approve, defer, or reject (in earlier years, the term "withdraw" was used in place of "reject").

Names of candidates were posted in the clubhouse, so members could review and comment if they wished. At least ten days after the posting, the committee would interview the candidate. Then the committee voted to recommend or not recommend a candidate to the board. Sometimes prior to a vote, the committee might ask the lead sponsor for additional information about the candidate. After receiving the committee's recommendation, the board of directors voted to elect or not elect the candidate.

By custom, if one member, and certainly if more than one member, of the admissions committee voted to defer a candidate, a member of the committee went to the lead sponsor and asked him to withdraw his proposal for membership. In this way, no proposal ever needed to be formally rejected. The process from proposal to election of a member took two to three months.

The Ford file went to the admissions committee in November 1968.

According to notes on the Fred Ford file folder, handwritten by committee chair Charles Albers, reference letters were to be back for the

December 6 meeting of the committee. The candidate's name was posted in the clubhouse December 4.

At the December 6 meeting of the committee, eight members voted to approve the candidate and one voted to defer. Ford's personal interview with the committee was set for December 13. Every member of the committee was so advised, stated Albers in a December letter to president Darr.

Turmoil reigned at the Club and it wasn't all sotto voce. "The Club was divided down the middle," recalled club historian Everett Barlow. "In all my years in the Club, this was the most divisive thing that ever happened in the sense of the language used, which was more abusive from member to member than even later over women membership."

"Feelings were running very high," said Ford. "I worried about Stan [Enlund] and Milt [Darr] at their banks. But they never flinched. I give them a great deal of credit."

"Taylor Hay was smart enough to stay out of this one," says Darr, "to my knowledge anyway."

At least four letters were sent to the board and committee prior to the December 13 meeting of the committee. Substantial verbatim extracts are provided here:

DECEMBER 11, 1968

I have been a member of the Union League Club of Chicago and have lived in the clubhouse for 35 years.

The proposal that Frederick C. Ford be admitted to membership in the Club is meeting with such opposition and is creating such serious problems that action on the proposal should be deferred until all club members are fairly informed and given opportunity to express their views by referendum or other democratic process.

Overwhelming majority of club members and club employees with whom I have discussed this matter would favor such a procedure.

It is the duty of the officers and directors of the club to reflect the desires of the majority—not the minority—of the members who elected them to their positions of trust.

DECEMBER 9

I notice in the December issue of Men & Events that a man by the name of Frederick C. Ford . . . is proposed for membership. . . . Furthermore, I understand that Mr. Ford is a Negro—or "black" as they say now. . . .

I have been a member of our fine Club for more than forty years and have served as a Director and Officer on several occasions. . . .

I feel very strongly, and I know my opinion is shared by others, that electing Mr. Ford to membership could result in great harm to our

Club. A good many of our finest members, in my opinion, would gradually drift away and eventually move elsewhere. I realize full well the situation confronting our Country today but on the other hand the Union League Club is a private organization and is under the direction of the President and Board of Directors. Their responsibility, as I see it, is to act in a way which will strengthen the Club, not weaken it.

I urge you to refrain from electing this negro to membership in the Club.

DECEMBER 10

[From a past president:] Although readily acknowledging the Board's sole responsibility under the By-Laws for direction of the Club's affairs, I cannot comprehend why, in the matter of such significance, it did not broaden the base for its apparent consensus by undertaking a determination of probable consequences through discreet consultation with a representative segment of membership. There is ample precedent for such a course in matters of far less moment.

I have been led to infer that the motivation for the contemplated action lies in a conviction of its necessity in further implementing the Club's Public Affairs program. If so, it is news to me that such a criterion should take precedence over traditional guidelines. In my opinion, to give it such is to risk a confrontation with the membership over the Club's future in public affairs.

DECEMBER 11

[From another past president:] Do you think it is fair to the membership of the Club not to disclose that Mr. Frederick C. Ford is a Negro, and while he may be representative of the outstanding characteristics that are found in some members of that race, on the other hand the Directors of the Union League Club have a responsibility in preserving the standards that have been our yardstick in the selection of members since the inception of our Club.

It is my personal opinion that to deviate from the hard and fast rules that have been followed in the past is not the privilege nor the responsibility of the Admissions Committee or the Directors of the Club, and if we are to change our attitude toward this type of applicant then such change should be in the form of a proposal that should be voted on by every resident member of the Union League Club.

Ten members of the committee attended the personal interview with Fred Ford. In his notes on the folder, committee chair Albers noted: "There will be some negative votes in all probability, as many believe that the principle [of allowing blacks to membership] should be first approved by Board."

In a letter to president Darr, dated December 13, Albers reported:

The entire admissions Committee with the exception of ——, who has been ill, has had every opportunity to fully peruse the Ford file, and every member of the Committee was advised that Mr. Ford would be interviewed today. Ten members attended, and I am satisfied that the absent members were unavoidably kept away. Of the ten present, three voted to defer the matter for further consideration, and seven approved. The consensus of opinion was that Mr. Ford handled himself very well and made an excellent impression. The deferrals noted were not at all because of the individual, but rather because they felt that this action represented a departure from established policy, which should first have been set by the directors. I thought the board should have these facts before it.

Handwritten at the bottom of the letter, in Albers' minuscule hand: "Three additional members *not* present—have since indicated for deferral [emphasis in original]."

On the front cover of a candidate's folder, a rubber stamp's imprint provides columns in which committee members are to initial under APPROVE, DEFER, or REJECT. On the Ford folder, there are seven sets of initials in the APPROVE column, six in the DEFER space, and none in REJECT.

The proposal folder was forwarded to the board for action.

Pressure now focused on the board. To provide some further, limited airing of the issue, but far short of a club-wide referendum, the board called a discussion meeting for the board, admissions committee, and, it appeared, past presidents.

Club presidents traditionally serve one year only, so there are always a number of past presidents who continue their club activity. Past presidents have been by tradition convened by a serving president to provide counsel based on their collective institutional knowledge and experience. They are a force within the Club.

There is no record of what was discussed at this meeting, other than indirectly, as in this letter to Darr from a past president:

JANUARY 16

It seemed to me after the meeting last Wednesday evening there was a more or less general agreement that the officers and Board would act on the application under discussion probably at the next meeting after obtaining the best information available as to the attitude on the question by the Club membership. There was a full realization that it would be difficult to obtain an accurate count of the membership and it would rest with the Board to take final action.

For the information of the officers and Board members at the suggestion of several of the past presidents I made a count of the opinions of approval or rejection of the application under discussion. For approval of the application: three [who are named]. For rejection: ten [who are named]. Joe Matter advises me that because he has been out of touch with affairs for about three years, he believes it would be unwise for him to do other than leave it to the good judgment of the officers and Board.

In the Ford folder, there is also a sheet with a listing of Club members who are designated as being FOR or AGAINST the application. The sheet is unidentified, but appears to represent a poll of former members of the board, for the benefit of the board at the time. Twenty-three members are indicated FOR and fifty-nine AGAINST.

The fifty-nine against approval became members of the Club, on average, around 1942; those in favor of Fred Ford's election entered, on average, about fifteen years later. This offers some support for the observation that older members of the Club tended to be opposed to the admission of blacks, while those elected almost a generation later were more inclined to support having a black member.

Past president Joseph A. Matter, cited above in a letter, also refers to a "change in the character of our membership" in this letter to president Milt Darr:

JANUARY 17, 1969

Let me say first that you have my fraternal sympathy for having this problem [Fred Ford application] to wrestle with. The only time it has been acute before was during my administration. You may remember when Percy Julian, a world-famous Negro chemist who had just received the award as "Chicagoan of the Year," was refused admittance to a luncheon in the Club. I was in California at the time. My first knowledge of what had happened came through a long three-page telegram from Roy Wilkins in behalf of the NAACP. I thought at first one of my friends was ribbing me, but unfortunately this wasn't so. It seems to me that every newspaper, news magazine and radio station in the country played the thing up and the incident of course badly marred the Club's reputation as a civic force. After several Board meetings we put into effect a new set of rules which prevented a similar recurrence. . . .

I do not believe that our rejection of this particular application, even though the rejection receives considerable publicity, is necessarily going to eliminate the Club as an active advocate of better government.

We have been so strong and frequently so potent an advocate of more honest and efficient government ever since our founding that I should be very unhappy to see anything done which would reduce our status to that of purely a social Club.

I am afraid that I would not have too much confidence of the outcome of a membership poll of the kind Bill suggests [of all the membership]. Twenty or more years ago I would have been quite confident of the outcome but the character of our membership has changed substantially since that time. As an alternative, it has occurred to me that there might be submitted to vote of the members at the next annual meeting, an amendment to the by-laws which would simply preclude the rejection of the application of an otherwise qualified person on grounds of race or religion. Presumably the present application is not going to be accepted. This would give us time in which to turn around and would be a relatively innocuous means of determining membership sentiment. I am quite sure that all members voting on the amendment would realize its purpose and would vote in favor of or against it accordingly. . . .

Purely as a personal matter, I would have no objection to Club membership by several completely well-qualified persons of non-Caucasian descent. I realize, however, that having once accepted a few such applications it might become a very difficult problem indeed to exercise our usual strict and impartial treatment in passing on similar applications. I also realize the necessity of preventing a deep-seated dissension which might result in fatal or near fatal Club financial maintenance. Even with membership requirements which are subject to criticism, the Club's efforts in behalf of better government would be of more value than those of a Club slowly subsiding into bankruptcy. . . .

I sympathize sincerely with you and the box you are in. There is no obviously completely satisfactory solution. . . .

John

On January 21, 1969, the board elected Frederick C. Ford to membership in the Union League Club. The vote was unanimous with one member absenting himself.

On February 12, Irv Kupcinet commented in his *Sun-Times* column: "Lincoln's birthday is the appropriate day to reveal that the very posh and, up to now, lily-white Union League club has accepted its first black member. He's Frederick Ford, vice president of Draper and Kramer. Time marches on."

Club president Darr received both bitter and congratulatory letters in response to Ford's election. The Club archives hold a dozen responses. Several are excerpted here. First the bitter ones:

[From a nonresident member in California:] It does not speak too well for the applicant himself that he should seek membership in a private all-white club through the back door, as it were, by the connivance of the Officers of the Club.

His admission constitutes a momentous change in the atmosphere of the Club. . . . What about our ladies? We have many social activities at the Club during the year, and are they going to be satisfied with an integrated attendance threat. And what about the temporary occupation of bedrooms by friends of the applicant. This is only the beginning in any event.

MARCH 21

[From a nonresident member from Wisconsin:] If you wish to admit Negroes, then submit that policy change to the general membership. Have a vote, then abide by what the majority wishes, or have we gotten so intoxicated with the drive to redirect the feelings of whites that they are going to have to be submitted to the will of the "reformers."

Congratulatory letters are found in the same proportion as those against Ford's election. The following excerpts are representative:

MARCH 6

[From a Chicagoan:] The mission of this letter is to congratulate the Board on having, at long last, brought our Club into the twentieth century. I felt such an abiding shame, a few years ago, at the Judge Parsons incident that I nearly submitted my resignation. Now, I am enormously relieved to know that the blot from that shameful incident has been at least in part removed.

I might add, in passing, that I have not, for more than ten years, urged any of my friends to apply for membership in our Club, simply because I was ashamed to hand them our printed application form, reeking as it is with racial and ethnic bias. Now that our Club has taken the right course—of judging applicants for membership on their individual merits rather than their ancestry—I urge that the existing application form be abandoned and replaced by one which a man can, without qualms, turn over to a friend whom he would like to have as a fellow member.

MARCH 13

[From another Chicagoan:] This is to confirm my unequivocal support of the action of the Board of Directors. . . . Let's get back to something important. Can't there be some improvement in the menus for luncheon.

[From an Evanston, Illinois, member:] Let me congratulate you. . . . Certainly the Club cannot indulge in the hypocrisy of having its origins in the Civil War and being a leader in civic affairs on the one hand and taking a racist attitude on the other. . . .

On the whole I think the Club is extremely well managed in every respect. However, as a member of the Athletic Department I have observed a distinct deterioration in the services available in that area.

The battle for tradition, or the status quo, over change now shifted to the annual election in March of the members' nominating committee. Each spring, the outgoing president and board present a slate of seven members to serve as the nominating committee, which in turn presents a proposed slate of officers and several new board members to be elected at the annual meeting in June. There are also provisions in the bylaws for an alternate members' nominating committee slate, accomplished by a petition of twenty-five members.

On March 6, a "Members' Committee" sent a letter to the membership indicating plans to run an alternate members' slate for the nominating committee:

By now, most of the membership has heard that the Board of Directors of the Union League Club, even knowing of strong protests from the few aware of the intent of certain members of the Board to change tradition with respect to membership of the Club, has nevertheless proceeded to make such a change. . . .

In the judgment of the members who have signed this letter [thirty-three], which includes several past presidents and other past officers of the Club, it is time that the membership is aware of what is happening in the Club, and is certain that the affairs of the Club be conducted in the future in a manner that reflects the will of the majority with respect to this and other matters.

The letter goes on to explain plans to present the alternate slate. In response, Club president Darr sent this letter to Club members:

MARCH 11

Many inquiries have reached the Club for explanation of the "Members Committee" letter of March 6, 1969. Accordingly, the Board of Directors has directed me to inform you of the circumstances.

In January, 1969, the Board of Directors elected to membership in the Union League Club of Chicago a highly qualified gentleman who happens to be a Negro. This action was taken following the normal processing by the Admissions Committee and the Board.

We invite your attention to Section 2 of article I of the By-Laws which provides:

Any male citizen of the United States of lawful age and good moral character shall be eligible for resident membership.

Your Board is committed to sustaining the "Condition of Membership and Primary Corporate Objects" as set forth in your by-Laws, including the obligation ". . . to maintain the civil and political equality of all citizens in every section of our common country."

One member returned the letter, with the following handwritten note: "I think the 'civil and political equality' have no relevance to the subject of your letter of March 11 to members. There is involved only a social policy adhered to for many years by the Club. That policy should not be changed without submission to and approval by the entire membership."

On March 20, the dissidents sent all members a four-page memo. The most pertinent parts follow:

For years there has existed a Union League Club tradition, which probably dates back 90 years to the Club's organization, that no man will be admitted to membership in the Club who is protested by existing members. . . .

With the single exception of the individual referred to in president Darr's letter of March 11, 1969, each and every member of our Club has had to survive the exactions of that tradition in order to be admitted to its privileges and, with that single exception, our board of directors has always honored that tradition. . . .

Six members of our admissions committee after due consideration voted against approval. During the short period remaining prior to date on which the board was to vote . . . more than 100 Club members, including 11 of our past presidents, objected verbally and in writing and asked that the views of Club members first be obtained. But this the Board refused. . . .

We respectfully solicit your support and urge you to vote for the 7 gentlemen proposed by the members for the 1969 Nominating Committee and return your ballot before April 10, 1969.

[Signed in typescript by six members on behalf of the Members' Special Committee.]

A "Volunteer Committee to Support the Board" was created to counter the memos coming out weekly from the dissident "Members' Special Committee" in support of the alternate members' nominating slate. The support-the-board group fired back with a letter, citing the above memo:

This unbridled and unprecedented attack upon the Club officers, directors and Admissions Committee contains gross misstatements of fact concerning Club policy and actions of Admissions Committee and the Board.

One of the examples of misstatement that our investigation has disclosed is the statement . . . that "Six members of our Admissions Committee after due consideration voted against approval." The facts are as follows: [three long, detailed paragraphs explain that the six members who indicated deferral of Ford's application did not do so because they found his individual qualifications lacking]. *No person ever initialed the "Reject" column provided for votes against admission to membership* [emphasis in original]. . . .

There is one issue only: Are we going to reject a membership proposal of any man, who is admittedly otherwise fully qualified, solely on the basis of his race? The adoption of such a racist policy could lead to wholesale resignations and the ultimate destruction of our Club. We urge you to reaffirm your belief in the heritage of the Union League Club by supporting our officers and the Board of Directors.

[Typescript listing two hundred members who comprise "partial list" of Volunteer Committee to Support the Board.]

Retort:

The communications from the volunteer committee for support of our present board confirms that six members of our admissions committee voted against approval of the applicant in question.

In the admissions committee a vote to "defer" is a polite way to voice disapproval. It gives sponsors an opportunity to withdraw an application. As stated by the volunteer committee there were originally seven votes to "defer" later reduced to six votes to "defer." . . .

Why was the applicant in question given preferential treatment?

[Signed in typescript by the MEMBERS SPECIAL COMMITTEE.]

When the ballots were tabulated in April, Milton Darr, his board, and the slate of their nominating committee were sustained by 1,197 to 1,237 (the range of votes in favor of the seven candidates) against 711 to 812 for the dissidents' slate. Two thousand four hundred and ninety resident members were eligible to vote.

As Darr said in an interview in 2001, "We had to win that vote. It took an incredible amount of work, but now I think it's one of the best things that ever happened to the Club."

And then the issue was over. "I knew there would not be a problem," recalls Fred Ford. "I have never had anybody say anything about it to me." Several Club members confirm this, saying that six months after the vote the question of black membership was no longer an issue.

Few dissidents resigned; Club membership did not decline. In fact, membership increased in 1970 to the authorized maximum of 2,500 resident members. Ford served as chair of the admissions committee from 1979 to 1981, chair of several other committees, president of the Union League Club in the 1984 to 1985 club year, and he continues as a trustee of the Boys and Girls Clubs Foundation.

The 1969 election of Fred Ford represented a clear changing of the old guard with the new. Club custom was consciously put aside by the board—six committee votes to defer action would in any other case in Club history have resulted in withdrawal of a proposed candidacy, and would do so today. However, once they became embroiled in a controversy more acrimonious and divisive than they had expected, Darr, Enlund, and McEnerny and their supporters determined to see their professional and civic colleague Fred Ford elected, even at the expense of breaking with Club tradition.

In 1974, Taylor Hay was forced by the board to resign several years earlier than he had planned. Old Crow and Jim Crow were history in the Union League Club of Chicago.

SOURCES

The primary sources for this chapter come from the meticulously organized and comprehensive Club archives, including board minutes and membership records, as well as from Chicago newspapers for the periods discussed.

Interviews with many Club members. Especially useful were those with Everett Barlow, club historian; Henry L. Pitts, Robert Bergstrom, Frederick C. Ford, and Milton F. Darr, Jr., past presidents of the Club.

The author also interviewed Doreen Thomas on August 23, 2001. Mrs. Thomas was the devoted secretary to Taylor Hay from 1956 until his retirement in 1974, when she also retired from the Club. Several interviews with Roger Henn were also of great value.

Chapter 11

THE SIDE DOOR

In response to the honor of being named in 1998 the first woman to the Hall of Fame Club in downstate Centralia, businesswoman J. Faye Wham recounted this anecdote to her fellow community leaders:

> There is a very exclusive men's club in Chicago, the Union League Club. In the past they had not allowed women to join but this year they have a woman president.
>
> Years ago we had a young lady from Centralia working at the club. Lea Riggs is now retired and lives in Centralia. Occasionally when it was difficult to get a room in Chicago, Lea would find one for me at the club. I well remember one cold day in December, just before Christmas. I had been shopping, came in out of a snowstorm, dashed through the front door and was apprehended by a bellboy. Looking around my packages, I asked if there was anything wrong. He said, "Yes . . . yes! I have been trying to intercept you for two days. You are not allowed to come in the front door."
>
> Of course I asked, "How do I get in?"
>
> "Ladies must go around to the Federal Street side door!"
>
> I immediately apologized and said: "You hold my packages and I will go out and come back through the right door."
>
> With that cold wind whipping around and the snow in my face, I thought, "This is foolish, but I am lucky to get to stay here."
>
> The bell captain was waiting with my packages when I got around. He pointed: "Now *there* is the ladies elevator. You have been going up and down in the men's, and you are not allowed to do that. You have a book of instructions as to what you can do. Did you not read it?"

"No, I haven't had time, but I will read it as soon as I get to my room. So sorry."

Now they have a woman president. We've come a long way . . . baby!

Similar stories abound, told by those who fell afoul of Club rules for women. In the 1880s, however, the Union League Club's "side door" was a symbol of special, sensitive treatment for ladies. A century later, it became a rallying cry for women trying to break down doors and other barriers to membership in men's clubs (and business leadership) around the country.

The opening of the present clubhouse in 1926 offered women in the Club special amenities. A ladies' elevator was provided to whisk the women to their second floor parlor and also to the "Ladies Floor" on the fifth floor, where the elevator terminated. The Oval Palm Room on the fifth floor was designed for teas and a painting of Venus reminded the ladies of their unique charms. There was a ladies' card room where they could gather to play bridge. From the Palm Room the ladies and their guests could go into the ladies' dining room.

Ladies were not permitted above the fifth floor except for special entertainments and, later, for evening dinners. Sleeping rooms were reserved solely for members and their gentleman guests. In 1933, women were admitted to sleeping room privileges because of the demand for rooms by nonresident members traveling with their families to the Chicago world's fair that year. Possibly even more important was the overall lack of demand for rooms caused by the Depression.

Hard times force change in even the hoariest traditions. When the ladies' elevator broke down and required expensive repairs, the Club delayed repairs until better times. As a result, ladies were allowed to use the front door until 1936.

When the Depression receded a bit that year, Club leadership also rescinded the ladies' sleeping-room privileges. Quickly, however, they rescinded their rescision because of protests from ladies and their member spouses. Privileges once accorded are only with great difficulty withdrawn.

One factor in this decision may have been the role of widows in the Club. In 1928, privileges for widows of members were extended for a period of two years following a member's death. (A person with privileges could use Club facilities, with respect to gender, without paying dues.) Soon the privileges were made lifetime. Club records are also replete with board actions that extended similar privileges to sisters and daughters of deceased members.

That is basically how things stood until the 1970s.

The battle for women's suffrage began in the 1840s and culminated in victory at the federal level in 1920. According to Linda Kerber, a historian who focuses on women in America, following 1920 there was a general retreat by women from feminism into domesticity. Kerber thinks this may have resulted from exhaustion or a sense that the vote would lead naturally to other elements of equality.

Like Myra Bradwell, Jane Addams, and Mrs. Potter Palmer before them, Amelia Earhart and Eleanor Roosevelt were celebrated as "exceptional women" in the 1930s, yet domesticity was endlessly romanticized. The predominant attitude in society held that a woman was feminine; a feminist was neurotic.

In the 1940s and 1950s high school home economics courses defined the normal family by "sex roles" with the lady master of all she surveyed—in the home. Law and professional schools generally limited admission of women to 5 percent of their incoming classes.

The proportion of women in college actually declined between 1920 and 1960. The "Cult of True Womanhood," contends Kerber, became so completely internalized that most women rejected any attempt to change it.

This began to change slowly after World War II. Women had kept the factories humming during the war and were shunted aside after. In 1955, a tired and determined Rosa Parks refused to give up her seat in the front of a Montgomery, Alabama, bus. The consciousness of blacks began to stir, and more slowly, so did that of women.

In the late 1950s and early 1960s, fraternity boys joked about the attractive sorority girls who were out to earn their "MRS." degrees and then the "Ph.T." (putting him through [law or medical school]). Soon, many women began to find that perception offensive.

"The pill" was introduced in 1960. Betty Friedan authored the *Feminine Mystique* in 1963. She declared that the suburban home had become a "comfortable concentration camp" for women. Friedan gave voice to the women's movement.

Between 1960 and 1985, the percentage of women lawyers jumped from 3 percent to 16 percent. Women in banking roles doubled, from 18 to 36 percent. Women became the majority in college.

The men of the Union League Club remained, however, stuck in the 1950s.

At first the jibes were lighthearted, though pointed. In 1961, a visiting newspaper columnist and his wife stayed over as guests at the Club. The separate elevators became the issue.

"The lady will use the ladies' elevator to the 5th floor," said the man at the front desk. "At the 5th floor, she will transfer to the main elevator. It

"Long John" Wentworth helped found the Union League Club of Chicago, in part to support Ulysses S. Grant's bid for the presidency in 1880.

Club members rented space in the Honoré Building until they built the first clubhouse in 1885. *(Courtesy Chicago Historical Society)*

Architect and member William LeBaron Jenney designed the 1885 Union League building.

(top) The Union League Club library in the old clubhouse, ca. 1910.

(bottom) While many men's clubs did not admit women at all, the Union League built a private entrance and designed interior space for member spouses. Shown here is the ladies' apartment of the 1885 clubhouse.

POLICE HEADQUARTERS

CHICAGO, *June 14th* 188 6

Arrest For Murder
and
Inciting Riot,

Rudolph Schnaubelt, about 30 years of age, 6 feet high, 190 lbs. weight, slightly stooped shouldered, light brown hair, usually wears full light beard, but was shaved off when he left here, and more light mustache.

Depend more on photograph than above description. Works at making matchmakers tools.

Schnaubelt was one of the leading Anarchists who caused the riot and massacre in Chicago, May 4th.

If found arrest him and wire me,

Fredrick Ebersold,
Gen'l Superintendent of Police.

The Haymarket Riot of 1886 occurred not far from the Union League Club, and the Club held Washington's Birthday celebrations beginning in 1887 as a patriotic response to the event. Shown above is a wanted poster calling for the arrest of a purported anarchist involved in the riot. *(Courtesy Chicago Historical Society)*

(right) Ferdinand Peck, visionary who promoted the construction of the Auditorium Theatre in 1887. Designed by Dankmar Adler and Louis Sullivan, the theater is in operation today. All were members of the Club. *(Courtesy Chicago Historical Society)*

View of the interior of the Auditorium Theatre, as it appeared in *Harper's Weekly*, December 28, 1889. *(Courtesy Chicago Historical Society)*

(left) Dankmar Adler, ca. 1916.
(Courtesy Chicago Historical Society)

View of 1893 World's Columbian Exposition. Exposition president Harlow Higinbotham served as the Club's first vice president in 1887.

Jane Addams in Chicago, 1916. Ms. Addams was a Washington's Birthday speaker in 1911, along with former president Theodore Roosevelt. At another time, Addams was offered a bribe in the Club—by a nonmember. *(Courtesy Chicago Historical Society)*

The second Union League Club building opened in 1926. Here it is decorated for the 1932 Republican Convention.

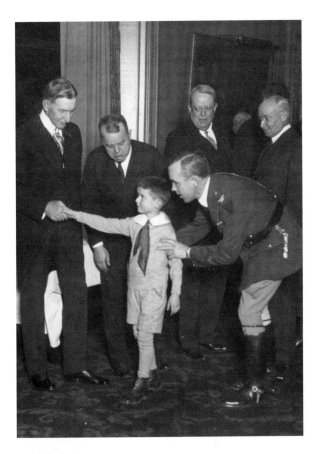

(left) Vice President of the United States and active Club member Charles G. Dawes greets a child at a reception held at the Union League, 1926.

(below) Early members of the Union League Club line up before the fireplace in the new clubhouse, 1926. Pictured left to right are Sidney Eastman, George Moulton, John Benham, Nelson Thomasson, Frank Aldrich, Harry Kelly, W. J. Jackson.

Students from Sullivan Junior High gather in front of the Union League fireplace to sing Christmas carols, 1927.

(above) The Washington's Birthday celebration attracted more than 800 students in poster contests, essay contests, band concerts, pageants, and other events. Here students from Senn High School are dressed for a dramatization "George Washington, the Friend," ca. 1930.

Two high school students display their Washington's Birthday celebration posters in a contest sponsored by the Union League, 1927.

The Union League Club dining room set for an event, ca. 1995.

(left) Director of the United States Mint Nellie Taylor Ross visits the Union League's "Million Dollar" room, papered with worthless stock certificates, 1935.

(below) Winston Churchill stands with British Consul Godfrey Haggard and members G. L. Richardson and W. Frank McClure on occasion of Churchill's visit and speech at the Club, April 1932.

(right) Women line up at the ladies' entrance, ca. 1940.

The ladies' cocktail room was not open to men, unless accompanied by women. Photograph ca. 1945.

(left) Percy Julian, shown here with Eleanor Roosevelt, was a world-renowned chemist named "Chicagoan of the Year" in 1950. He was denied access to a luncheon meeting of chemists at the Club in 1951 because he was African American. *(Courtesy Chicago Historical Society)*

While most programs for women dealt with fashion or home-related topics even into the 1980s, aviator Amelia Earhart (third from left) made an appearance at the Club in 1936.

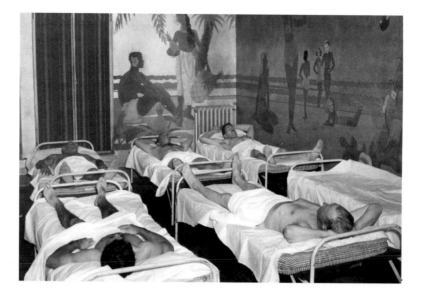

(right) Members enjoy sun lamps in a "tropical" setting, winter 1941.

During the debate over the admission of women, integration of athletic facilities was a major issue. Here, members line up for a swimming event on a hot day, while their friends have lunch by the pool, 1940.

(top) The Union League first Boys Club (later Boys and Girls Club) building raised to make room for a swimming pool, 1919.

(bottom) The Dining hall at the Union League Boys Club (later Boys and Girls Club) camp, Salem, WI, ca. 1925.

(top) "The Four Horsemen of Notre Dame" pose with four Boys Club members, ca. 1950. The "Four Horsemen" (Don Miller, Elmer Layden, Jim Crowley, and Harry Stuhldreher) gained fame in the season of 1924.

(bottom) A small contingent of the Chicago Children's Choir performs at the Club in 2002. The Club Civic and Arts Foundation has supported the choir annually since its beginnings decades ago as a small neighborhood group. The choir is now a major Chicago cultural institution.

(top) *Trees in Blossom* by Monet, 1872; from the collection of the Union League Club of Chicago.

(bottom) *A Summer Visitor* by Edgar A. Rupprecht, ca. 1921; from the collection of the Union League Club of Chicago.

(above) Club President John E. Scully (1999–2000) and his wife Judy Scully with honory Club member and former president George H. Bush on the evening of Mr. Bush's address to the Club's Washington's Birthday dinner, 2000.

(right) Honorary Club member Elizabeth Dole with Michael Chioros (Club president 2003–4), when she spoke for Washington's Birthday, 2001.

is not permitted that she ride all the way down through floors five and one. . . ."

"I wonder what goes on between the fifth and first floors?" asked the wife.

"Oh, the usual thing in a club."

"And what is the usual thing?"

"Oh, probably a bunch of men running around without clothes on. You know, swimming, steam room, barbells, pushups, Indian wrestling, and comparing tattoos. Things like that."

In 1970, a *Chicago Tribune* columnist weighed in on the issue. A reporter for the paper was required to go around to the side door at the Chicago Athletic Association club (most of the clubs had separate entrances for women; the exception was the Chicago Club, which didn't allow women to darken their door, period).

"Would it not be possible," wrote the popular Bob Cromie, "since Miss Wolfe is rather petite and—I believe—has no claustrophobic tendencies, for the doorman to pop her into a burlap bag and simply carry her thru the lobby, thus preventing contamination of whatever susceptible male members happen to be present? She could then be shaken from the bag in the elevator and make her own way thereafter."

Reporter Wolfe responded to the effect that next time forget the bag; she would bring a club.

"Chaps, you have been warned," concluded Cromie.

In 1972, the Club rescinded the requirement that women use the side-door entrance. Too little, too late. Female activists brought out the club of the lawsuit.

A year later the Professional Organization of Women for Equal Rights (POWER) brought suit in Chicago, demanding that the state revoke liquor licenses to nine downtown clubs, including of course the Union League, that discriminated against women. Though ultimately unsuccessful, the suit was in the news for three years.

Arguments by lawyers for the clubs as reported in the press often affronted women. Don Reuben was the lead lawyer for the Chicago, University, and two other clubs (but not the Union League, which was represented by Carole Bellows). Prominent and acerbic, Reuben was quoted in the *Chicago Daily News* in 1975, before a court hearing began: "I can't use my best defense. I'd like to tape the Women's Athletic Club dining room at lunch time. It sounds like the bird house at Lincoln Park Zoo."

In Springfield, the Illinois General Assembly defeated proposals to amend the U.S. Constitution to add an Equal Rights Amendment for women, first in 1972 and again in 1976. In that latter year, in a highly charged atmosphere, a majority of lawmakers—but not the extraordinary majority required by the Illinois Constitution—supported the proposal. Governor Jim Thompson, a Club member, favored the Equal Rights Amendment.

By 1976, the University Club of Chicago (probably the Union League's primary competition for members) and several other clubs had dropped the bar to women membership. Late that year, *Business Week* surveyed the women's membership issue nationwide and concluded that twilight was coming to the all-male business club. Legal challenges were being mounted across the country, the magazine observed, and the Internal Revenue Service was under pressure to deny tax-exempt status to clubs that discriminated by sex.

Club president John Pennell (1976 to 1977) appointed a committee to consider women membership. The committee recommended women membership by a 5–2 vote. In November 1977, the board of directors concurred by an 11–2 vote and asked approval of the Club membership. The special committee sent out a request for comments from members. Proponents were heartened: 194 resident members supported women membership and only 38 opposed.

Such a change, however, required amendment to the Club bylaws, which referred to "any male citizen" as a prerequisite for membership. Bylaw changes required the affirmative vote of two-thirds of resident members voting in person.

The vote was held December 13, 1977, in the main dining room. Those present rebuffed women membership resoundingly, 178 against the bylaw change, 104 in favor.

The unsuccessful vote almost immediately created a flap in Governor Thompson's campaign for reelection the following year. Rather than resign his Club membership in the face of pressure from the National Organization for Women, Thompson had promised to try to change Club policy by working from within. But he was in England vacationing when the unsuccessful vote occurred.

Chicago Sun-Times columnist Roger Simon blasted Thompson for his hypocrisy on the issue, detailing earlier quotes by the governor in which he supported restrictive clubs: "Any group of Americans has the right to have its own club" and, "I'm not sure the women are all that hot to use the men's bar anyway. My wife tells me that the women's bar is much better than the men's bar."

Politically, Thompson felt he had to do something. He resigned his membership in the Club in a two-page handwritten letter to Club president Herb Brook:

Dear Herb—

For many years now, it has been my privilege to enjoy the companionship of the members of the Union League Club; to have the greatest respect for the proud record of civic betterment that the Club has so rightfully earned, and to applaud the philanthropic contributions to our city which the membership so generously makes today.

My fellow members have decided that the Club shall not be open to women as full members. I regret that decision. I regret even more that I did not follow through on my promise to attempt to persuade my fellow members to open membership to women on an equal basis with men. That omission was inexcusable and I offer no excuses. Whether the members knew of my position from news accounts, or whether, in view of the size of the vote my voice would have made a difference, is irrelevant.

I have simply concluded that it is not right for the Governor of the State of Illinois to accept membership in a club which excludes women from membership solely because they are women. Acceptance of the governorship of this state carries with it great power and great privilege, but also great responsibility. My responsibility is clear—I cannot participate as a member in organizations which exclude over half of our people for reasons of sex. I freely accepted, indeed sought, the mandate of our people to be their Governor and so I must accept, freely and voluntarily the duties of the moral leadership inherent in that position as well.

I leave with all best wishes to my fellow members and with great thanks for their comradeship, help and support. I look forward to the day when, if a majority decide that equality shall prevail in considering applications for membership, I can return.

With best regards,

Jim

The 1977 vote lost because the Club leadership had failed to take into account the feelings up on top of the clubhouse in the Athletic Department, a "club" within the Club.

Get off the Club elevators at the twentieth floor and you enter a world of sweat, steam, mahogany lockers, coarse locker-room talk, horselaughs. A labyrinth leads to three levels of handball, racquetball, squash, and basketball courts, weights, an Olympic-size pool (with poolside restaurant for breakfast and lunch), saunas, showers.

The Athletic Department is a fun place where everybody is equal, whether they are tycoons or just lost their jobs in a corporate merger and have few prospects.

Catholic League rivalries are big among some of the regulars. "We even have heated arguments," Athletic Department director Jim Lynch chuckles, "among guys from the same school who argue over which team was better. 'My team was sure a helluva lot better than your team.' 'Oh yeah! Let's suit up and see!'

"These are guys in their sixties, getting their old teams together, to go out on the basketball court. I love it.

"I like this place 'cuz we sell the same wrinkled gray shirts and shorts to everyone, right out of the tumbler.

"We make this a fun place. Tom holds court at the front desk at six A.M. By the time the guys get to my door they are already laughing. Tom or somebody has already messed with them. I'm pretty good at recalling jokes and telling them to the next guy, so guys come to my office with their latest."

In *The Selfish Gene,* a popular assessment of evolutionary driving forces, Richard Dawkins describes a "war between the sexes." He believes men and women are in basic conflict with one another. At the least, thinks the author of this book, they like to be able to get away from one another. Where better than the sanctuary of a men's athletic club, with all the sweat, steam, profanity, and competition that "make a man a man."

The facilities are excellent, certainly on a par with and generally better than most clubs in town, according to Lynch. Not so extensive as those at the trendy for-profit East Bank Club, but that place is in part a showcase for young professionals hoping to meet others like themselves. You don't wear gray shorts and wrinkled T-shirts at the East Bank Club.

Much as the public affairs committee touts its distinctive civic role, the Union League Club of Chicago—and the civic mission—wouldn't exist without a top-notch athletic facility. Sixty percent of the 2,500 resident Club members pay an extra forty-five dollars a month to belong to the athletic department. It's open from 5:00 A.M. until 8:30 to 9:00 P.M.

Many, if not most, members join the Club for its athletic facilities and for the energy in the Rendezvous Room bar. "The guys up here never read *Dateline* or *State of the Union* [Club publications]," declares Lynch, "but their wives do. The wives say, 'Let's go to this, and that.'"

Pretty soon some of the guys from upstairs are involved with the Boys and Girls Clubs and maybe even public affairs. Several past presidents and activists in the Club who were interviewed for this book, such as Bob Rylowicz and Jack Higginson, said they joined the Club for the athletic facilities and only later became involved in the foundations.

About 300, maybe 350, of the 1,500 or so members of the athletic department use the facilities almost religiously. About the same number never use them but wouldn't for their lives give up their mahogany lockers. The rest come in once a week or so.

In 1980, Lynch started an annual awards banquet. A hundred guys go to have fun and hear Lynch as emcee insult all those present for their personal and athletic deficiencies. Drink and eat boar meat. The banquet is now a tradition.

Nineteen eighty was also the year of the second vote on women membership.

In 1979, Club leadership geared up again. Former Club president Henry Pitts headed an "Ad hoc By-laws Change Committee" co-chaired by Samuel Witwer, president of the 1970 Illinois Constitutional Convention, and Donald Graham, president of Continental Bank. The committee would seek another vote on the issue of women membership—if there was sufficient positive response to a postcard survey of membership. A letter that made the case for women membership and the response card went out in the fall of 1979. Support was overwhelming: 1,132 returned signed cards in favor; only 97 indicated opposition.

The vote was set for early 1980.

"All the members in the athletic department were totally negative," recalls Jimmy Lynch. "The men in the athletic department did not want women members. Period. Some of the old-timers disliked having to put on swimsuits. Their right to skinny dip was a big issue to them."

Opponents slipped a letter against women membership through the vents of each locker.

Frank Voysey responded to the ad hoc committee by letter that was widely circulated:

> Dear Mr. Pitts:
>
> As a member of nine clubs and four financial trade associations, I am well up on the legal aspects of the pros and cons for women members of all-male "bastions." . . .
>
> You must know that most members don't give a damn whether we have female members or not—except for one large, active, club-supporting group which is, of course, the Health Club members. Women are all over the place anyway, so if as members, who cares?
>
> Well, almost one-half the Club will care. . . . Once a member has been accepted the person has access to all of the club rooms and facilities. Chances are you would have less than 100 women members anyway and perhaps 30–40 would want to use the Health Club. Disturbing over 1,300 men from their exercise routines for a handful of women seems unnecessary to say the least. . . .
>
> [Voysey went on to explain that the real "nitty gritty" problem was the major cost that would be required to refit the athletic department facilities for women, an issue Pitts did not address.]

In response to a similar statement such as that which you and your friends are saying, "It is inevitable," [an old Southern philosopher] replied, "Death is inevitable but I'm damned if I'll vote for it."

Very truly yours,

Frank E. Voysey

Club leadership worked hard, however, to achieve a vote that reflected the postcard survey results. An all-day vote was set for April 30, 1980. Proponents made an assumption that athletic department members would not make the effort to vote in person (as bylaws require) if the vote were held away from the Club. Orchestra Hall on Michigan Avenue was selected as the site for the election.

Wrong. Members from the Board of Trade hired limousines and ferried members across the Loop to vote. Many came to vote wearing sneakers under their suit pants. They ignored the privacy of polling booths set up by member Dick McKay, president of an election-supply business. Instead, they proudly put their ballots up against posts and crossed the "No" box with a flourish for all to see, like John Hancock signing the Declaration of Independence.

Final tally: 349 in favor of admitting women; 721 opposed.

Henry Pitts, surprised by the vote, recalled later that many younger members sent back their signed cards in favor of women in order to please their bosses at their law firms and banks. In the privacy of the voting booth, however, they voted their feelings. The emphatic rejection put the issue to rest inside the club, for a couple of years.

Outside the Club, the issue festered. A few months following the 1980 vote, Susan Getzendanner was appointed the first woman to sit on the federal district court in Chicago. One of her first actions was to hold a press conference to spurn publicly the Club's standard offer of privileges in the clubhouse in her role as a member of the federal judiciary. The news media gave big play to her rebuff of the Club.

"I think the discriminatory policy of the Union League Club is outrageous," Getzendanner declared. She recounted numerous incidents where, as a corporate attorney, she had been excluded by Chicago's clubs, including her exclusion from a law firm celebration of a court victory in which she had played a part. "White men do not understand what it is like to be discriminated against because they have never had doors slammed in their faces."

Club leadership cast about for ways to defuse the issue. They quietly approached the Women's Athletic Club, which then and now excludes male membership, to explore the concept of reciprocal membership. The WAC was not interested.

The Club instituted a series of "Programs for Ladies" in 1982 to 1983. Unfortunately, the programs appealed to the 1950s woman and would have appalled those pounding on the doors for admission. Among the luncheon offerings: "Elizabeth Arden presents the latest styles and colors for the fall," "Rare, glamorous, elegant and fun furs are highlighted in a fashion show by York Furriers," and "What every woman should know about financial matters."

There were suggestions from the ranks of the membership that the Club change its name to the Union Athletic Club of Chicago and thus become solely a health club. This was dismissed out of hand by Club leadership, who cherished the civic mission and the commitment to boys and girls.

In 1983, Terry McCarthy raised the flag of women membership again, suggesting classes of membership. This would include a class for both women and men who would have all privileges except those of the health club. Member George Martin, a graduate of all-male Wabash College and a stalwart in the athletic department, led the charge for the opponents.

In a series of widely circulated letters to McCarthy, Martin took on the proponents point by point. Martin found the Class B membership idea worse than disallowing women totally. "Once members, they are in a much more strategic position to shout 'foul' because they are being denied an integral part of membership, while men will still be able to avail of either Class A or Class B membership."

Martin also pointed out that, contrary to concerns about membership levels, the Club had a waiting list. He added: "Every time someone like [newspaper columnist] Mike Royko gives the ULC a chiding, as he did this week in a column on [Chicago lawyer and politician] Bernard Epton, he boosts rather than minimizes our prestige, image and reputation."

Martin closed his final missive in the series by chastising Club leadership for waving in front of members the threat of future government action against clubs that discriminate. "The suggestion that we take action 'before being inevitably forced to do so on terms dictated by governmental policies' is embarrassing. Are we to sit around and wonder what the 'government' might, some day, decide to be our fate. Or, are we to inform the government what we believe to be our prerogatives and let them—for they are our representatives—know what we expect. This democracy was not built upon a citizenry who waited for instructions from officials."

Martin's tone carried over to a special membership meeting called by president McCarthy to discuss the women's membership issue. The tone of the meeting would determine whether the Club proceeded to another vote of the membership.

The meeting was reported firsthand in the *Chicago Sun-Times* by a

Club member who enjoyed freelance reporting. His name was not used because, as the reporter said, "The repercussions of such frankness about this delicate matter could have widespread ramifications in his business life." The paper headlined its July 14, 1983, story with bold type the size used when war is declared: NO WOMEN: THE QUEST TO PRESERVE THE LEAGUE'S CENTURY-OLD UNION.

"I go into the Wigwam [a dining room at the club]," declared one member, "and there's a bunch of men talking *men's talk*. There are no women *chattering*." He spat out the final word, reported the newspaper, as if it were a poisoned spoonful of mousse. "Then I go downstairs to the second floor and see no women—it's *great*," the man continued.

The *Sun-Times* story also continued: "An uproar of laughter and cheers filled the room. For an eerie second, the scene was reminiscent of some ancient brotherhood of bachelors, vowing on their honor to remain free and single."

For proponents of women membership, the meeting went downhill from there. The matter was not taken to a vote.

The Club may have been strong internally, as George Martin observed, yet opposition to women was taking its toll in the outside world. Civic organizations began to shun the Club when coalitions were constructed. "As a civic organization, which the Club had always been," noted former president Henry Pitts, "you can't have much credibility if you are in effect against the Nineteenth Amendment [women's suffrage]. Groups didn't want our name on their endorsement listings."

In Washington, D.C., Supreme Court justice and Club member John Paul Stevens was continually chided by his colleague Sandra Day O'Connor about belonging to a club that wouldn't admit women. "I may have to resign," Stevens told friends in the Club.

The Illinois State Bar Association voted in 1983 to prohibit meetings in clubs that engaged in racial or sex discrimination. The American Institute of Banking, which often used Club facilities, warned the Club by letter in 1987 that its next scheduled gathering for 250 in the Club would probably be its last. Many banks and major law firms in the city created informal policies against using facilities of clubs that discriminated.

When Tony Batko appeared on radio talk shows in 1986 in support of the Club's efforts to stop the city from rehabbing a shuttered department store for use as its new central library, he was sometimes distracted by interviewers who wanted to razz him about the Club's all-male policy.

Often on the defensive because of its policy, the Club barred media from the clubhouse.

The federal government also began weighing in on the side of women. In 1984, the U.S. Supreme Court upheld a Minnesota statute that required the Jaycees (a service club) to admit women to full membership in that state. Also in 1984, a bill was introduced in Congress that would disallow business-tax deductions in clubs that discriminated on the basis of sex.

Robert Rylowicz devoted his term as Club president (1986 to 1987) to winning membership for women. "Rylo," as everybody calls him, was and is a big, hale, and hearty guy, as well known and liked as any member in the Club. A successful insurance executive, Rylo was born on Wolcott Avenue, four blocks from Club 2 of the Boys and Girls Clubs. As a child, a fire in the factory next door engulfed his family's home as well.

"We lost everything," Rylo recalled. "The *Tribune* ran a photo of us in 1934, with the headline, 'Can you help this family?' "Northwestern University's Settlement House took us to a used furniture place and also paid rent for a month in an apartment they found for us.

"So I had deep feelings for organizations like Club 2. And so when I was asked to serve on the board of the Club and later be president, I said, 'Yes, and Yes.'"

But Rylo didn't have strong feelings about the women's issue leading up to his Club presidency. "I asked my wife. She said as the wife of a member she had all the privileges of membership, so why?"

Nevertheless, Rylo and the Club manager took a trip to visit the Union League Club of Philadelphia (whose only connection with the Club was its historical origins in a different Union League during the Civil War).

The Philadelphia club had earlier approved women membership. That club, Rylo recalled, had done its homework and had sold the policy to its membership. He decided it was the right thing to do.

Rylowicz shifted his focus as president from that of increasing occupancy in the Club's sleeping rooms to the women's issue.

He took another survey of membership and found, again, that more than two-thirds said they favored women members, though some respondents would deny athletic privileges for them.

Rylo put his heart and soul into the effort and his popularity on the line. A born salesman, he organized a series of forums in the Club on the athletic, economic, and government regulatory issues that swirled around the women's issue. In summary, Rylo contended that future prospects looked dim unless the Club acted to admit women.

Rylowicz called a vote of the membership for March 17 through 20 in the clubhouse. "I spread voting out over several days so people could come in from afar." Members could vote throughout each day of that week. A letter signed by seventeen former Club presidents urged the membership to support women membership. Rylo, his board members, and other proponents worked the phones like a campaign for the U.S. Senate.

Prior to the opening of the polls, a special meeting was held at which former president Everett Barlow spoke for the proponents and Dick Meyer for the opposition. The meeting was taped for audio and is archived. Barlow extolled the rich contributions of the Club over its history and of its early inclusion of women into the life of the Club. "In 1987, the Club has a responsibility to include women as members, as part of the Club's long tradition of including the leaders of our community as leading members of the Club."

Dick Meyer reviewed the finances and membership of the Club. He saw huge additional expense and little gain if women were admitted, but he concluded with a more fundamental argument: "The character and environment of the Club will be radically changed forever if women are admitted to membership."

Of the 3,150 members eligible to vote, 1,841 cast votes in the clubhouse: 1,183 voted for the change to allow women to membership; 658 voted against. This represented 64 percent in favor, just 44 votes shy of the two-thirds majority required.

For the third time, the Club had rejected women membership. Rylo was crushed.

Women activists were outraged. Gloria Scoby, publisher of *Crain's Chicago Business,* resigned from the board of the Chicago Council of the Boy Scouts of America because the scouting officials met regularly at the Club. Scoby wasn't alone in her anger. Fifty-nine members of the Club resigned in protest against the Club's continuing exclusion of the other sex.

A week after the vote, Scoby's influential publication reported that activist Gale Cincotta, head of the mayor's commission on women affairs, declared that she might propose to the city council an ordinance that would deny liquor licenses to certain clubs that discriminated against women.

Two months later, in May of 1987, Don Harnack became president of the Club. After the annual dinner meeting at which new officers are installed, there is a perfunctory board meeting. At this meeting, however, as recalled by new board member Jack Wiaduck (later a Club president), Harnack declared: "Gentlemen, we have a problem [women membership]. *We* are going to admit women!"

"What am I getting into?" thought Wiaduck.

In June, Chicago aldermen David Orr and Edwin Eisendrath introduced the ordinance. Harnack needed some time. He went to city hall and pleaded successfully with council staff to delay the effective date of the ordinance, which was expected to pass unanimously, for thirty days, to the end of July.

Harnack is a lawyer—burly, decisive, impatient, sometimes undiplomatic. "We had been debating this issue almost continuously since 1979," Harnack recalled much later from his lakefront home in Winnetka, Illinois. "I just decided we had to get the issue behind us—somehow."

At first Harnack and his board planned yet another vote, even drafting a memo to members that set the week of July 14 for casting ballots. But they pulled back. What would they do if they lost yet again, but now in face of violation of a city ordinance that would deny the Club its liquor license?

Instead, "I just went ahead and did it!" Harnack said. That is, he decided to interpret the City's ordinance as trumping the Club bylaws. Henceforth, he and the board would interpret their bylaw membership requirement of "any male citizen" as meaning "he or she." But Harnack needed cover.

"I went to legal counsel [Bob Bergstrom, a member and strong proponent of women membership] to get an opinion as to whether the proposed ordinance was constitutional. And I got Larry Coles to opine that the legislature superseded our bylaws."

Armed with their opinions of Yes and Yes, Harnack went to the chair of the athletic department committee to get the best possible lowball estimate on the cost to bring the facilities into compliance with the ordinance, which gave the Club just six months. Earl Hagberg came back with a figure of one hundred thousand dollars. He missed the actual cost only by a factor of five: five hundred thousand dollars.

Harnack sent a letter to all members on July 23 that he would recommend to the board, at a special meeting of all Club members, that on July 30 the Club begin accepting proposals for membership without regard to sex.

At that meeting, Harnack declared there would not be another vote of the membership on the issue. He explained the Club would attempt to meet the city requirement for equal access to all facilities within six months.

"I was not universally popular at that point," says Harnack. "I think Charlie Strobeck was ready to hit me with his crutch."

Harnack adjourned the meeting. And it was over.

At the conclusion of his one-year term as president, Don Harnack gave his farewell valedictory. During his speech he began to hyperventilate. He finished his talk, barely, and collapsed from an embolism. Harnack recovered, but it was an emblematic conclusion to a difficult, often miserable year for him.

Harnack remembered a Christmas party a decade later at Indian Hills Country Club on the north shore. "I walk into the john. There's another guy in there. I've never seen him in my life. He looks at me and spits out, 'I know you. You're the guy who let women in.' And he storms out."

Shortly after the issue was over, a woman was sitting in the Rendezvous Room. An older member, red in the face at the sight, got off his bar stool, marched over to the lady. He got down in her face and shouted: "Don't you understand! You're ruining one hundred years of tradition."

Years later, a member commiserated with another male at the Rendezvous bar. Two women were also sitting at the bar. "Can't they at least sit at tables, like women should?"

The battle wasn't really about the cost of fixing up the athletic facilities. It was a battle between conservatives and those who think of themselves as progressive. It was a battle between an old way of life (which many younger members also liked) and a new way of doing things.

Opponents of women membership knew the change was coming someday, but they didn't have to be for it. Making the stand was more important than the outcome.

Once it was over, things at the Club got back to a new kind of normal rather quickly. There were resignations, but most came back, as did those who resigned earlier in protest of the losing vote. George Martin is still a member. Charlie Strobeck became somewhat reconciled.

The Club had a good financial year under Don Harnack. He and others paid calls on organizations and law firms that had stopped using the Club. Business improved. The board allowed any member who had resigned over the issue to come back for only a hundred dollars. A hundred or so members from both sides of the issue rejoined.

There have been physical and personal changes in the Club. "The best part of the Club was the Women's Lounge," recalls Angie Higginson, who is the spouse of a member. "We could enjoy ourselves there." The lounge is gone.

"Women were treated like queens in the past," recalls another spouse of a member who herself became a member. "Now we're treated like members."

"After women were admitted," says Jim Lynch, "they wouldn't come up to the athletic facilities. But when women came to realize that the staff treated them the same as men, they started coming up. And they're great. They never complain, the way men do. And I'm as likely to have a woman sitting in my office telling me a story as a guy. Two of my favorite members are ladies. One is seventy-eight and the other is seventy. Great ladies."

Lynch has 175 women members, including spouses of members.

Women members represent about 10 percent of those on the Club rolls, which is a disappointment to Harnack, Barlow, Rylo and others who pushed so hard for their inclusion.

After going through the chairs of board service and vice presidencies, Laura Hagen was elected president of the Club in June 1998. The inaugural address by the incoming president is a big deal in the Club, given at the annual meeting and dinner before three hundred or so members. Hagen devoted just two paragraphs of her twelve-page speech to the issue that made her presidency special:

> It is indeed an honor to stand before you not only as the 109th president of the Union League Club of Chicago, but also as the first woman. Are the founding fathers turning over in their graves today? I don't think so. For this Club was founded by men of strong principles and values. One of them, James Bradwell, was even a feminist! In 1868, his wife, Myra Bradwell, was the first woman to apply for, and be denied, admission to the Illinois bar—despite passing the qualifying exam. After taking her case all the way to the U.S. Supreme Court and losing, she was finally admitted almost 20 years later when the legislature lifted the ban on women at the bar.
>
> Today, we celebrate our ability to carry forward our founders' "Commitment to Community and Country" in a Club that does not discriminate on the basis of race, sex, creed or national origin. . . .
>
> In this rapidly changing, turbulent world, the Union League Club is more important than ever. The Union League Club is our sanctuary, where we can escape from the stresses of everyday life.

A sanctuary, as always—but now for women, not from women.

SOURCES

The Club archives hold several document boxes of Club records and press clippings related to the women's membership issue. These include an audiotape of the special meeting and debate that preceded the 1987 vote. There is also an oral history by Don Harnack of his role in the issue.

Interviews with Henry Pitts, Everett Barlow, Don Harnack, Ardell Arthur, Angie Higginson, Fred Ford, Frank Whittaker, Bill McDermott, and Paul Dillon.

Books consulted include:

Dawkins, Richard. *The Selfish Gene.* New York: Oxford University Press, 1976.

Henn, Roger. "History of the Union League Club of Chicago." 1980. ULCC archives, #2001-30.

Kerber, Linda, and Jane Sherron De Hart, eds. *Women's America: Refocusing the Past.* 2nd ed. N.Y.: Oxford University Press, 1987.

Light

Chapter 12

"IF 20 DEAD GANGSTERS
COULD BE BOYS AGAIN"

The 1971 murder of Miguel A. Barreto was no big deal in itself. Murder in Humboldt Park in the 1970s was commonplace. It still is on this near northwest side of Chicago, intersected by the grand park and Division Street. Gangs like the Warlords, Latin Kings, Cobras, Disciples, Latin Jivers—the list goes on—had taken deep root in the sprawling Humboldt Park neighborhood. The gangs' roots still go deep there.

Barreto was a program director at the Latin American Boys Club and president of the club advisory board. The club had been started by the Spanish-American action committee in the early 1960s. By 1967, the club had fallen on hard times. Community leaders asked the Union League Boys Clubs to take it over, which they did.

Barreto's murder happened later the same evening he had been honored by the community for his boys-club work. Details on the murder are murky. Some think the Latin Jivers were trying to take over the club. The Jivers controlled the drug trade at the corner of Crystal and Washtenaw streets, a hundred feet from the front door to the club. They still do.

An ex-Franciscan priest named Al Mackin ran the boys club. Community activists came to Mackin and pleaded: name the club after Miguel Barreto. The request made sense; there weren't many good role models in Humboldt Park in 1973. Today, the Barreto Boys—and now Girls—Club continues the good fight against gang domination of youngsters in East Humboldt Park. The club wins some, loses some.

Mackin made the club a "safe house" from the gangs. Gang members could then and now belong to Barreto but they can't enter the club wearing gang identification or display their gang affiliation inside the club. The club is a safe place today for little Marianela, who steals your heart with her dancing dark eyes and infectious grin, and for her many cousins and friends.

They spend almost every summer day in the club, and after school and Saturdays the rest of the year. So do many of the 1,200 members, ages six to sixteen.

The club isn't much to look at. Originally, the structure housed a three-flat and the community room of a former synagogue. A gym was added later. A three-million-dollar renovation and expansion of the club was under way in 2003, courtesy solely of the "big kids club" downtown at 65 West Jackson.

The community is fiercely supportive of Barreto. So are the members of the Union League Club of Chicago.

Early Club members were suckers for kids, especially street urchins. Many had been on those same streets when they were younger. In 1920, when the first Union League Boys Club opened, most Union League members would have been born between the Civil War and the 1880s. Few kids in that era, including Club members, clutched silver spoons at birth.

In 1890, speeches to schoolchildren became a part of the Club's Washington's Birthday celebration. That year, eight thousand children packed the Auditorium and another four thousand the Central Music Hall, where they fidgeted through patriotic songs and declamations. By 1910, the program had been expanded to include immigrants, who clearly needed, or so Club members felt, lectures setting forth American ideals. That year Theodore Roosevelt and Jane Addams addressed both school children and immigrants—kids in the morning, adults in the afternoon—in a crowded First Regiment Armory.

Following several meetings in the Club over the years on topics such as "A Rational Method for Dealing with Delinquent Boys," the Club invited Edwin Hall of Washington, D.C., to come to Chicago. President of the Boys Club Federation, Hall gave a sobering talk to civic leaders in the clubhouse:

> The underprivileged boy—of whom there are six million in this country—has no place to go from the time he gets through supper until bedtime—except the street. And going into the street he joins a gang. And the only place the gang has to go is into pool rooms, or to an old stable, or a cave under a sidewalk.
>
> The reason they leave the home at night is their parents are tired, or there may be five or six children packed into tight quarters, so naturally he seeks the street, where he flirts with minor forms of delinquency, then more serious offenses, then the police, and the boy becomes a marked man.

Too many of these boys will fill your penitentiaries and reform schools. And so the great question is whether men like you, who have met with some degree of success, are willing to devote a little part of your time and money to see that these boys are given a fair chance and a square deal!

The Club rallied to the cause. In 1920, the Club created the Union League Boys Club. Club 1 opened that year in a tough, white-ethnic southwest side neighborhood called Pilsen where fourteen hundred boys had been arrested the previous year. The Union League turned a one-time saloon and whorehouse, known as the "Bucket of Blood" for its violence, into a gym, library, game rooms, study rooms, and later a swimming pool, for a thousand boys. Forty-three Club members contributed one thousand dollars each to get the club off the ground. (To this day, many old-timers refer to their neighborhood as the Bucket of Blood.)

That summer, the boys were taken to a camp in Wisconsin—city boys need the fresh air, Club leaders thought, and a chance to see another world. That tradition continues to this day. A year later, members of the Boys Club presented Shakespeare's *As You Like It* in the Union League Club, the "big kids club," as some boys referred to it. Soon there was a Boys Club Band and top athletes who were winning boxing and wrestling matches across the city.

A juvenile court judge came to the big kids club in 1922 to declare that delinquency in the eighteenth police district, where Club 1 was located, had fallen dramatically.

Complaints about children had fallen from 1,344 in 1919 to 592 just two years after the Boys Club opened its doors. Youngsters brought into juvenile court plummeted from 145 in 1919 to 46. And there had been a 50 percent drop in the breakage of lamps in the area where the club was located. According to Boys Club minutes, police records indicated the district had gone from the highest rate of juvenile crime in 1920 to the lowest rate of juvenile crime in the city by 1923!

Union League Club members became true believers. Members donated dental chairs for a clinic, band instruments, and labor at the summer camp; Drs. William and J. S. Jack provided medical attention, even performing operations, for the boys at the club. Union League Club members and Boys Club staff began finding jobs for the youngsters—1,100 jobs from 1920 to 1925—as they still do.

Never, to this day, has any activity of the Union League Club generated more enthusiasm, commitment, and affection than the Boys and Girls Clubs. For example, just before his death in 1924, Boys Club trustee David Goodwillie requested that eight boys from the Boys Club serve as his pallbearers.

The Club also had an opportunity to establish a club in the African

American section of Chicago on the south side. In 1920, as the first club was being established, philanthropist and Club member Julius Rosenwald offered to help fund a club in the district. The Boys Club trustees demurred, however, saying the first club should be well established before taking on another one. This even though the terrible Chicago race riots of 1919 were fresh in the minds of members; or maybe because the riots were fresh in their minds. The cultural chasm appeared to be a street too wide to cross.

When discussion of a second club surfaced in 1924, there is no mention in the minutes of possibly locating it in the African American part of the city. In 1925, however, Britton Budd and other trustees of the Union League Boys Club helped south side leaders found a club for black boys, modeled along the lines of the Union League's club. Budd and two other Club members also served as trustees of this Boys Club on the south side.

Club 2 opened its doors in 1927 at 524 North Wolcott on the city's near northwest side. In 1929, the foundation bought a lot for Club 3 but plans to build a new Club building were set aside because of the Depression. A year later, when Capone and his henchmen ran the streets of the city, the Union League Boys Clubs issued a plea to support the foundation's summer camp in Wisconsin with a pamphlet headlined, IF 20 DEAD GANGSTERS COULD BE BOYS AGAIN.

The summer camp is a jewel in the crown of the Union League's operations. Since 1920, more than fifty thousand poor kids have spent two weeks at camp along Lake Francis in rustic southern Wisconsin. The camp is one of a relatively few nonreligious camps in the region devoted solely to underprivileged kids.

Until 1941, the Union League shared Lake Francis with the American Communist Party (!)—which also operated a summer camp and training grounds for the proletariat on another shore. That year, the foundation bought the 120 acres owned by the Communists.

Nearby Kenosha Post 21 of the American Legion immediately awarded the Union League its Certificate of Distinguished Merit for "removing this blight on Kenosha County" and for pulling the red star down from over southern Wisconsin! Each year without fail at the annual Camp Day, when two hundred Union League Club members join in the fun with the campers, Legion representatives return to express their gratitude.

In the 1920s, the mostly Polish, Central European, Italian, and Irish campers took the train to Salem, Wisconsin. Club 1 member Henry Bekier described camp in 1927 for the Union League Club *Bulletin:*

> On arriving at camp, we see the sun going down over the beautiful lake.
> After supper, we are assigned to our shacks, get our bedding—and a talk

from Mr. Klees [the first Boys Club director]. Later we gather around a camp fire where stories are told, songs sung, games played.

The next two weeks are spent hiking, observing birds and their habits, and studying trees. Twice a day we go down the hill to the lake where we learn to canoe, swim, and save people from drowning. And there's plenty of fishing to be done, cuz there's plenty of fish in the lake.

"War" is the biggest thrill for the boys of 1927. The campers are divided into two "armies." The armies set up camps in the tall trees. In the middle of the night, spies are sent out, skyrockets burst above, the bruised and wounded are sent to a "hospital" up the hill. Great fun.

At the annual Boys Clubs' dinner later that year at the "big kids'" clubhouse, camper Johnny Babor delights the audience of three hundred members with an impromptu report on summer camp:

> It's the most wonderful place in the world. There's a big lake up there—and it's pretty muddy but that's all right for boys from the West Side.
>
> We have a big mess hall. It's not as nice as this one, but it's nice and we get good eats—and we don't have to pay $1.50 a plate for them, either.
>
> I will always remember this night because I am sitting at the same table with my boss. It's wonderful to be at this dinner but I like better to eat at the summer camp because you can eat there the way you want to and you don't have to look around and watch how other people eat before you can eat yourself.

Conflict resolution may have replaced "war" at camp, but the day's ritual is unchanged. Every morning without fail since the 1920s, boys—and now girls—have gathered at 7 A.M. at the steel pole in the center of the camp to raise the flag and recite the Pledge of Allegiance. Then it's off to the mess hall for breakfast, followed by cleaning of cabins, chores, and inspection.

"The camp provides a complete change from the home environment," says former clubs' director Jay Markle. "We offer a regimented environment with discipline. We used to have some hard nuts who weren't used to discipline, but they came to like camp anyway. It was good for them."

In July, the "big kids" come up from Chicago for Camp Day. Two hundred Club members and spouses arrive early on a Saturday by chartered bus and auto. Boys and Girls Clubs trustee Ron Rascia and his wife rode up on their Harley.

Rascia attended camp from 1962 to 1969, along with his brothers. Three generations of Rascias are up for this Camp Day; the rest came by auto. As they walk by a clutch of brown, black, and white campers, a brother whispers that it wasn't integrated in the late 1960s. Now an attorney, Rascia runs into lawyers in court in Cook County who went to the Union League summer camp.

Rascia's father was a member of Club 2. "It was the center of life for us youngsters," the Rascia patriarch says. "The Club kept us in line, because we didn't want to lose privileges for the swimming pool and gym."

The younger Rascia beamed as he talked about his camp experiences, past and present. "We had a pellet-gun range then, which wouldn't be politically correct today, but was it fun. I couldn't wait to go back each summer. I want to see the clubs and this camp do well, based on my great early experiences. Some organizations are top-heavy with administration. Not this one. The dollars are well spent."

Later in the morning, new Club members Keith and Kathy Cardoza sit in the E. T. Wilkes Chapel, a basic concrete-block affair with a stunted steeple. They wait for all 150 campers to file in for chapel service. All sing "This Land Is Your Land" and "The Battle Hymn of the Republic."

From the East, the Cardozas are not long out of graduate school at the University of Chicago. Now money managers, the young couple was attracted to the Union League Club because of its foundations. This was their first Camp Day. As of 2003, Keith Cardoza is a director of the Union League Club and a trustee of the Boys and Girls Clubs.

Outside, the Secret Service director for the Chicago office and a number of his colleagues drive onto the grounds in a spit-shined new presidential limousine. The kids' eyes bug out. With all gathered round, instruction is provided in protecting the president with a young black girl playing the president. That same year, the Secret Service held a golf day that raised ten thousand dollars for the Boys and Girls Clubs. The "president" and her entourage drive off toward the mess tent, where campers and guests gather for steaks grilled outside.

The Kenosha American Legion commander thanks the Club for its fine service at the camp. It is not clear if this is continuing gratitude for buying out the Commies or reassurance to the members that recent local grumbling about the "kinds of kids coming to camp" is just that—local and not representative of the larger area.

Awards night at Club 1, in the city's now Mexican-American Pilsen neighborhood, is a big deal for the kids and for the busload of Union League members who come out to the little kids' clubhouse to join in the celebration.

The Union Leaguers descend from the bus, the men in pinstripes and the women members in power suits, straight from the office. To the boisterous kids in white shirts or whatever was clean that day, the members look as if they just landed from Pluto.

Pandemonium reigns at Club 1. Three hundred kids from age six to the mid-teens mill around in cacophonous bedlam in the crowded old gym, smelling of sweat and fun. Mothers and volunteers from the neighborhood bustle over supper in the kitchen.

Members present trophies to successful basketball teams, meritorious computer club members, "smart girls," "super stars," dance troupes, and gymnasts; hundreds of trophies glisten on folding tables behind the speaker's podium.

The evening is a great success. Initially, a couple of members new to the annual awards night grimace at the endless rows of trophies. Will they make it home by midnight? But the presentations move expeditiously. Achievement is rewarded and so is simple improvement; each winner comes forward to receive applause, cheers, and a trophy awarded by a Boys and Girls Clubs trustee.

The printed program for awards night at Club 1 lists each "Honor Boy [now Youth] of the Year" from 1927. The ebb and flow of peoples is easy to follow. Casimir Jania (1928), Edward Kolodziej (1949), Frank Quilici (1953; former player and manager of the Minnesota Twins). By the 1970s, the names have shifted to Ricardo Almendarez, Sergio Gonzalez, Steven Kaczmarek, Juanito Resendiz.

Craig and Labus, trustee and treasurer of the Boys and Girls Clubs, makes the service awards. In the 1960s, Labus was a member of Club 1. Laura Hagen, first woman president of the Union League Club, and in 2001 the first woman president of the Union League Boys and Girls Clubs, presents the "Youth of the Year Award" to Cynthia Valdez, the first female recipient.

Ed Kolodziej. Hmm, this writer thinks. The same name as a distinguished professor of international relations at the University of Illinois at Urbana, a colleague of the author. Ed responds to an inquiry:

> Yes, that's me. I spent over a decade in the 1940s and 1950s in the Union
> League system, including as program director at their wonderful camp
> near Kenosha, Wisconsin. I developed a friendship with the librarian at
> the club—yes, a librarian for Polish kids in the ghetto who were illiter-
> ate in two languages.
>
> The friendship with librarian Alba Biagini has lasted 56 years. She
> was a biology teacher in the Chicago system with a master's degree from
> the University of Chicago (where I took my doctorate following her
> model). She legitimated reading and thinking when these were equated
> with being a "fairy" by the kids on the block. I always had to hide books
> from the kids at school and even from aunts and uncles. No Union
> League, no friendship—well, only in America.

Club 2 is above Grand Avenue, the dividing line in the 1960s between whites who lived north of Grand and blacks below. In 1962, several black families moved into an apartment building in the local Italian neighborhood north of Grand. The building was torched and most blacks vacated. One family was not touched by the fire. The intrepid father brought his two sons to Club 2 to enroll them. Strong feelings percolated in the club's immediate vicinity.

Jay Markle, executive director of the Union League Boys and Girls Clubs from 1956 to 1984, was called to the scene. Markle met with the father. "This may be difficult for your boys, but if you want to enroll them, I'm all for you. But I will want to take the issue to my board downtown, as this is new for us."

The trustees voted unanimously to support Markle (though one prominent member expressed his opposition after the meeting). The boys became members and had no problems in the club. White gang members did spray paint on the street outside the club, "Segregation Yes, Integration No." Markle went to the street corners where the gangs hung out. "If you guys make problems, you will have black groups protesting all over this neighborhood and life will become miserable for you." The approach worked. There were no more problems.

The Club 2 neighborhood is gentrifying. The old four-flat building catercorner from Club 2 has been transformed into a single-family manse by an "urban pioneer," as prosperous young professionals are often called. This type of change leaves fewer boys and girls in the neighborhood. In the years to come, Club 2 may have to move west to follow its boys and girls.

Nevertheless, the public high school that serves the present Club 2 still has one of the highest dropout rates in the city. Indeed, fewer than half the youngsters in the neighborhoods served by the Club's four Boys and Girls Clubs graduate from public high school.

The Barreto club serves 1,250 kids six to sixteen years old who live in the neighborhood. The smallest kids pay a dollar a year for their membership card, which they must show each day to get into the old two-story brick building; the older teens pay five dollars for the year. Two weeks of summer camp in Wisconsin costs from nothing to five bucks total, based on family income, for an experience worth a hundred times more than the five dollar bill.

The club opens at 9:30 in the morning in the summer. Outside, twenty kids of varying ages and colors jostle playfully, waiting for the club to open. Inside there is a gym, weight room, games, computer lab, art room, plenty to keep many of the kids busy all day. At noon every day, the city Department of Human Services serves a cold lunch to everyone. Not bad for a buck a year.

Barreto is in a working-class Puerto Rican neighborhood with many poor families. In the winter, says the club director, some kids come without coats. The neighborhood of narrow one-, two-, and three-story brick houses chopped into apartments isn't fancy, but it doesn't look like a slum either.

The community is deeply infected with gangs. On the east side of Humboldt Park (the Club is one block east of the park) are the Cobras, Disciples, Dragons, and the Jivers. The Jivers control the street corner outside, where they sell crack cocaine to customers who drive by. These gangs are all affiliated with "the Folks." On the other side of the park are the Warlords, Latin Kings, and other gangs, all affiliated with "the People." Gang members cross the park onto the others' turf at great peril.

The business of the gangs is selling drugs, especially crack cocaine.

"I know a fourteen-year-old girl in this club who is hooked," a club staff member says. "She has become a prostitute to pay for her habit." It costs about $150 a day to maintain a crack habit and the only way most kids and adults can come up with that kind of money is by robbing or prostitution.

The gangs represent status, recognition, authority, position, and protection. Young girls think gang members are cool.

"I was paying a part-time worker $5.15 an hour," the staff member continues. "He told me he had joined the Jivers. I told him he couldn't work here any longer, which he knew. It's hard for me to compete on money terms. He can make $200 a day selling drugs through the Jivers. One of the Jivers drives a Lexus."

Talk of drugs leads, maybe naturally, to talk of violence.

This Club is in the heart of a violent area. "In the seven years I've been director, I have lost eight club members, including one staff member, who was stabbed to death. I have quit going to funerals."

It sounds so matter-of-fact.

According to staff, the chief of the Disciples used to bring his youngsters to Barreto; gang leaders are often in their mid-twenties. This Disciple was gunned down, dead.

Gangs kill by driving by in a car and spraying an area with bullets. Or they put their gun hands around the corner of a building and blindly spray the alleyway. That is why so many innocent people are killed. Not long ago, just down the street from Barreto, a four-year-old was killed on his Big Wheel by a gang bullet sprayed from three blocks away.

One Barreto staff member carries a police scanner so he can tell the kids not to walk down this or that street on their way home.

The Union League Boys and Girls clubs fight this evil with good people and a mix of fun and serious learning.

The afternoon program during the school year is highly structured. Kids rotate among games and academics, so that every kid has some tutoring, computer room time, and art every afternoon. Many kids never join the gangs; Barreto is a refuge for them.

Barreto has ten Macintosh computers and a computer instructor throughout the school year. The demand from the kids is overwhelming.

The twenty-two staff people at Barreto function as surrogate parents for many of the club members.

"Tío Edwin" (Uncle Edwin) Castillo runs the education programs at Barreto. There is "Catch Up" for five-to-seven-year-old youngsters. There is "Math for Fun," "Teen Reach," and "Street Smarts." These last two programs are about helping teens find out about themselves, their potential, and maybe convince the girls that getting pregnant is not cool. There is also tutoring and homework help.

"Who's winning this struggle for the hearts and minds of the kids," Barreto staff are asked, "the gangs or the club?"

"Right now, the gangs are," a young man responds, grimacing. "But we're winning with some of the kids."

Tío Edwin deserves a biography. He started as a member at Barreto but was lured away by the Jivers. He was arrested for selling LSD. One thing led to another, including "aggravated assault with a weapon." Castillo was in and out of prison from 1984 to 1995. He was never out for more than a year before he ended up back behind bars—Cook County jail, and Stateville, Pontiac, and Big Muddy state prisons.

Each time Castillo came out, he returned to Barreto staff—Miguel (now state senator) del Valle, Johnny Cisco, Johnny Morero. They counseled him and told him each time that he's always got the club.

In prison, Castillo "got religion," literally. His female attorney also proved he was innocent of firing his gun in the aggravated-assault conviction. He may have been framed by a "dirty cop" who wanted in on the drug action.

Out of prison, Castillo took a part-time job at Barreto, married his one-time sweetheart, and entered community college. Later, he applied for the full-time education job. Because of his background, Boys and Girls Clubs trustees interviewed him several times at the downtown clubhouse before giving the go-ahead to hire him. Tío Edwin (his nieces in the club call him "uncle," and so now does everybody at Barreto) is doing a fine job.

"The buy-in of the members is incredible," declares Mary Ann Mahon-Huels, executive director of the Union League Boys and Girls Clubs. "We started a $6.4 million capital campaign in 2000. In less than a year we met the goal. The average gift from the seventy-three foundation trustees was $30,000. That doesn't include a million bucks given anonymously by a long-time activist who also rolls up his sleeves for the kids." And not all of these men and women are high rollers, not by a long shot.

Two thousand six hundred Club members (out of 2,500 resident and 1,500 nonresident members) contribute annually, most through the voluntary checkoff of nine dollars that comes with their regular Club statements.

In 1978, when money was tight, members' spouses created a women's board. For a quarter-century, the women have put on an annual ball that nets about a quarter-million dollars.

You see them in the lobby of the Club, putting the arm on members to buy twenty-five-dollar tickets or to sponsor a page in the benefit's program. Women also spend time at the clubs, working with the arts programs and even pitching in to repaint walls in the old buildings.

The message from the women is always the same: "Our three clubs and summer camp offer six thousand inner-city children academic, arts, and sports programs in an environment free from drugs, gangs, and violence. Our clubs provide positive alternatives to help these youngsters become responsible citizens." Four thousand of the youngsters are Hispanic, 1,200 African American, and 800 Caucasian.

Each club fits the needs of its neighborhood. Club 1 has twenty-three baseball teams. The local Catholic school had no gym, so it used the Club 1 gym. Barreto emphasized weight training and has had national champions, which goes a long way for Club pride out on the mean streets. When the girls at Barreto wanted to become cheerleaders, Barreto created a cheerleading program.

Emil Syngel preceded Mary Ann Mahon-Huels. For forty-one years at the Union League Boys and Girls Clubs, Syngel was a tough, authoritarian Greek American who kicked tail when necessary and got the job done. He says:

> I have a simple approach to this: All children want to play, have fun, be safe, understand the rules and have someone care, be responsible and learn.
>
> The neighborhoods are tougher now. Kids used to get jumped for a quarter—now they could be shot, as various gangs maneuver for favorable status in the community. Today, we emphasize more educational programs and work very closely with the schools to supplement and reinforce what they are doing.
>
> We have lost the family structure and the traditional values families project. Our job is to keep kids away from negative influences but, more important, give them a place to belong and make sure they are cared for. Youngsters are looking for that lost family and its structure within a safe environment—and that is us.

Syngel and Mahon-Huels have focused the clubs on the objective of getting as many youngsters as possible through high school. In the clubs' neighborhoods, where the dropout rate from freshman to senior year is more than 50 percent, that's a daunting task.

From the first year, eight decades ago, the minutes show that monthly board meetings always have had twenty-five or more trustees present. Experienced in board work, the trustees are deeply involved in committees but they don't micromanage.

The Union League Boys and Girls Clubs operate with a three-million-dollar budget that supports twenty-two full-time staff at the clubs and camp and scores of part-timers. The budget comes primarily from members and the five-million-dollar endowment they have built; the remainder comes from the women's fund-raisers, corporations, foundations, and government grants.

At the end of the last century, the trustees and staff took a long look back at their old clubhouses and a look into this century. They decided to create a fourth club but only after renovating the camp and three clubs. That's where the $6.4 million from the capital campaign has been spent.

The camp renovation committee met in May 2001 at the camp, sixty miles north of the city, to hear an architectural firm's presentation. All twenty on the committee were present. They included Bob Patterson and Dick Gavin, retired senior partners of Sargent & Lundy, the nation's largest nuclear power construction company; Fred Ford, vice chairman of Draper & Kramer, one of Chicago's major real estate development companies; and Reinhard Jahn, a major manufacturer of roofing products. The architects were on their toes for this meeting.

The lead architect trumped his high-powered audience by introducing his young colleague, Hilarion Amaro—a former camper and member of Club 1. Big smiles all around.

The senior architect didn't mention, maybe he was unaware, that Amaro had been a recipient of the Reinhard H. Jahn Scholarship, which provided him two thousand dollars a year for each of his five years at university. Nor did he note that Amaro returned to Club 1 frequently to tutor in math and computers.

"Fifteen years ago," begins camp director David Lira Leverone, "I was told that today's generation at our camp would weigh less and exhibit more attention-deficit problems and learning disabilities. I didn't believe it then, but it's true.

"Girls are also changing," he continues. "They are more aggressive. Now we have classes for the campers on conflict resolution and violence prevention."

The director's point: More security is needed at the camp, for instance, motion-activated lights. Telling stories about nasty "swamp man" nearby won't keep today's kids in the camp at night.

"I'd also like electronic toilets. Kids rarely flush them."

There is discussion among the trustees about whether to commercialize the camp so as to generate revenues at other times of the year. Fred Ford is opposed. "That would take us down another path and cost more. We should focus on kids we serve and their needs."

Everett Barlow, another Club past president who has committed much of the past three decades to the Club and its missions, agrees: "Many years ago—and half of us here were trustees back then as well—we went to see another camp. It was fancy and nice, but it wasn't any longer a camp for real kids. We should never lose sight of the poor inner-city kids. I don't think our contributors would go for commercialization."

The subject drops.

In the fall of 2002, the LaFayette Union League Boys and Girls Club opened in the LaFayette Elementary School, one of four hundred Chicago public schools. Located on the northwest side between Division Street and Chicago Avenue, near California Avenue, the school's enrollment had dropped because of gentrification; the school principal had space and needed help.

In 2002, LaFayette School was located in a pocket between gangs. The Latin Disciples north of Division, the Cobras south. There were no services for youngsters in the pocket: no library branch, and the Barreto club is north of Division, which youngsters crossed at some risk.

This was the first marriage of a school and club for the Union League Club Boys and Girls Clubs. The collaboration makes sense. The club is open from the end of school until 6:30 P.M., with plans to extend those hours until 9:00 P.M.

The creative club director loves the idea. Many of the club members attend the school; the parents feel comfortable having their kids there; the teachers and principal help recruit members because they see the benefits of an after-school club that mixes fun with arts, music, and education programming.

This may be the wave of the future. The cost of operating a school-based club is a fraction of that for maintaining a physical clubhouse for boys and girls. Yet there are drawbacks. There is no pool, which is a magnet, especially in the summer. The club is dependent upon the principal of the school, who could kick the club out. But then why would a principal want to do that?

For example, at about the same time that the LaFayette opened, the Barreto club to the north moved its operation into the nearby Von Humboldt public school during the four years required to demolish and rebuild Barreto. The principal at Von Humboldt publicly credited Barreto and its after-school educational programs for dramatically increasing the reading scores at her struggling elementary school.

The trustees face difficult strategic decisions about how to get the most in varied benefits from limited resources. For example, the go-ahead to build a basically new clubhouse at Barreto at the cost of more than two million dollars was agreed upon as much to improve and anchor the neighborhood in a positive way as for the kids.

From what the author has observed over two years at trustees' meetings and at all the club locations and the summer camp, the trustees bring admirable passion to their work.

Lois McCullagh served for decades as administrative secretary for the Boys and Girls clubs and was a driving force in their successful development. She married a Club member and became the first president of the women's board of the Boys and Girls Clubs. She recalled that during World War II, a fellow named Gus Camata came into the Club and to her office.

"I came to the Club to thank someone."

"Fine," responded Lois, "but why?'

"You see," responded Camata, now a veteran Chicago policeman, "I was on the USS Hornet when it was torpedoed. I ended up in the water. Now where do you think a kid like me from Race and Wolcott could learn to swim if it wasn't at Club 2!"

SOURCES

The primary sources for this chapter include:

Minutes of the Union League Club Foundation for Boys and Girls Clubs.
ULCC monthly publications: *Bulletin, Men and Events,* and *State of the Union.*
Author's numerous visits to Boys and Girls Club facilities and the summer camp during 2000, 2001, and 2002.
Author's interviews with foundation trustees, staff, and additional Club members.

Chapter 13

IT'S A GRAND NIGHT FOR SINGING

Teens in red blazers fill the marble staircase that rises from the first floor lobby of the Club. In the main lounge on the second floor, the Chicago Youth Symphony Orchestra is playing a lively Rossini overture. Later that evening in October 2002, international opera star Samuel Ramey and jazz legend Ramsey Lewis both perform and receive "distinguished privilege holder" status in the Club. It's a grand night for music in the Club, and not that unusual.

In their signature red jackets, the thirty teens on the staircase are but a small representation of the Chicago Children's Choir. Their sophisticated repertoire this evening includes Bach, spirituals, and haunting African folk melodies. At one point a young man, a recent émigré from Macedonia, steps forward to sing from *The Lion King*.

To the side, in contrasting black as always, is their charismatic director, Josephine Lee. At twenty-seven, she is by all accounts a musical genius who might not be headed for stardom were it not for the Civic and Arts Foundation of the Union League Club.

The Civic and Arts as well as the Engineers foundations of the Club award three hundred thousand dollars a year to talented young people from Chicago who can use help to reach their dreams. As organizations, foundations are intrinsically less interesting than the objects of their beneficence. This chapter focuses on a few of the groups and individuals such as Josephine who might not be at the forefront of the Chicago performing arts scene other than for the foresight and support of these two Club foundations. (For a more formal statement of the mission and accomplishments of the Civic and Arts Foundation, prepared by the foundation, see Appendix D.)

A second focus is on several individuals in the Civic and Arts Foundation, selected from among many activists, who have provided yeastiness and leadership to the organization.

Josephine Lee is artistic director of the Chicago Children's Choir. The CCC is fifty-five choirs from seventy Chicago public and parochial schools that otherwise would be without musical programming. These choirs feed five performing choirs and a crème de la crème concert choir that astounds hearers from Vienna to Johannesburg. The CCC now has its own charter school, just like the Harlem Boys Choir. This helps accommodate both schoolwork and evening appearances, such as with the Lyric Opera and the Chicago Symphony.

At an afternoon rehearsal on the top floor of the Chicago Cultural Center, the domain of the choir, Lee commands all she oversees. The high schoolers have been gathering from around the city by bus and CTA trains for the 4 P.M. rehearsal. Lee enters the rehearsal hall with a flourish, replaces one of the assistant conductors at the podium. All is instantly silent. She speaks briefly, in the kids' vernacular, about their appearance the night before at Navy Pier and how former president Bill Clinton had later praised them all.

Then, Lee leads her instrument, that is, the choir, through a soaring Bach cantata and then an African folk melody. "That's an A-flat," she admonishes the sopranos over the singing, "not an A-natural!" The guilty singers wince. It won't happen again. They revere Lee.

The author is overwriting this, readers think. But no. Absent the sustaining support over forty-five years from the Union League Club Civic and Arts Foundation, neither the CCC nor Josephine Lee would likely be just where they are today.

"I remember when the choir was a neighborhood group from Hyde Park," says Rose Ann Grundman, a longtime director of the Civic and Arts Foundation. "They were really quite mediocre. At Christmas, they would come to the Club to carol us. The children stood like sticks, singing without emotion."

Yet the foundation stuck with the choir year after year, providing annual grants of five thousand dollars—when five thousand dollars was real money—to keep the choir going, improving. The CCC is a big deal now, its multimillion-dollar budget now also supported by big name foundations and donors.

Other beneficiaries of financial awards from Civic and Arts, now accomplished pros on the world stage, know that they also owe a lot to two remarkable women—Rose M. Grundman and her daughter Rose Ann. These women were central to the Union League Club long before women were allowed to membership. The artists return the favor. "Several years ago before the Club's annual meeting and dinner," Rose Ann Grundman continues, "when Phil Wicklander was stepping down from his presidency, Phil asked me if there were any chance in the world I could get his absolutely favorite violinist, Rachel Barton, to play at the dinner."

At the time, Rachel Barton was recovering from a terrible train accident that almost took her life. Grundman called Barton's mother to inquire. Unfortunately, the mother said, Rachel is having another operation that day. Otherwise she would love to do it.

Wicklander understood, of course, but was disappointed.

Two days later, Rachel Barton called Rose Ann Grundman to say, yes, she would be delighted to accept—she would simply postpone her operation!

"We kept this a secret from Phil and the dinner gathering. What an emotional evening. This incredibly gifted violinist, then without the use of her legs, playing heavenly music for Phil and all of us."

Rachel had been the C&A's young violin scholarship award winner in 1990. At the dinner, she told Phil Wicklander and Club members that the award and several thousand dollars in prize money had been critical to nurturing what has become a sparkling career.

Another organization of the Club, the Chicago Engineers Foundation, directs its awards to high school students from Chicago's public and parochial schools who have been accepted into accredited university engineering programs. In addition, the foundation rewards these students as they continue their studies.

In 2002, the Chicago Engineers Foundation awarded nearly $71,000 to students, $700 each to thirty young men and women graduating from high school and $600 to each of eighty-three continuing university "engine school" students. Students may use their awards in any way they see fit, which makes the scholarships nice bonuses for many minority and first-generation American students.

The Club inherited this program in 1975 when it absorbed the Chicago Engineers Club, which had occupied a narrow seven-story building immediately to the south of the clubhouse since 1910. The small clubhouse had been a focal point for professional engineering societies in the region and had been headquarters for the Western Society of Engineers.

Robert Isham Randolph, who gained fame in Chicago and beyond as the swashbuckling head of the Secret Six of the Capone era, had been a member.

The convivial but small group of engineers enjoyed a dining room and grill, the latter decorated with, among other artifacts, a whale penis which hung from the ceiling. Unfortunately, the small, cramped nature of their edifice and small roster made continuation of their club unlikely.

The Union League Club accepted 140 Engineers Foundation members onto its own rolls and took ownership of the building and its $40,000 mortgage, plus the scholarship program.

In 2003, however, the Club had still not figured out what use to make of the Engineers building other than for storage. Illustrative of the problems with the twenty-foot-wide space, the floors of the acquired building are not level with Club floors.

Fortunately, the scholarship program for Chicago students has continued to expand through the Club's voluntary membership monthly dues checkoff for foundations as well as special generosity from Club members.

Engineering students from struggling urban families face major financial and scholastic challenges. For the young, committed performing artist, however, the climb toward the top is somewhat different—often scary, lonely, and threadbare.

Young musicians need money for private lessons and two hundred dollars each time a good accompanist is required. They also need to be heard and to be tested repeatedly in competition. With this preparation, they can face with some confidence the brutal audition process that opens the door—or blocks passage forever—to chairs in the Chicago, Philadelphia, and other world-class orchestras, as for several C&A scholarship winners, or a leading place in the opera company at London's Covent Garden, as for C&A winner soprano Nancy Gustafson.

Rose McGilvray Grundman knew this in 1938 when she became music chairman and later president of the Conference of (Women's) Club Presidents and Program Chairmen of Chicago. In its heyday in the 1940s and 1950s, there were a thousand women's clubs in the area. Most had money for musical programs and speakers. Every Thursday at 10 A.M., conference members gathered at the Art Institute of Chicago to hear local artists gathered by Rose M. Grundman. Each performed for eight minutes, which gave them much-needed exposure and the chance to be booked by local clubs.

In 1976, when Rose M. Grundman was a mere eighty-one, the Civic and Arts Foundation asked her to chair its small high school musical scholarship competition. Not a member, of course, Grundman had been made an honorary member of the C&A because of her extraordinary service to music in Chicago. Her husband Paul was a member of both the Club and the C&A. Rose Ann Grundman soon became her mother's aide-de-camp and in short order they and the foundation created the largest musical scholarship program in Chicago.

Rose Ann Grundman looks and acts like the professor of mathematical biology she was at the University of Illinois College of Medicine in Chicago—serious and focused on her work. She favors solid brown suits and matching solid brown winter coats.

Her passion lies with serious young musicians regardless of their backgrounds. She lives for their professional futures and does everything in her power for "her children."

The life of an aspiring classical musician is today tougher than ever. There used to be hundreds of women's clubs in the Chicago area with budgets for musical programs. Now but a handful remain. And there are fewer places to perform.

Each year the Civic and Arts Foundation awards $50,000 in musical scholarships, from $3,000 for winners in the high school category to the $12,000 Rose M. Grundman Scholarship for Women's Voice, for which Rose Ann is a cosponsor.

The scholarship competition requires fifteen judges, three each for five divisions. Fortunately, Rose Ann Grundman has a Rolodex of top-notch musicians who could staff several full orchestras and opera companies, which includes the music faculty and teachers for many of the best universities and studios in the Chicago region.

As a result, the C&A competition gets the best as judges, which adds to its prestige. The judges include principals from the Chicago Symphony Orchestra and James Palermo, artistic and general director of the Grant Park Music Festival.

Contestants must live and study within one hundred miles of Chicago—and be American citizens. "That is important," says Josephine Lee. "It prevents a few prodigies from around the world from swooping down and carrying off all the prizes, as happens in many competitions."

"The competition is highly anticipated by area musicians," Lee adds. She speaks from experience. Lee won the $6,000 young-adult piano competition in 1995, important help for a young woman from the family of a Korean-American Methodist minister.

All the competition winners agree in advance to perform at the Union League Club. This is done as much for the musicians as for the Club. The young musicians need to be heard by people who might make a difference in their careers. And they need audiences.

It doesn't hurt the Club ambiance, of course, that rich, live music—possibly from a future Nancy Gustafson or Rachel Barton—fills the Club for the Washington's Birthday Dinner celebration and other galas.

Like Auntie Mame, Angeline Higginson is as colorful as Rose Ann Grundman is professorial. Higginson has been another key to the success of the Civic and Arts Foundation—she raises the money. Angie and husband Jack are fixtures in the Rendezvous Room and part of the Club family.

Angie Higginson became a director of C&A in the mid 1970s and president in 1990 to 1992, although to this day not a member of the Club;

instead, she is the spouse of a member. A majority of C&A directors must be members of the Club, but seven may be nonmembers. In her first year as director, she didn't go down all that well with the more reserved types on the board. Soon, however, she was climbing the rungs with wide support. Higginson gets things done and she has a big heart.

With assets of little more than $1.5 million, C&A has to raise significant dollars each year to meet its $250,000 programming budget.

The C&A Board meets at the Club, where it has free office space. For years, Angie Higginson has been the chief fundraiser for the annual benefit dinner and auction, which nets more than a $100,000.

"The home-run hitters are the twenty-five-hundred-dollar contributors," she emphasized at a C&A monthly meeting for directors. "This year we're also going after increases from the lower levels of contributors."

The twenty around the table were put on notice as to their ticket and auction item responsibilities. Higginson will see to it they fulfill them. Finished with her sales pitch, she sat down. Husband Jack, president of C&A from 2001 to 2003, continued the meeting.

Jack and Angie married in 1959; he joined the Club in 1962. Like many at the time, Jack joined because the Club had waived the initiation fee and offered inexpensive athletic department fees and dues for men under thirty, in an effort to infuse the Club with more energy. Later he became a committee member, then a board director of the Club and chair of the entertainment committee. That led to the foundations. In 2002, he was not only head of C&A but the longest-serving trustee (since 1968) of the Boys and Girls Club Foundation and a past president of that foundation as well.

The Higginsons are illustrated to represent many other past Club presidents and directors who along with their spouses become active—and then stay active—on one or more of the three foundation boards. For example, in 2003, half of the twenty-four directors of C&A were also trustees of the Boys and Girls Clubs.

The Club created the C&A Foundation in 1949 to receive tax-deductible gifts of art and money; the Club itself cannot offer the deductibility benefit. The foundation also later provided a modest sinecure for Dr. Edward Martin, who became the first full-time executive director of C&A in 1960. Ed Martin retired from the Club that year with a lousy pension after thirty-six years of devoted service as executive director of the public affairs committee. Martin was an institution in the Club. He deserved better and the board realized this, belatedly.

Since 1949 C&A has boosted the careers of artists who practice in a wide array of media. In recent years, C&A has awarded more than thirty thousand dollars annually to promising young visual artists, poets, and short-story writers in the Chicago area. Additional thousands go to museums and for programs to help poor kids do better in school and in life.

As is not unusual among eleemosynary entities, the board squabbles over how to allocate limited dollars across civic, cultural, and musical categories. Angie and Jack Higginson want to focus on poor kids. "Can't we find talented kids," said Jack Higginson, "in our own Boys and Girls Clubs and support them as well through Civic and Arts?"

In 2002, Jack Higgins won approval from C&A trustees for a major shift in foundation funding. Instead of funding other organizations, C&A will put most of its dollars in programs operated directly by the foundation such as the music competitions. The revered Chicago Children's Choir may be an exception. The Higginsons believe this will make it easier to raise money and also generate more attention to the Club and the foundation.

Somewhat at odds is Rose Ann Grundman. She advocates support for talented Chicago artists regardless of background.

And Grundman also digs in her heels when she hears talk of diluting her musical scholarship awards and support for the Chicago Children's Choir. "They are the crown jewels in our tiara. I fight for every dollar we can get for them."

A squabble was brewing in late 2002 over whether to continue a ten-thousand-dollar annual grant to the Chicago Youth Symphony Orchestra, which is headquartered a few blocks away in the Fine Arts Building.

Located on South Michigan Avenue, the Fine Arts Building is a throwback to the late nineteenth century, when Chicago was struggling to knock the rough edges off its image. Black and white tile floors and heavily varnished wainscoting lead down dark corridors; office-door windows in milk glass announce, in small black letters: Elizabeth Bernstein, Teacher of Violin, and so on down the hall—teachers of voice, piano, horn, anything musical.

The elevators are the original, run by wizened operators who may have come with the building. At the eighth floor, this visitor carefully steps down half a step from the elevator to the hallway floor. "Nice try," the author thinks to himself, doubting the dour operator would appreciate the humor.

The cacophony of an orchestra warming up reaches out to the corridor. At the end of the floor, a small rehearsal hall is filling up with tiny people, all carrying instruments their size or bigger. A mother helps her son the cellist with a special bench to sit on, the standard chairs being too big. The tyke is but six (true), the youngest in the Chicago Youth Concert Orchestra. Others range up to fifteen.

A full-of-the-devil white boy talks animatedly to a black violist. A young Thai, about ten, in an oversize Cubs cap, warms up in the reed section. Next to him is a much larger twelve-year-old blond girl who may be from the suburbs.

A lanky young black man approaches the podium. The noise dies. A black teen and her bassoon slip in, in the nick of time for the rehearsal; her CTA bus may have been late. The conductor calls for Tchaikovsky's "Swan Lake," lifts his baton—and beautiful music issues forth.

The conductor stops the music and holds a colloquy with a grade-school boy trumpet player wearing an oversize football jersey. "You came in late. Let's try that again."

Late again.

"Where are you?" the football jersey asks the conductor, with all the confidence in the world.

The conductor asks the trumpeter to play the passage by himself, which he does without blinking, making a rich, authoritative sound. The two are now in accord. The orchestra continues.

The eighty-seven members of the Chicago Youth Concert Orchestra represent the training orchestra for the Chicago Youth Symphony Orchestra, which is a pre-professional training orchestra for ensembles around the world. Eleven graduates of the latter have chairs in the fabled Chicago Symphony; three are in the Philadelphia Orchestra; the last conductor of the CYSO left to become the assistant conductor at Philadelphia.

The newer concert orchestra might well not exist if it hadn't been for a major grant from the Union League Civic and Arts Foundation, which began its support for the youth symphony in 1971. In 1988, CYSO president Jeannette Kreston saw a need to reach out more to inner-city children, whose parents and schools are less likely than elsewhere to encourage and develop interests in classical music.

The concert orchestra makes special efforts through the public schools to identify and nurture that talent. The best go on to the Youth Symphony, and then, for some, to professional careers with major orchestras.

That first year and since, C&A has provided key five-figure grants to get the ball rolling. Now the concert orchestra has its own conductor, music scholarships for the poor kids who need the help, and a concert schedule of its own.

A week after this rehearsal, Rose Ann Grundman is in her center box at Symphony Hall to hear the senior group, the Chicago Youth Symphony Orchestra, in its first concert under its new maestro, Allan Tinkham. Tinkham leads his new charges through a challenging program of Bartok, Webern, Grieg, and Resphigi. On Sunday, *Chicago Tribune* critic Jon Von Rhein raves: "Three former music directors of the high school-age training ensemble—Rossen Milanov, Daniel Hege and Michael Morgan—now hold conducting posts in Philadelphia, Syracuse and Oakland, respectively.

Allen Tinkham, it is safe to predict, will one day follow their example and garner a major U.S. podium of his own."

There are other connections between this orchestra and the Civic and Arts Foundation. In 1999, for example, in the symphony's fiftieth anniversary program, the Chicago Youth Symphony honored the Club this way:

> The Chicago Youth Symphony Orchestra is proud to recognize the Union League Club of Chicago for its commitment to supporting young people in the city and furthering the careers of young artists. Through its foundations, the Union League Club has made a difference in the lives of hundreds of thousands of children and teens. As evidence of the Club's impact, all of this afternoon's eight soloists for Mahler's Symphony No. 8 are former winners of the Union League Civic and Arts Foundation voice competition and now perform with major opera companies.

The Club has never embraced the C&A Foundation the way it has the Boys and Girls Clubs Foundation. C&A origins may be a factor. The group was created largely to be a repository for tax-deductible gifts of art, and a place for the beloved Dr. Edward Martin to hang his hat and supplement his meager Club pension. C&A focused initially on patriotic histories and important but un-Club-like poetry writing awards via *Poetry Magazine*. It was hard for some of the fellows in the Club athletic department to warm up to poetry.

Even today, many members have little awareness that C&A is an integral part of the Club, even though Rose Ann, Angie, and Jack and others are, almost daily, in and out of C&A offices on the ninth-floor administrative level of the Club.

"When I was president of C&A (1987 to 1989)," says Club historian and former Club president Everett Barlow, "we needed money to build our assets, but damned if we could pry it from the members."

This is reflected in the disparity in the Club's allocation of income from the members' voluntary monthly checkoff of fourteen dollars to the foundations. Nine dollars is directed to the Boys and Girls Clubs Foundation, $3 to Civic & Arts, $1.50 for the Engineers, and $.50 for the Club art collection.

Seventeen hundred and fifty of the Club members participate in the single monthly checkoff for the foundations.

Five hundred forty contribute $150 or more each year to the Civic and Arts Foundation, the minimum for membership in C&A.

In the late 1980s, in an effort to increase its assets, C&A president

Everett Barlow and his board proposed a trade to the Club: C&A would sell to the Club its collection of fifty-five works of art, already hanging permanently in the Clubhouse, in return for one painting, *Return of the Kermos* by the Russian Leon Gaspard. Barlow had inside information: when he served as Club president (1984 to 1985), he had received an offer of $250,000 for the painting. The Club agreed to the trade.

"Sotheby's tried to knock our price down, so we sold the painting through a Santa Fe gallery," Barlow relates, with a satisfied smile. C&A continues to hustle for revenue any way it can.

In 2002, the Chicago Children's Choir and the Chicago Youth Symphony Orchestra gave a joint concert at Carnegie Hall in celebration of their combined one hundred years of performing for Chicago and beyond. The performance was sold out.

That same year, the Chicago Children's Choir honored the Union League Club at its annual benefit. The Choir presented the Club one of their signature red jackets.

SOURCES

In addition to Club publications and numerous archival files and Chicago newspaper files, this chapter was informed richly by interviews, which included the following: Club members Everett Barlow; William McDermott; Jack and Angeline Higginson; Rose Ann Grundman; Hugh Schwartzberg; Charlene Williamson, president of the American Opera Society; Nancy Carstedt, president of the Chicago Children's Choir; and Jeannette Kreston, president of the Chicago Youth Symphony Orchestras.

Chapter 14

ART ALONE ENDURES

The Union League clubhouse is known foremost for its art collection. That a men's club (until 1987) should have an art collection worth many millions of dollars is unusual. In the gilded 1880s and 1890s in Chicago, however, art in the Club made eminently good sense to a core of sensitive as well as practical members. In 1886, there was the new clubhouse to decorate, designed by active member Major William LeBaron Jenney, Club members often noted proudly. Jenney is the architect credited with the first skeletal frame "skyscraper." Further, the Calumet Club boasted of its "select collection of modern paintings." Located south of the business district in the fashionable Prairie Avenue district, the Calumet was a primary competitor of the Union League for up-and-coming prospective members.

In addition, women were to play a significant role in the new clubhouse—truly unusual for a men's club—and they appreciated the civilizing touch of art in the clubhouse.

To build a collection that would, maybe not so incidentally, shame that in the Calumet Club, the Club amended its bylaws in 1891 to set aside 2 percent of dues "for purchase of paintings and other pictures and works of art for the Club."

Architects like Jenney were drawn to Chicago after the Fire in 1871. The most illustrious of these builders and designers were arguably the first great artists, defined broadly, to be identified with the City. Major firms in Chicago included those headed by Jenney (1868), Dankmar Adler (1871), John Wellborn Root and Daniel Burnham (1873). Burnham and Sullivan each worked in Jenney's atelier before striking out on their own, as did William Holabird and Martin Roche. These architects all followed Jenney's lead in joining the Union League Club.

An engineer in the Civil War, Jenney was active in the Club from the beginning. The Union League was his only club affiliation, which is somewhat unusual for successful men at the time who would belong to several social-business clubs. A bon vivant and marvelous raconteur, Jenney is likely to have gathered or attracted his fellow architects frequently for lunch at a round table in the clubhouse, as was the fashion of the day among the professions, according to early Club member Nathaniel Sears. After all, Burnham and Root were occupied just across a narrow street from the Club with work on their now famous Monadnock Building (1891), and Adler and Sullivan along with Club president Ferd Peck were busy four blocks away with the Auditorium Theatre and Building (1891).

The architects also had more practical concerns at the Club. There are notes in Club archives about Burnham and Jenney in the bowels of the clubhouse poking at the boilers, trying to reduce smoke emissions, a problem that plagued the city.

The most important stimulus, however, to works of fine art in the Club was the coming World's Columbian Exposition. The colorful cultural impresario Ferd Peck was to be president of the Club in 1893. Peck became a magnet and host for the world's elite. Thus, the Club had to look the peer of clubs the world around, as well as offer the uplifting spirit of fine art. As noted in the introduction to the Club's second catalog of its art, in 1907: "Whenever men of education and taste meet together . . . there is a demand for harmonious surroundings and desire for pictures and statuary to satisfy the aesthetic sense."

The fair also showcased the best in art. Unfortunately, according to Jenney's partner William Mundie, later a chair of the Club's art committee, the first clubhouse was not fireproof; otherwise the Club might have purchased more from the fair's artists for display in the clubhouse.

Clubs in Chicago were learning how to be clubs from clubs in the East, which opened earlier. The Union League Club of Philadelphia had, for example, an art association within their club. In 1887, a catalog of their art collection reached Chicago and circulated among members along with a suggestion from the circulators that a similar activity be formed in the Club. In addition to Peck, the group that encouraged the Club to develop a collection included four remarkable and active members—Charles Hutchinson, Martin Ryerson, William M. R. French, and John Barton Payne.

Benjamin Hutchinson, his family, and young son Charles brought little to Chicago from Massachusetts in 1858. "Old Hutch" quickly applied savvy, skill, and ruthlessness to grain trading, meat packing, and banking. By 1888, for example, Hutchinson cornered the market on wheat and walked off the trading floor one afternoon a million dollars richer. Old Hutch and his unmistakable slouch hat were inseparable on the exchange floor, where he was first to arrive and last to leave, and in the barrooms where he drank as hard as he worked.

Old Hutch was of the generation that made Chicago wealthy. Cut from more refined cloth than his father, son Charles and his generation smoothed the city's rough edges. Father refused his son's desire to go to college, insisting that Charles join him in the family businesses. Son met father halfway, serving as president of the Board of Trade and of the Corn Exchange Bank. Yet he saved his true passion for his love of art, if only as an amateur and a patron.

Old Hutch was contemptuous of his son's interests. "Think of him, a son of mine!" he declared dismissively. "He paid $500 apiece for five painted sheep when he could get the real article for $2 a head."

Charles Hutchinson paid no heed, paying his father back for rebuffing his interest in higher education. In 1882 at age twenty-eight, Hutchinson became president of the board of the new Art Institute of Chicago, a post he held uninterrupted for forty-two years. Young Hutchinson committed himself to culture with greater zeal than Old Hutch had to business.

Over his lifetime, Charles Hutchinson was a contributing member or an officer of seventy organizations, treasurer of twenty, and director or trustee of forty. The beneficiaries included the University of Chicago, the Chicago Symphony, and the Field Museum. Of course, almost everyone at the Club was involved in the world's fair, as was Hutchinson, who headed the fine arts department and was a guarantor.

Neither Hutchinson nor Ryerson was enormously rich by the standards of the gilded age. They conserved their money and devoted themselves to cultural philanthropy. They traveled frequently to Europe and the Orient, where they immersed themselves in the art and artists of the day, at the Louvre, in Mary Cassatt's studio, on guided tours in search of the exotic art of the East.

At the Club, Hutchinson, Ryerson, and William M. R. French pushed and guided the development of the Club's fledgling art collection. A lumber fortune heir, Ryerson was vice president of the Art Institute and Hutchinson's inseparable friend. French ran the Art Institute for them.

The three helped create and served on the art committee at the Club; French served as chair from 1897 to 1901. They had help in the Club, of course, from Ferd Peck, lawyer-judge John Payne, and commodities trader Frank Logan. Later secretary of the Interior under President Wilson, Payne was president of the art committee in 1895 when the Club's Monet was purchased. Logan served on the committee for twenty-two years. Payne and Logan were also on the board of the Art Institute and Logan endowed a major prize for American artists.

The foundation of the present Club collection was formed by these men during the 1880s and 1890s and in the first decade of the next century. In 1895, the committee purchased a Claude Monet, *Pommiers en Fleurs,* for five hundred dollars. This created a flap in the Club; after all, it was modern. According to Club lore, president John Hamline reputedly scoffed, "Who would pay five dollars for that blob of paint?"

On the other hand, the irrepressible Bertha Honoré Palmer was a strong advocate for Monet and owned many of his paintings, a number of which she bequeathed to the Art Institute for its world-famed impressionist collection. It appears that Payne may have purchased the Monet in 1895, the same year as an exhibit of the artist's works in Chicago, and soon thereafter sold it to the Club at a price well below those set for Monet's paintings at the exhibit.

The Palmer connection may have played a part as well in the committee's purchase soon thereafter of American impressionist paintings, including *Blossoming Time,* by Mary Fairchild MacMonnies Low. Low and another American, Mary Cassatt, painted murals for the women's building at the 1893 world's fair, an edifice created at the insistence of the remarkable Mrs. Palmer.

French, Hutchinson, and Ryerson were also open to the avant-garde. That doesn't mean they appreciated it. For example, the famous (or to conservative tastes, infamous) Armory Show of 1913 in New York City introduced Picasso, Kandinsky, Matisse, Duchamp, and other modernists to America. Organized by artists, the show was held in an armory rather than the New York Metropolitan Museum of Art, which wasn't interested.

A smaller version of the controversial Armory Show was displayed at the Art Institute without incident. William French pointedly left Chicago during the show, however, commenting privately that the exhibit displayed "a large element of hoax and humbug, and another large element of laziness and incompetence." In public, Hutchinson was more diplomatic, noting the show represented "talented and competent artists who are sincerely experimenting in the craft of their profession . . . [yet] the great artist never ignores the public."

Under the trio's leadership, the Club collection was to develop along lines of conservative quality, offering stimulation and comfort to Club members. Unable to afford the European masters, the Club soon began to use its limited patronage to select, as it does today, from the best works of American art with a favorable attitude toward artists in Chicago.

Unfortunately, from 1910 until about 1950, the Club failed to sustain active, aggressive interest in contemporary American art. The Club became preoccupied with financing and erecting its new clubhouse (on the same site as the one it replaced), designed by member William Mundie of Jenney and Mundie and opened in 1926. Then came the dark days of the Depression and the challenges of keeping the Club solvent and of course World War II. In 1929, the Club eliminated the 2 percent dues set-aside for art. During the period, the art committee did acquire several fine pieces, including works by Walter Ufer and Victor Higgins, artists of the Taos School, and Thomas Hill's *Yosemite Valley*.

The issue of just what were "the best works of American art" became problematical as well. The surge of interest in nonrepresentational modernism among arbiters of fine art became bitterly controversial. Frank Logan's wife reacted adversely to the modernist work of several Logan prizewinners at the Art Institute. She went on the warpath against "moronic grotesqueries of so-called modern art" via her self-developed Society for Sanity in Art. Needless to say, the Club stuck with representational art.

Club members also supported local artists by helping create other opportunities for Chicago artists. In 1899, Hutchinson, Payne, Sullivan, Burnham, and Adler were among Club members who helped launch the Municipal Art League of Chicago. The League conducted an annual juried show to support Chicago artists and purchased many of the pieces exhibited.

Paul Schulze, Sr., served as chair of the Club's art committee from 1929 to 1948. Schulze rose from a hardware clerk in South Dakota to become founder of a successful baking company in Chicago. In 1924, he donated fifteen of his paintings by American impressionists to the Art Institute and two years later donated Charles Hawthorne's *The Shad Fisherman* to the Club.

In 1936, when also president of the Municipal Art League, Schulze arranged for the league's collection, which had no home, to be displayed at the Club. Ultimately, the Club purchased the complete collection. The fifty-five pieces acquired include works by Pauline Palmer, Edward Potthast, Edgar Rupprecht, Walter Ufer, Guy Wiggins, Frank Wadsworth, and Adam Emory Albright.

By the end of World War II, the Club collection suffered from neglect. The Monet hung between the banks of elevators on the fifth floor, unprotected and uninsured. The Club had incomplete documentation for its collection of five hundred pieces of art, not knowing what it owned.

The Club caught its collective breath after the war and again turned some attention to the art collection. In 1955, the Club launched a series of biennial exhibitions open to area artists. Over three decades, the exhibitions provided a counterpoint to the Art Institute's taste for contemporary art. Or, as public affairs director Roger Henn put it: "I ran regional art shows to offset the offbeat shows over at the Art Institute." Frank Young of the art committee and others in the Club pitched in. Young was president of his own American Academy of Art, a school for artists and illustrators.

For conservative artists, the show quickly became a major event. As Henn said, "Many artists who belong to the realistic school felt this show was their only opportunity for recognition." Seven hundred fifty artists submitted work to the first jury and twice that many came forward to vie for selection in the second exhibition.

Local art critics were not overwhelmed. The *Tribune* minced few words: "The Union League Club's biennial art shows go their own serene way, entirely unconcerned with vogues and rages of the day." The show offered "something for everybody," so long as everybody is totally unconcerned about "assessing the art trends of the mid-1960s."

The shows probably reflected popular tastes more faithfully than did the Art Institute exhibitions, as well as the Club's strong belief that good traditional art needed expression and support.

The best way to appreciate the Club's collection is to take a tour with one of the docents. There is fine art on all of the Club's floors with the exception of the athletic facilities.

Docent and art historian Ardelle Arthur has been familiar with the art collection since the 1940s, first as a "career girl" who arranged meetings at the Club for her company, then as the wife of a member, and now as a member herself.

"This is a Richard Hunt." Arthur begins her tour in the first-floor lobby. The tangled mass of glistening bronze emanates strength and energy. The piece is a perfect greeter to busy men and women on their way to meet luncheon guests.

"Hunt is a well-regarded African American Chicago sculptor," Arthur observes. "His soaring works can be seen at Sheffield and Lincoln on the north side."

Later, on the fifth floor, the docent reflects, "This is the former ladies' cocktail lounge. When I was the spouse of a member, I loved this room, where we ladies could be to ourselves. It's now called the fifth floor parlor." She turns to a large canvas, "This is a Vera Klement. I love it." On the canvas, a woman with her back to us is framed by a window, the colors all soft shades of cream, yet striking in their contrasts.

The massive cherry conference table in the boardroom is softened by art on every side, neatly highlighted by focused beams that illumine the paintings without spilling over to the frames.

"This is a Guy Wiggins, a famous American impressionist . . . and this is by Frank Virgil Dudley, the 'painter of the Dunes.'" The colored shadows suggest impressionism; vivid but unbroken brushwork informs the viewer it is not.

Art dominates the grand Main Dining Room, with its formal continental presentation and beamed ceilings high above. After reviewing works by Irving Ramsey Wiles, Pauline Palmer, William Henry Howe, and more than a dozen others, largely from a century ago, the docent brings us to a dramatic seven-by-ten-foot painting that screams to be seen. We are before *Night Fires* by James Valerio. The Club raised forty thousand dollars in 1994 to purchase this piece. Vivid, almost electric colors light a night sky behind a haunting female figure.

"In this one piece," the docent continues, "you have a portrait in realism, a still life, and the surrealism of the forest fires in the distance. Technically, this work is superior. Look closely at the crystal pitcher, the water inside, and the cellophane [part of the still life]. Tell me how," she exclaims, "he painted water that looks absolutely like water, and cellophane that looks like cellophane!"

On first view, the work looks out of place among the often academic paintings of an earlier era. On the other hand, the Valerio makes a statement for all to see that Club art committees of late (membership changes somewhat every year) are becoming sensitive to Midwestern artists whose work is au courant, if not cutting edge. And as another docent observes, "The Valerio absolutely lifts the whole dining room."

Later, in the library, *Sheridan's Ride* by Thomas Buchanan Read is pointed out for its historical interest. The dashing general Philip Sheridan was an honorary member of the Club in the nineteenth century and graced the club frequently for meals. Read was both painter and poet, the author, for example, of the poem "Sheridan's Ride." His poem, in an original copy, accompanies the painting. Painters said Read was a better poet than painter; poets thought him a better painter than poet. The painting fits the Club's patriotic tone nicely.

The docent stops at a Potthast beach scene, which she admires. Nearby are two of four pieces by the Armenian American Hovsep Pushman, whose family was drawn to Chicago by glowing reports of the World's Columbian Exposition of 1893. Pushman's works are still lifes of Asian objets d'art encased in ornate frames.

The docent is asked about the nude above the bar in the Rendezvous Room. "Oh, the sanctum sanctorum!" she responds. "I never feel right going in there. It was always the men's bar. Ladies never went in there!"

The nude is a fixture above the gleaming mahogany bar. George Haight, a prominent lawyer and Club president, remarried in 1942. When his new bride saw the nude above the Haight fireplace, she reportedly declared: "Either it goes or I do." The painting, entitled *The Captive,* has graced the Club bar ever since.

The Captive was painted by Charles Frederick Naegele in 1898 and exhibited at the Art Institute the following year. The reclining figure of a full-bodied woman faces away from the viewer. When the painting was sent out of the Club in 1995 for conservation, it was learned that the veil over the figure's derriere was not original. The veil has been removed.

The Blashfield mural *Patria* over the fireplace in the main lounge created a stir when it was unveiled to celebrate the opening of the clubhouse in 1926. All the figures in the piece are women! There was a movement in the Club to have the mural replaced, which was unsuccessful. After all, Blashfield was an internationally known muralist, if quite traditional in style, who oversaw much of the mural work done at the World's Columbian Exposition.

The docent and her tour group, one of several art tours each month, walk to the marble stairs and down one level to the lobby. They pass the Monet; a white marble bust of Daniel Webster by Hiram Powers; a small sculpture, *Squirrel Boy,* by Lorado Taft's assistant Leonard Crunelle; and two large, sunny canvasses by Edgar Rupprecht. The art overflows, and yet the tour group has seen but a fraction of the 750 pieces in the collection.

"You bought that piece of crap!" Dillon Hoey of the art committee exclaimed to former Club president John Scully. The indecorous observation was prompted by a first viewing of what has become known in the Club as the *Ike* portrait. Eisenhower is depicted in his eponymous jacket aboard a landing craft. Behind him, Ike's men are landing on Omaha Beach.

Eisenhower was in his London headquarters, of course, on D-Day. The portrait by Chicago artist Richard Willenbrink brings to mind romantic paintings of Napoleon and other great warriors overseeing their battlefield triumphs. The artist used broad brushstrokes and rich, sharp contrasts in his colors. The portrait steps forward to the viewer. Club art curator Marianne Richter calls it, diplomatically, "not to my taste." Scully, a banker and retired Army Reserve general, loves it. Another member, a woman, remarked—half approvingly, half in mild derision—that the Ike gives forth a good "guy feeling."

"The public affairs committee wanted to celebrate Eisenhower's one-hundredth birthday," explained Scully. Dick Rauch, Bob Fitzgerald [past presidents also], and I selected Willenbrink, who has taught at the Art Institute, from many artist proposals. The art committee insisted, however, that it be put in the library, out of the way.

"By tradition, Club presidents are asked what their one wish for the Club would be. I said, 'Put Ike in the stairwell off the Rendezvous [Room],' where everyone can see it. It's still there," Scully notes with obvious pleasure.

"And that's what's great about the Club. We're like family. We can have our spats, and still be great friends."

The third-floor gallery is outside the Wigwam, another of the Club's dining rooms. For years, curators have presented exhibits here by artists whose works have often not been shown in galleries. The works are often for sale, another way the Club supports local artists. The curator and art committee take this exhibit space quite seriously. On the other hand, some philistine Club members might mutter that there may be a reason the artists haven't been shown anywhere before—as they harrumphed in 1981 about the New West show.

"There was this Plexiglas box decorated with chicken feathers," recalls veteran dining rooms manager Carl Madsen. "Inside was a marionette with three faces, bouncing around, accompanied by incessant, loud, twangy country music. The music disturbed the diners and drove the waiters nuts after a while. We pulled the plug on the music whenever we got the chance.

"Finally someone complained to Dick McKay, the Club president at the time. He came down, took a look at the chicken feathers and said, 'Get this piece of crap out of here [McKay wasn't the same fellow who couldn't stand *Ike*].' So it was put in the athletic department!"

Not consulted, the curator at the time resigned in a huff. The art community commented acidly on the Club's primitive understanding of art.

"If the New West exhibit were displayed today in the gallery," says Madsen, still at his post two decades later, "members would think the exhibit cute, kitschy—but we'd still pull the plug on the music when no one was looking."

In fact, the third-floor gallery represents an important opportunity and space for Chicago artists to have their work seen by those who often buy and also spread word of an emerging talent. Supporting Chicago artists in an art world dominated by the two coasts has been a theme throughout the history of art in the Club. Phil Wicklander exemplifies this passion for Chicago artists. An artisan himself, he has headed Wicklander Printing, a major producer of high-quality, high-end six-color printing. Schooled in art by the late curator and artist Dennis Loy, Wicklander is a former chair of the art committee and president of the Club.

As Club president in 1995 to 1996, Wicklander pressed successfully for reinstitution of the allocation of part of member dues (0.5 percent) for art acquisition, which generates about twenty-five thousand dollars a year. He helped create the Distinguished Artist Program in the Club, which has honored a number of major Chicago artists such as Richard Hunt, Vera Klement, and Ed Paschke. During Wicklander's chairmanship of the art committee in 1993, the Club surveyed art professionals in Chicago to identify the city's leading artists and then mounted a show of their works. The survey and show were conducted again in 2003.

Then there is the Monet. Why, today, have a solitary Monet, its worth in the millions, when the Club has developed an American collection? In 1957, the art committee voted to request the board's authorization to investigate the possibility of exchanging the Monet, then valued at twenty thousand dollars, for a number of works owned by the Art Institute that would enrich and fill holes in the Club's American collection.

Nothing came of the idea. Again in 1985, when the Monet had been appraised for nine hundred thousand dollars, former art committee chairman Iver Olsen pleaded with the committee to sell the painting for similar reasons. Nothing came of it. Monet will probably be part of the collection forever. Everyone has heard of Monet, even when they might not recognize Bellows, Inness, Ufer, Wiggins, Klement, Paschke.

Overseeing, conserving, and shaping a collection of 750 works of art by a committee whose membership changes every year is challenging and expensive. The chair of the art committee is always a member of the Club board of directors, whose terms are limited to three years. The chairman determines the size and makeup of his committee.

Another committee, the house committee, is responsible for the clubhouse and how it looks; its membership changes each year as well. In addition, since the clubhouse literally belongs to the members, some have strong feelings about the presentation and feel of their mansion in the city. Given all that, there has in fact been relatively little conflict over the management of the collection.

Displeasure over an exhibit in the third-floor gallery has been mentioned, yet that gallery continues to be a vibrant and stimulating space. The house committee asked that a Roger Brown piece, *Cathedrals in Space,* be moved from its placement in the fifth-floor parlor because its seeming phallic representation made some uneasy. But that is the only such request in recent years.

The process of "deaccessioning" (selling) works from the collection has been fraught with controversy. Following an inventory of the collection in the early 1980s, a number of works were sold at a silent auction in order to generate funds for acquisition. This caused distress among some members who felt the sales diminished the collection. At present there is a multistep process that involves staff, art committee, and even members before any work can be sold. To avoid conflict of interest, members of the art committee and the board of directors are prohibited from purchasing works to be sold.

In addition to a full-time professional curator, part-time assistant curator, and part-time conservator, the Club is one of only two local institutions to have a paintings conservation laboratory; the other is at the Art Institute.

Loan requests from museums must be dealt with. The art committee and staff have also collaborated with the Chicago Cultural Center on exhibits. In 1980, the Club took part of its own collection on the road in a "Centennial Exhibition of American Art," which celebrated the Club's own centenary.

What has been wrought over a century and a quarter of collecting?

The Club collection is a delight for those who appreciate American art, especially works by Chicago and regional artists. Art cognoscenti in the East might sniff that the collection is rather provincial, but the art has been collected for the pleasure of the members, not for museum critics. Even so, the Club collection rivals that of the public galleries in many medium-size cities.

The collection is strong in American art before 1910, weak in modern American art after 1913. Fitting the patriotic principles of the Club, there is a strong representation of portraits of public figures by respected practitioners in that field. The collection includes several fine examples from the Taos School.

Since the mid-1980s, the art committee has become more progressive in its tastes and aggressive in its pursuit of fine art. In 1997, the Club purchased at Sotheby's a Roger Brown, *Chicago Taking a Beating*, the first work the Club has purchased at auction since 1895. The Club has acquired a number of other Chicago imagist works as well.

For the future, there are questions about the best strategy for acquisitions: Save the dues allocation for art until it reaches, say, a hundred thousand dollars and then purchase a significant piece to fill a gap in the existing collection? Or try to identify emerging Chicago artists and buy several works with the same amount of money?

The art collection confers a widely known distinction upon the Club. "Oh, the Union League Club. They have the art collection, don't they?" Members, including some who may not have seen a painting outside the clubhouse since their college art appreciation course, act like doyens of the art world as they point out to guests pieces on the wall in the dining room or along the broad staircase that reaches to the sixth floor.

To help them, a piece of art is featured regularly in full color in *State of the Union,* the Club magazine, with a tutorial essay by the curator about the artist and the work.

Not that members always accept what they are told. In 1926, a member lent the Club a large canvas entitled *Artemisia Drinking the Ashes of Her*

Husband, which hangs in the main lounge on the second floor. The painting on a wood panel is signed, "P. P. Rubens" and was so proclaimed to be for many years. There must have been some doubts, however, even in 1926. The Club newsletter, edited then by the diplomatic Dr. Edward Martin, notes that the painting "bears in its original paint the name of P. P. Rubens and shows in figure, form, and coloring the characteristics of that great artist."

A controversy developed over the authenticity of the "Rubens." The weight of evidence from art experts over the decades holds it not to be by Rubens, although one art critic called it "one of the few originals painted by Rubens' own hand." Later, however, the critic was revealed as a "complete fake" in the field.

Club members Clark and Joan Wagner have traveled to Potsdam and Madrid to see the two other extant "Artemisias" as part of their sleuthing of the provenance of the Club "Rubens." Clark is a former chair of the art committee and Joan is author of a detailed history of the Club art collection. In a paper given to the Chicago Literary Club in 1996, Clark Wagner concluded: "There is nothing presently known by us that would definitively tie our painting to the hand of the master, and there is much that suggests that such a tie does not exist. . . . Based on the available evidence, I believe that the most we can presently claim for our painting is that it is a workshop piece and that it should be assigned to the Studio of Rubens."

For many members, however, it will always be a Rubens.

SOURCES

A History of the Art Collection of the Union League Club of Chicago by Joan Wagner, June 2000, gives a highly detailed and valuable history of the Club collection and is available in the Club library and archives.

I benefited as well from lengthy interviews with a number of persons knowledgeable about the collection, especially Marianne Richter, curator of the art collection, who was a remarkably patient tutor; Joan and Clark Wagner, Roger Henn, Everett Barlow, and Ardell Arthur, a docent for the collection.

Richter also provided well-written essays about works of art that appears in *Union League Club of Chicago Art Collection,* published in 2003.

Quite helpful have been essays by Neil Harris, "Art and the American Club: Chicago's Union League Club as Patron," in *Union League Club of Chicago Art Collection* (2003); and "Art in the Union League Club," by William B. Mundie, from *The Spirit of the Union League Club,* 1926. Mundie was chair of the art committee at the time.

Culture and the City by Helen Lefkowitz Horowitz (University of

Chicago Press, 1989) provides a thoughtful analysis of the roles and motivations of Chicago's leading men, many of them members of the Club, in the development of Chicago's major cultural institutions.

Also, Clark Wagner, "Is It a Rubens?" presented to the Chicago Literary Club, May 6, 1996.

Craven, Wayne. *American Art*. New York: Harry N. Abrams, Inc., 1994.

Morrison, Hugh. *Louis Sullivan*. 1935. Reprint, New York: W. W. Norton, 1998.

Randall, Frank A. *History of the Development of Building Construction in Chicago*. 2nd ed. Urbana: University of Illinois Press, 1999.

Sears, Nathaniel C. "Reminiscences," June 12, 1929. ULCC archives in General Historical Files #1999-2.

And, of course, the earlier catalogs of the art collection of the Union League Club of Chicago, available in the Club library.

Chapter 15

A "DONE DEAL" UNDONE

The *New York Times* described the Chicago Public Library in 1985 as a disaster, a mess, an embarrassment, and a laughingstock. One of the most extensive library systems in the country, with a main library and eighty-three branches, the Chicago Public Library nevertheless for decades ranked near the bottom in per-capita expenditure, book stock, and circulation. For years, its central library books had been stored in a warehouse.

Daniel Boorstin, the Librarian of Congress, called the Chicago library situation "nothing less than scandalous, a public disgrace," as reported in the *Times* piece.

Paul Stack is a tough, visceral trial lawyer who loves libraries. He had long known of the disaster called the Chicago Public Library system; all people interested in libraries did, including Anthony Batko, an intense, cerebral publisher of educational materials for youngsters. Each served at different times on the library board in Riverside, a leafy suburb west of Chicago where they reside. The two met as members of the library committee of the Union League Club.

The following sounds unlikely, but Paul Stack swears it to be so. Stack had been reading a previous history of the Union League Club, which detailed the Club's early exploits in taking on the city's and state's corrupt political systems. Stack lamented the lack of similar civic assertiveness in his day. He called Batko: "Help me put together a committee to look at the Chicago Public Library. Let's see if we can do something about it." Batko agreed.

They created the Chicago Public Library Group, which became a subcommittee of the public affairs committee. "We needed the prestige of the Club," says Stack. They attracted five other Club members, including another lawyer, an architect, and a computer expert. Stack wanted to break the sprawling Chicago system into small library districts and eliminate the huge main library. Others in the new group disagreed. They spent several months talking with library experts from Chicago and across the country.

All were critical of the Chicago Public Library and many questioned its plans to renovate the handsome but shuttered Goldblatt's building on State Street as the new main library. One Chicago-based expert was especially passionate in his criticism of the Goldblatt idea. This expert was later appointed to the Chicago Public Library board by mayor Harold Washington, where he voted for the Goldblatt site. But that's Chicago politics and another story.

The experts helped convince Stack and Batko that Goldblatt's would be a colossal mistake and that a world-class downtown library was key to revitalizing the eighty-plus branches.

But the skids had long been greased for Goldblatt's. It was a done deal and don't anyone muck it up at this eleventh hour. In the Club, some members tried to dissuade the duo. "Get off it. Don't you guys know that nobody in Chicago cares about the library. Chicago cares about the Bears and the Cubbies—but not the library!" There was also sincere concern, inside and outside the Club, that opposition to Goldblatt's could ruin the city's best shot—and maybe last shot for many years—at getting a new central library. Others in the Club had vested interests in seeing the deal go through; one member had a contract pending for twenty-five million dollars in architectural work and interior finishings.

The stately eight-story, white terra-cotta Goldblatt's department store had been designed almost a century earlier by the well-known Chicago architecture firm of Holabird & Root (the original principals had been members of the Club). By 1982, however, Goldblatt's was on the ropes financially as was the south Loop area in which it was located.

Goldblatt lawyers figured if they could sell the building for ten million dollars they could stave off bankruptcy. Mayor Jane Byrne liked the idea of south Loop revitalization, which is how the Goldblatt lawyers marketed their idea. Goldblatt and Charlie Swibel, Byrne's political deal maker, did a deal. "The next thing we knew," an alderman said in early 1982, "out of the blue we were 'given the word' to vote to buy Goldblatt's." The new library could be fitted in later somehow. After all, it was a big building.

The City Club, another veteran Chicago civic organization, said it didn't like the aroma of the deal but the deal went through without a hitch, as most do when the mayor wants it.

By 1985, everybody was for the new library in Goldblatt's—the *Tribune, Sun-Times*, the television stations, new mayor Harold Washington, the library board, the south Loop merchants, and important museum and college leaders, whose many institutions were anchored along South Michigan Avenue.

Undeterred, the small committee at the Union League Club continued its analysis. From April to July it met and met—and became more and more appalled by the idea of Goldblatt's as the new central library.

Stack and Batko asked the public affairs committee to recommend to the board that the Club publicly oppose Goldblatt's. This has been the standard operating procedure since the earliest days of the Club, when the board worried the activist political action committee (later public affairs) might go its own way and get the Club in trouble.

Stack and Batko backed up their request with solid information to indicate that Goldblatt's could never be anything but an incredibly expensive, second- or third-class library. It was a department store, after all. There were, for example, scores of pillars on each floor of the narrow, rectangular building, all in the wrong places for bookshelves, the handicapped, and other users.

Board members had been hearing from people outside the Stack-Batko committee. "Don't screw it up. The city has been without a downtown library for more than a decade. The Club will get its ears boxed for coming in at the final hour with the recommendations of two guys nobody has ever heard of. This is nutty."

Fred Ford was Club president in 1985. He was executive vice president and comptroller of Draper & Kramer, a big Loop property manager and developer. A company like this is vulnerable when the powers that be—commercial and political—get their noses out of joint.

Ford and his board backed Stack and Batko.

Delighted, the two held a press conference in the clubhouse the week before Labor Day 1985 to announce the opposition of the venerable Union League of Chicago to the city's proposal to transform Goldblatt's into the new library. Two reporters showed up for the press conference. The next day, the city council reapproved the Goldblatt's proposal, 50–0. Four days later, in a lead editorial, the *Chicago Tribune* called for full speed ahead on the Goldblatt's project.

After the board committed itself to oppose Goldblatt's, top city and library officials came to the Club for lunch to make their pitch for Goldblatt's. The visitors put on a big show in favor of Goldblatt's for Fred Ford and his board and brought the implicit pressure that comes with such a display.

Ford never flinched in the face of pressure, whether from Club members who had interests in the project or from the city.

Discouraged but undaunted, Stack and Batko scrambled to find support. Tony Batko remembered a friend from his air force days whose family back in Ohio was very close to Cardinal Joseph Bernardin, head of the Chicago Archdiocese. The Roman Catholic bishop of Chicago is a major player in the city's politics when he wants to be.

In late September 1985, Batko's friend came through. Batko and Stack met with Monsignor James Roach, Bernardin's street-savvy right-hand man. They reminded Roach that a strong Chicago Public Library was important to the cardinal. Few of the Catholic schools could afford their own libraries and their pupils were heavy users of the city's branches, which were often just down the street from their schools. Dropping Goldblatt's, the two crusaders argued to the priest, is an absolutely essential first step to reforming the Chicago Public Library system.

A linkage had been made. Batko kept Roach updated on their efforts; the connection could be helpful later. At that moment, however, the two fledgling crusaders desperately needed some positive press for their almost invisible efforts.

Frank Whittaker came up with a brilliant public relations gambit. A former lobbyist, Whittaker was the Club's full-time director of public affairs. The Union League is the only city club in the nation with a professional public affairs director. Whittaker proposed that the Club sponsor a competition between the city's two schools of architecture to design a new main library for Chicago. The competition would make it clear the Club had no hidden agenda of its own in blasting the city's proposal. Displayed in the Club lobby, the stunning architectural models from Illinois Institute of Technology and the University of Illinois at Chicago transformed the Club from a naysayer into an advocate for creative change and also provided great visuals for both the newspapers and television.

The competition and a slew of press releases from Batko and Stack, all under the Club's imprimatur, kept the issue alive in the press. In December, the *New York Times* ran the piece, POLITICS, LOST BOOKS AND BUDGET WOES VEXING CHICAGO LIBRARY, cited at the beginning of the chapter. The piece castigated the library system and prominently mentioned Stack and the Union League Club efforts. When the *Times* deigns to run a piece on an issue, anywhere in the country, the issue becomes cloaked with credibility and importance.

But the *Times* fazes neither local politicos nor the *Chicago Tribune.* Lois Wille, the *Tribune*'s deputy editorial page editor, didn't like the Union League Club and its policy against women members. She said so in her several editorials in support of Goldblatt's. Wille called the Club a fuddy-duddy, silly old men's club. More important, she said the Union League Club efforts could derail a long-delayed effort to achieve, finally, a new library in a part of town that could use a major improvement to its shopworn image.

Grasping at straws, in late January 1986 Paul Stack called Ed Gilbreth at the *Sun-Times* in response to an editorial that vaguely related to the library issue. "We've got a lot on this Goldblatt's proposal," Stack told the veteran Gilbreth, "and it'll be a monumental disaster if it goes through." The *Sun-Times* expressed interest; a meeting was set.

Stack and Batko took Warren Burmeister of the Civic Federation with them to the *Sun-Times* meeting.

The federation, created a century earlier by Club leaders, had often been a civic partner of the Club. The federation had been studying the library issue, prompted by the work of Stack and Batko.

The trio walked into a packed editorial board conference room. The squat *Sun-Times* building overlooks the Chicago River; just to the east is the skyscraping tower of their chief rival, the *Chicago Tribune*. The *Sun-Times* has long been No. 2 to the *Trib;* with a staff half the size of the *Tribune,* the *Sun-Times* has to try harder.

This day the *Sun-Times* was primed. New editor Frank Devine, fresh from New York City, was already offended that Chicago stored its library books in a warehouse and one right behind the Tribune Tower at that.

Stack and Batko covered the conference table with documents and unloaded all they knew. After ninety minutes, Devine told the two he was assigning veteran investigative reporter Charles Nicodemus to lead a *Sun-Times* assault on the Goldblatt's proposal. For decades, Nicodemus had been rummaging into the dirty laundry of Chicago and Illinois politics. He doubted everything he ever heard from a politician. Nicodemus was a bulldog who never let go of his prey.

After a subsequent five-hour interview with Stack and Batko, Nicodemus wrote a February 1986 front-page story, NEW CITY LIBRARY: WHITE ELEPHANT OR CROWN JEWEL?

A month later, the *Sun-Times* ran a rare front-page editorial right under their banner: LIBRARY LUNACY. "Chicago," the editorial intoned, "is teetering on the brink of a colossal blunder."

The cavalry had arrived. The embattled Stack and Batko could continue stalking their white elephant.

It was almost overkill. Political junkies in town thought the paper was becoming hysterical. But early proponents of Goldblatt's were beginning to abandon ship. Counting its kill, the *Sun-Times* crowed, KEY ALDERMEN URGE JUNKING LIBRARY PLAN, and a headline story the next day, MAYOR ON LIBRARY: IT'S BAD—BUT. . . , quoted the mayor as saying that a recycled Goldblatt's would be less desirable than a new building but it was too late to change plans.

The Civic Federation disagreed, urging the city to "avoid the costly Goldblatt's rehab plan." The Club had some allies, finally.

In March 1986, the Club held a press conference to unveil the models created in five weeks' time by the architecture students. This time the press showed up in force. Bathed in light in the Club's stately, huge main lounge, with the mural *Patria* presiding over all who enter, the models glowed—perfect visuals for the 6 P.M. television news shows. The talented students, bleary-eyed from all-nighters, had outdone themselves.

When Paul Stack finished his remarks, he took questions from the press. One came instead from an uninvited architect from Goldblatt's project team. "Have you ever been in Goldblatt's?" he asked. Stack, the quick trial lawyer, shot back: "Hundreds of times. I used to buy my underwear there."

Stack and Batko tried the *Tribune* editorial board again, accompanied by Civic Federation director Burmeister. Pulitzer Prize winner Lois Wille and Stack tangled almost immediately. According to Batko, Wille called Stack a fool for trying to block Goldblatt's. Stack returned the volley in kind. Batko kicked Stack under the table in an unsuccessful effort to calm him. The gentlemanly Burmeister refereed. Positions hardened. The *Tribune*'s Mike Royko called the Club a "political has been" in his nationally syndicated column.

In May, the city council held its first real hearing on the new library issue, four years after the purchase of Goldblatt's. The Chicago Public Library presented a dazzling documentary narrated by Studs Terkel, the city's icon for all things good and progressive. Stack and Batko were armed with only a carousel projector.

Goldblatt's proponents curtly denied them use of their prime front-and-center space to show their slides.

The hearing was devastating for the Goldblatt's side. No librarians or outside experts supported them. In contrast, the head of the Dallas Public Library wrote a letter for the hearing, calling it "appalling to me that Chicago is giving serious consideration to housing a central library in a converted department store. . . . It's incomprehensible." His remarks carried extra weight because he was president of the national Public Library Association.

By now Nicodemus had looked into the original sale of Goldblatt's and found file drawers of documents missing. This brought the Better Government Association into the fray. Club member Terry Brunner and the BGA he headed were the watchdogs, often attack dogs, for Chicago's good-government forces.

The city was becoming concerned for Goldblatt's. The mayor's office wanted to sell the bonds for the project as soon as possible to lock in the deal. The vote was set for July 29, 1986.

The *Sun-Times* kept blasting away. Contrary to library contention that the sprinkler system was in perfect condition, Nicodemus learned that the system had been allowed to freeze and crack; contractors would have to tear up floors to inspect for leaks. The fire escapes were unacceptable; additional stairwells would be necessary.

Good friend Monsignor Roach scheduled an early July breakfast with Cardinal Bernardin for Stack, Batko, and the BGA on the day he was to leave for Rome. Stack hammered at the importance of the central library to the health of the branch libraries that served the Catholic schools.

Later in the day, a representative of the cardinal joined the BGA for a meeting with the mayor's top people. The staff finally said they would recommend to Mayor Washington that he appoint a blue-ribbon committee to study the feasibility of an alternative to Goldblatt's.

Two weeks later, however, the mayor decided to dump the blue-ribbon group idea and go ahead with a July council vote on the sale of the library bonds. The cardinal was infuriated; he set a press conference to voice his displeasure. So did the Club and its allies.

Meanwhile, city and library officials met with the *Sun-Times* to voice their concerns about the paper's coverage of the issue. Their hope that the sprinkler story would be its last proved naive. The *Sun-Times* editors told the visitors the paper had stories coming up on major problems at Goldblatt's—asbestos, aisles too narrow for the handicapped, and insufficient floor support for the weight of the books. Stack and Batko had provided the paper with much of the background for these stories.

Stunned, the mayor's office put off the sale of the bonds for another month. By now, library board members worried they would be the ones to look the fools. And for unpaid board members, looking the fool may trump loyalty even to the mayor.

The mayor appointed a blue-ribbon panel. The blue-ribbon panel concurred with the Union League coalition. The group diplomatically put the blame on Mayor Washington's predecessor, Jayne Byrne: "The rehab of Goldblatt's was ill-conceived, poorly thought out and never honestly presented to Chicagoans by the Byrne Administration. . . . Goldblatt's is a tired, worn out hulk."

About a month later, the library board's facilities committee completed a lengthy hearing and prepared to write a report on the Goldblatt's situation. John Waner, the committee's chair, was an old political warhorse from the Midway Airport bungalow belt. He could see that Goldblatt's was a bad deal. Aware that a report was needed, Stack presumptuously offered to write it.

To the amazement of Stack and Batko, Waner told them to go ahead.

Waner asked the two to meet him that same night at his "office" at the Dancing Wheels Roller Rink near Midway to drop off their report. Waner presented the report to the library board the next morning without changing a word. "Not in the best interests of the Library to go ahead with Goldblatt's," concluded the report.

The *Tribune* editorial board continued its criticism of the Goldblatt's opponents, but it was too late. The paper's own Pulitzer Prize–winning architectural writer felt compelled to write a column in his space rebutting his colleagues. Paul Gapp declared: "Clearly, relocating the library to an abandoned department store on State Street is unthinkable. The current fixation on that proposal must be broken quickly, cleanly and permanently."

Goldblatt's as a library was history. One stone at a time, the weight of the evidence had become too heavy for the city to bear.

"Public citizens can have more impact than elected officials," declared Paul Stack in retrospect. "We represented the public. We had no hidden agendas."

They also had the Club. "We couldn't have done it without the Club," added Batko. The Club put an estimated hundred thousand dollars into the library effort: to fund the architectural design competition, for consultants and travel for library experts from around the country. Club members who were leading architects, contractors, development, and finance experts volunteered valuable time to Stack and Batko. Club public relations work countered, almost press release for press release, those churned out by the mayor's office and at the library and also kept each new Stack-Batko finding in public view.

Nor would the Club have taken up the initiative absent the pleas of two men with quixotic commitment who weren't even members of the public affairs committee.

Nor could Stack, Batko, and the Club have accomplished their objective without the *Sun-Times* and vice versa. Stack, Batko, and Nicodemus were in almost daily contact for a year, sharing information and intelligence.

The partnerships formed with the Civic Federation, BGA, and the cardinal added authority beyond that of the Club and their involvement provided a critical mass.

This was a classic case of citizen-generated coalition politics where, as is so often under-appreciated, good information and analysis were the most effective weapons. And two citizens, who didn't even live in the city but wanted the best for it, who worked to exhaustion to transform a potential civic embarrassment into a cultural treasure.

Mayor Harold Washington decided to locate the new library in the south Loop, near the Goldblatt's building, rather than in the north Loop, where others including Stack and Batko had focused.

It was a smart decision. The Harold Washington Library Center, named posthumously for the mayor, who died in office in 1987, opened in 1991. The postmodern design by Hammond, Beeby and Babka was inspired by Louis Sullivan's Transportation Building at the 1893 World's Columbian Exposition. The Harold Washington Library is the largest and quite arguably the best of its kind in the nation. The Washington Library is the anchor for a recent concentration of new and expanded college and university campuses in the heart of the city. And, critical to the original objective of Stack and Batko, most of eighty-plus branch libraries have been replaced or renovated.

"When Tony and I started out," says Paul Stack, "we were told nobody cared about the library. We didn't buy into it. Now people do care about this library. Now—you don't ignore libraries."

SOURCES

Once again, the ULCC archives must be credited as the most important and valuable source. In addition to Club documents and meeting minutes of the board and public affairs committee, the archives include an extensive set of newspaper clippings and press releases on the library issue from the period 1980 to 1993. See the Chicago Public Library Collection #1999-11.

Tony Batko has written an excellent paper on the issue, "Crucial Decisions," presented to the Chicago Literary Club in 1987, revised in 1998, available in the archives.

The author also interviewed Paul Stack and Anthony Batko at length.

Chapter 16

PUBLIC AFFAIRS IN A PRIVATE CLUB

From the politics of sewage treatment a century ago to the reform of the Illinois death penalty in recent years, the Club public affairs committee has pursued better government. This chapter illustrates several of the issues in which the Club has been active, even central—certainly persistent.

In the 1880s, Lake Michigan served as both Chicago's drinking water supply and sewage repository. Unpleasant to contemplate, even in retrospect. Charter Club member Frank Aldrich chaired the civic committee that steered legislation through Springfield in 1889 to create the Sanitary District of Chicago; Club members and other civic leaders made many trips to Springfield that year.

The new district's charge was no less than to construct a sanitary and ship canal to reverse the flow of water and carry sewage backward down the Chicago River to the Illinois River, where its effluvium would dissipate as it moved away from Chicago. The engineering innovations necessary for this task of unprecedented scale were adopted a few years later in constructing the Panama Canal. The "Big Ditch" is twenty-eight miles long, much of it cut through solid rock.

Politicians rubbed their hands in anticipation of the big money to be made in contracts and political jobs for grateful precinct workers. In opposition to grafters slated for election to the first board by the two political parties, the Club put up its own successful slate of six candidates for election to the first nine-member board.

By the 1920s, however, the sanitary district had become a haven for "ghost payrollers" who showed up on the payroll but not on the job. Club president (1916) Frank Loesch filed suit against the board and top employees in

1928. He charged them with squandering five million dollars in payroll padding, booze parties, and exorbitant contract pricing in what the newspapers labeled the "Whoopee Era" at the sanitary district. The law department of the district went, for example, from 38 attorneys in 1926 to 126 in 1928. Loesch won: the former president of the sanitary district and others were convicted. Scores of lawyers were disbarred or suspended.

In 1962, in the wake of yet another round of scandals at the district, hope for real reform of the sanitary district arrived when outsider Vinton Bacon was chosen as general superintendent of the district. Bacon was mistaken by many for "Mr. Peepers" of a 1950s television show—short, slight, bespectacled. He was, however, tough as nails. So was his nemesis, Frank Chesrow, president of the board and reputed by most close observers to be a member of the Chicago mob.

Chesrow even bucked the legendary "Boss," Mayor Richard J. Daley, to win the presidency of the board in 1958. Daley had backed Marshall Korshak. A prominent Chicago Democrat, Korshak reportedly lost interest in the post after a well-known gangster pressed a revolver into Korshak's stomach to emphasize his suggestion that Korshak would not want to contest the presidency with Chesrow.

Chesrow was also a patron of the arts. An owner of three small pharmacies, he somehow acquired a collection of Renaissance paintings that included works by Tintoretto, Van Dyck, Poussin, and Michelangelo. Chesrow sometimes mixed with the Club's Civic and Arts set.

Upon his arrival, Bacon was briefed in the Club by its special subcommittee on the sanitary district, headed by John McEnerney and staffed by public affairs director Roger Henn. Active Club members George Mahin and Harland Stockwell also participated. Mahin and Stockwell headed the Better Government Association and Civic Federation, respectively; their organizations were longtime partners in reform with the Club.

Contract fraud at the sanitary district was obscene, subcommittee members declared. Ghost contractors who were intimates of district trustees won bids and subcontracted the work out, pocketing millions in the process. First Ward boss and mob lieutenant John D'Arco had a direct pipeline to jobs in the district.

From the moment reformer Bacon became the district's top employee, he clashed with Chesrow and his board. He was overruled time and again. The Club, BGA, and other civic groups turned to Springfield for legislative reform of the district. Henn drafted legislation, and Club president (1971) Bob Bergstrom served as unpaid counsel to special investigating committees of the legislature. Club member and Senate president Russell Arrington pushed the legislation, and the Club served as the setting for frequent civic coalition planning and strategy sessions.

By this time renamed the Metropolitan Sanitary District of Greater Chicago, the district fought with bare knuckles against reform efforts to strengthen Bacon's role, limit that of the elected trustees, and enforce civil service rules. Two lobbyists for the sanitary district, both members of the Club, threatened unsuccessfully to have Roger Henn fired.

The nation was shocked in 1966 when a bomb was found under the hood of Bacon's sanitary district automobile in peaceful suburban Wilmette. A service station attendant, asked by Bacon to check the rough-running engine, found enough dynamite to blow Bacon across Lake Michigan.

The bomb was probably planted in the district's garage while Bacon was at a meeting called by Chesrow. The mob-style attempt on Bacon's life, foiled by an improper connection to a spark plug, outraged the Club.

The Club board met the next day, posted a five-thousand-dollar reward for information about the bombing, and called all civic organizations to a meeting in the club's Steel Room. The seventy-plus who came included Club member, Cook County sheriff, and later governor Richard B. Ogilvie, as well as the heads of every group that counted in Chicago. Club public affairs activist and later president (1973) John McEnerney took the chairmanship of Citizen Leaders for Ethics and Reform of the Sanitary District (CLEAR). Roger Henn was assigned full-time to staff the coalition. They demanded Bacon himself lead the investigation at the district.

Chesrow and his colleagues on the board were unimpressed. At their next meeting, they refused money for an investigation. Visibly angered, Club president Douglas Schwantes took the rostrum to press the case for money for a Bacon-led investigation. He was interrupted time and again with catcalls by angry trustees.

Schwantes, McEnerney, and CLEAR turned again to the legislature for action against the sanitary district. In testimony before a state Senate committee, Schwantes and the Club came under attack. "Your Roger Henn is a partisan obstructionist, a defeater of all the principles of the Democratic Party," bellowed Daley's Senate leader Art McGloon.

Worse, African American senator Charles Chew and Democratic colleague Bernie Neistein attacked the Club's racial and religious policies. Republicans sprang to the Club's defense. The meeting ended in disarray.

CLEAR and Republican legislative leadership forged a bill that gave Bacon control of day-to-day operations of the sanitary district, including contracts. The sanitary district trustees ignored the legislation. Bacon was fired.

The day Bacon was fired, Roger Henn stormed the podium at the sanitary district meeting to shout, over angry protests from trustees, "This is illegal. You can't do this!" Guards dragged Henn, kicking and screaming, out of the room. Henn, arms pinned back by the guards, was the lead photo in the next day's newspapers.

The Club and CLEAR could have taken to court their case against the district's refusal to comply with their reform legislation. In 1968, however, their reform effort was running out of steam, Henn's efforts and theatrics notwithstanding. Newspapers turned to new issues. Vietnam protests and the infamous altercations that year between hippie war protesters and Chicago police pushed sewer politics off the evening news. Civic Federation leader Harland Stockwell died. George Mahin left the BGA to become state revenue director for Governor-elect Ogilvie. The Club had been burned by the public attacks on its own membership policies. Some Club leaders were becoming nervous about the publicity and the big blocks of time a nonprofit club was spending on direct political action. Henn reined himself in. "Club president John Pennell became deeply concerned," recalled Henn, "that the Club was becoming too anti-Chicago Democratic Party and that the Daley people would go to the Democratic U.S. attorney general in Washington to try to rein us in. Nobody ever told me to back down, but I got the feeling."

For two years following the clash with the sanitary district, neither Henn nor his wife ever started their car without first looking under the hood. After meetings of the Club board of directors, a Club officer always drove Henn home.

The Club decided to shift its energies to another issue the Club had been championing for three-quarters of a century, state constitutional change. The issue was perfect for a club with a commitment to "good government" reform and a public affairs committee filled with lawyers and civic leaders who loved to study, debate, and then push their findings into the public arena. But the public cared not a whit about the sexless issue of rewriting a state charter. And so it took the Club and its allies eighty years to achieve their objective. The Club was with the issue every studious, unsuccessful step of the way.

In 1890, the Club held three membership meetings to discuss major issues of the day. The topics were "The Smoke Nuisance in Chicago," "Future Relations with the Sandwich Islands [Hawaii]," and "How to Amend the Illinois Constitution."

The Club put up money and effort to establish a constitutional convention in 1920. The work bogged down in regional conflict and the issue of representation for Chicago in the legislature; downstaters were against it, that is, against Chicago getting a fair share based on population. The convention was about to collapse when the Club invited all delegates to meet in the clubhouse with the state's business, civic, and political leaders.

After two days, an unwieldy compromise was reached, the convention reassembled, and members voted to adopt a new constitution, but in 1922 voters overwhelmingly rejected the tortured document.

In 1947, young lawyer Samuel W. Witwer went to Springfield to plead for a new constitutional convention. "Gentlemen," Witwer might have begun, in his starchy courtroom manner, "the Illinois Constitution of 1870 is a straitjacket of prohibitions written for a horse-and-buggy era. Illinois requires a modern, flexible charter to serve a growing state in a nuclear age."

The General Assembly promptly rejected his pleadings.

A serious fellow, Sam Witwer was not the first choice of fellow Club members to share a late afternoon highball. Yet he was admired for his intelligence, unyielding support for his beliefs, and integrity. And he would not give up.

In 1950, Witwer and many others achieved adoption of a compromise. Instead of a new constitution, the charter was made easier to amend. The Club supported this "Gateway Amendment."

The compromise wasn't good enough for Witwer. By the 1960s, most state constitutions had become turgid, detailed constraints on the executive branch, local governments, and economic development. The Illinois Constitution of 1870 was one of the worst.

In 1967, the legislature approved a call for a new constitution, which Witwer, Club public affairs activist Bob Bergstrom, and the civic community had been pushing. The Club went to work. Bergstrom was named chair of a special public affairs committee that convinced the Club board to get firmly behind a constitutional convention.

Described as a gaunt Norseman with piercing eyes, Bergstrom wrote *Con-Con—Why a Constitutional Convention Should Be Called.* Twenty thousand copies of the readable document circulated among the state's public officials and policymakers. The piece became influential in generating support for the required and successful 1968 public referendum to proceed with a convention.

Witwer was by then well known statewide as "Mr. Blue Ballot." Since 1947, he had been at the heart of the many efforts, some successful, some not, to modernize the state charter. He ran unsuccessfully for the U.S. Senate in 1960.

This was an era before the vicious thirty-second campaign television spots, which now often destroy rather than burnish reputations. A man of great integrity, Witwer burnished his reputation in a losing effort.

Witwer was elected delegate, then president, of the 1969 Illinois Constitutional Convention and became "Mr. Inside." Bergstrom was "Mr. Outside," badgering delegates continually with his progressive position papers on court modernization, legislative restructuring, and revenue reform, among others. Some found Bergstrom's writing and arguments compelling; others went along, exhausted, just to get the dogged Bergstrom off their backs. His position papers were often seen on the desks of delegates in the

Old State Capitol in Springfield, where Lincoln gave his "House Divided" speech and where this convention did its work.

Sam Witwer's stately leadership was complemented effectively by fellow Club member Elbert Smith, a convention vice president. After wrenching conflict and compromise, the convention enacted a new constitution and the following year voters approved this new state charter.

In early 1971, the Club celebrated adoption of the constitution with a great dinner. Everyone of public importance in the state showed up. Most probably didn't know the Club had been with the issue for eight decades. Those present included the president and vice president of the convention, the Illinois governor, and immediate past governor, all members of the Club.

Club president Bob Bergstrom also beamed that night. The indefatigable Bergstrom had become so involved in the convention that he married a delegate.

After the Con-Con success, the Club turned much of its public affairs energies toward the military. Beginning in the early 1960s, the costly and controversial Vietnam conflict had turned much of the country against both the war and the military.

The military focus was a natural for the Club. Founded by supporters and veterans of the Civil War, the Club has always had a deep military affection and it has been returned. From the days of swashbuckling honorary member and Civil War hero Philip Sheridan to the present, the sharply creased uniforms of senior officers of the armed services are a frequent sight in the Club.

Controversies over membership policies also induced the Club to turn toward the military. The Club had no blacks as members until 1969 and its bylaws restricted membership to males. The public affairs office was under pressure to bring authoritative speakers to the Club, yet many elected officials and leaders of civic and social organizations demurred when invited because of these well-known policies. On the other hand, war heroes like Green Beret Sergeant Barry Sadler, who wrote and sang a best-selling tune about his famed fighters; Medal of Honor winners; and general officers provided an appreciative pool of speakers.

Military affairs has been a subcommittee of public affairs for decades, since the Club raised and equipped a brigade of three regiments of volunteers in 1898 to offer service in the Spanish-American War.

Member Frank Lowden electrified club members with a speech that reviewed Spain's "inhumanity and misrule" and the role of her agents in the sinking of the USS *Maine* in Havana's harbor. Lowden was named by acclamation to lead the volunteer soldiers.

Military officials in Washington were, however, slow to see the need for the Club's brigade at the front. Through fellow Club member Charles Gates Dawes, then comptroller of the currency, Lowden gained access to President McKinley to press the case for an active role for the unit, to no avail.

As noted earlier, after World War I, Lowden appointed thirteen Club members to a commission to rebuild the Illinois National Guard. A Union League company, Company E of the First Infantry, sprang from the members, their sons, and Club employees.

In 1934, Post No. 758 of the American Legion was created within the Club as a meeting place for Club veterans of World War I. The Legion post in the Club is still active today.

In the dark first months of World War II, with U.S. forces at embattled Corregidor, the Club elected Douglas MacArthur to honorary membership. By the time word reached the general, he was on a submarine headed for Australia. Nevertheless, the general found time to reply via wireless:

FA 443 VIA RCA F MELBOURNE 23 25

1942 MAR 25 AM 9 32

FERRE C WATKINS-

UNION LEAGUE CLUB CHGO-

WILL BE DEEPLY HONORED TO ACCEPT

HONORARY MEMBERSHIP IN UNION LEAGUE

CLUB OF CHICAGO

MACARTHUR

Henn thus found the Club supportive, as he and his successor Frank Whittaker played key roles in bringing the Chicago-area armed services at Fort Sheridan, the Great Lakes Naval Training Station, the Glenview Naval Air Station, and elsewhere in the region, into an Armed Forces Council. Military balls in the Club and other venues in the city, with the resplendent epaulets and decorations of senior officers and their ladies, became one manifestation of the joint council.

More important, beginning in 1977, with the antiwar, antimilitary demonstrations of earlier in the decade still resonating, the Club served as the catalyst for an armed forces parade in Chicago on Armed Forces Day. Henn found that not one such parade had been held anywhere in the country the preceding year. The parade and ball that followed were big successes and became an annual Chicago affair.

Drawing on his public relations skills, Frank Whittaker moved annual open houses from military posts in the region to the same public plazas where antiwar protesters earlier held forth. The major plazas—the Civic

Center, 1st National Bank, the federal buildings, Illinois Center, and Pioneer Court—were filled simultaneously to highlight the several services, their histories and traditions. All this was accompanied by stirring martial music provided by bands from the military services as well as the Coast Guard.

The Club waved the flag where others had burned it.

In 1986, the navy went to Mayor Harold Washington to ask support for the men of the new nuclear submarine the USS *Chicago* (SSN 721), yet to be commissioned. "We don't believe in atomic weapons! No help from us," Mayor Washington reportedly told the navy.

The Club stepped up and created the 721 Club. For a donation of $721, members and nonmembers could become a part of the 721 Club. More than four thousand people turned out for the commissioning of the USS *Chicago* at Norfolk, Virginia, in September 1986, many times the normal gathering for christenings. Charlton Heston came. So did Mayor Washington.

The 721 Club has its antecedents in World War II, when the Club sponsored the navy's *LST 816,* and support later for the U.S. Air Force Reserve 928th Airlift Command, which was stationed at O'Hare Airport for many years.

In subsequent years, the 721 Club has hosted all 160 crew members of the USS *Chicago* at dinner dances held at the submarine's home port. Duffle bags for each crew member are filled with Christmas goodies and delivered each year to the ship and presents are sent to the children of crew members.

The Club now also supports the 502nd Regiment of the 101st Airborne Division at Fort Campbell, Kentucky. The military tradition lives on at the Club.

More than tradition, the broader public affairs mission of the Club is considered by Club leaders to be the conscience of the Club. Over the decades, the mantra has consistently been—corruption is bad and civic reform is good. Each Club president would love to score a major civic accomplishment on his or her watch. Generally, however, the gestation period for major policy change outlasts them. Bob Rylowicz devoted a year of his life as president (1986 to 1987) to achieving membership for women, only to see his failure turn into success the following year.

Unique among city and country clubs in the nation, the Club has since 1924 had a full-time public affairs staff, registered to lobby in the political arena. These directors have not, however, served as alter egos for Club leaders. Instead, the public affairs committee and its many subcommittees deliberate, sometimes agonizingly, until policy positions and programs are approved, first by the full committee and then by the board of directors.

Each of the four public affairs directors has put a different stamp on Club initiatives. The professorial Dr. Edward Martin (1924 to 1959) focused on governmental structure and process. The Illinois city-manager law, finally passed in 1955, was his baby, you might say, along with election reform, and was typical of his focus on process and management reform.

This stamp of process over politics is reflected in the charge Club president Benjamin Affleck gave the new public affairs committee membership early in his term in June 1928, as recorded in the minutes of the committee:

> Mr. Affleck impressed upon the members the Committee's important position in the Club, pointing out that it is the mouthpiece of the Club on public matters, and is the only committee of the Club whose field is not specifically limited by the by-laws. With a membership such as that which constitutes the Union League Club, he said, it is often difficult for a committee to adopt a course which shall meet all counsels. It is his thought, that if the Committee were to take up broad subjects such as the defense of the ballot box against fraud, amending the State Constitution, the school situation, state and national reapportionment, that its action in such and similar matters would not be subject to difference of opinion among the members.

These important yet "safe" reforms suited the social members of the Club just fine. The Club as an institution has, from time to time, imposed a governor on the public affairs mission. The "social club" versus "political club" tug-and-pull that defined the early club and made it both—but not too much of the latter—was clearly evident during the sanitary district scandals of the 1960s.

The feisty Roger Henn (1959 to 1978) wanted to be a political street fighter, but the broader Club preferred the high road.

Henn and Frank Whittaker were also hobbled from the 1960s to the 1980s by membership issues, first about exclusion of blacks and then of women. Longtime civic partners became hesitant to ask the Club to become part of their coalition efforts and the number of civic meetings held in the Clubhouse declined. Whittaker (1978 to 1994) focused his energies on military affairs and in providing creative thinking for the Club's signal role in the Chicago public library controversy. Former state legislator and public affairs director from 1994 and 2004, Diana Nelson brought a strong background in education reform to her role.

Nelson rebuilt alliances, which had deteriorated during the Club's membership controversies, with the Civic Federation, Metropolitan Planning Council, Civic Committee of the Commercial Club, Metropolis 2020, the League of Women Voters, among others.

The Club is once again host to continual meetings of civic coalitions and the public affairs committee has convinced the board to adopt positions on controversial issues such as expansion of O'Hare Airport (for) and a moratorium on the death penalty (for).

William Nissen is a partner at Sidley, Austin, Brown, and Wood, the huge Chicago law firm built in part by Club president William P. Sidley (1911) and his father before him (also a Club member).

Nissen was the court-appointed lawyer for serial killer John Wayne Gacy, not Nissen's typical client. In the process, Nissen became concerned about imposition of the death penalty when thirteen men on death row in Illinois in the 1990s were found to have been not guilty.

A member of the public affairs committee, Nissen convinced the committee of the importance of the issue. An ad hoc committee on the administration of justice was created in 1999. Nissen spearheaded the committee's research. He convinced public affairs and then the board that Illinois must impose a moratorium on the death penalty while further analysis and proposals for reform were considered. In 2000, the board agreed to this rather radical proposal, radical at least when coming from a conservative club in a society that appeared to strongly favor the death penalty.

George Ryan, Republican governor of Illinois from 1999 to 2003 and a Club member since 1977, favored the death penalty as a candidate in 1998 for the state's top office; he even campaigned on the issue. In office, however, when faced with the reality of "pulling the switch" on men and women whose time had run out, he couldn't do it.

Just two weeks after the Union League Club adopted its resolution in favor of a moratorium on the death penalty, Governor Ryan also called for a moratorium on the death penalty, to the uproar of conservative Republicans. Ryan created a blue-ribbon panel to evaluate the Illinois death penalty statute and process. Nissen and Nelson testified before the commission. Two years later, the panel's recommendations for reform of the death penalty process echoed those of Bill Nissen and the Club.

George Ryan didn't embark on his death penalty odyssey because Bill Nissen and the Club told him to do so. His club's unusual and controversial policy in support of a moratorium did, however, give Ryan—at a critical time—food for thought, authoritative support, and a palatable option to that of pulling the switch. In January 2003, just before leaving office, Governor Ryan commuted the death sentences of all one hundred-plus inmates on "death row" in Illinois.

Nor could Bill Nissen alone have given his issue the credibility and visibility that the Club and its moratorium proposal received. Ryan's primary legacy as governor will be his unwillingness to use the death penalty in Illinois. Ryan's ever stronger feelings against a flawed capital penalty process gave a spark worldwide to opponents of the death penalty. Bill Nissen and the Club are a part of that legacy.

The Chicago Riverwalk subcommittee of public affairs was meeting in April of 2001. It was typical of the scores of public affairs subcommittee discussions held every year in the clubhouse. Co-chairs Kathleen Spaniak and William Gardner called the meeting to take action on their proposal that the Club "help create and implement, along with the City of Chicago, a management entity . . . for the River."

The 156 miles of the Chicago River, once a bubbly cauldron of simmering sewage and toxins, was being reborn under the leadership of Mayor Richard M. Daley. Residents who had for decades turned their backs to the filthy river were now turning toward this potential "second lakefront" in their backyards.

But change comes slowly. Ward committeemen demanded control of the river portions coursing through their fiefdoms. Developers, residential owners, business, and citizen interests clashed intensely over access to and protections for the river. The mayor's office sought the help of civic groups. Should the Club become involved with the mayor, and how much?

Three men dominated the luncheon discussion that day. They weren't even members of the subcommittee or the public affairs committee at the time, but they had been. Club membership on a committee is limited to six years. After that, former members may become nonvoting "senior counselors."

Frank Covey joined the Club in 1960, went through the committee chairs including chair of public affairs, and became president for 1990 to 1991. Hugh Schwartzberg had also been chair. More important, he had a long history as a liberal reformer. His Loop law office walls are replete with photos of himself with the Kennedys, Martin Luther King, Jr., Nelson Mandela, and other icons of change. Jeff Ladd is the conservative of this trio. A young delegate to the Illinois Constitutional Convention of 1969-70, the political insider Ladd is chairman of METRA, the region's impressive commuter transportation system. All three are lawyers.

"I'm skeptical of Union League Club involvement in managing the Riverwalk," opened Ladd. "Something doesn't ring right here."

Taking up the challenge, Covey retorted: "Like other good projects such as civil service reform and the library, it's important to support this good initiative. It's not high on the pecking order of the Daley administration and the aldermen feel they own their wards. So it's tough to get an overarching management entity in place."

"But the Club could end up being used by the mayor and his office," worried Ladd. "Be careful."

"Yes, we should be careful," inserted Schwartzberg. "But this mayor doesn't turn blue every time he sees me the way his father did." Schwartzberg smiled and continued. "Every time I go to war with the city, I like the idea of the public having a voice through a separate entity."

"Yes," said Ladd, not really agreeing, "but when you separate organisms from the nervous system, they are unconnected." Ladd worried about the Club becoming a part of something that has responsibility without authority.

The others wanted to take that risk.

Ladd suggested the resolution be changed from "management entity" to "management structure." The subcommittee adopted the amendment and then the resolution, unanimously.

Schwartzberg smiled puckishly, "Jeff and I agree ultimately on everything." Nobody believed him, but the two along with Covey proved valuable senior counselors that day. Spaniak, Gardner, and others became more sensitized to the challenges of dealing with City Hall.

Schwartzberg added a coda: "Ten years from now the Club will give a prize to the first person who swims the length of the river."

The trio of senior counselors will be on to other issues by then, but the Club and the city will still be there with the issue of the Riverwalk, maybe together, maybe at loggerheads.

As Dr. Martin said to members passionate about issues that will outlive them: "Don't worry, the Club will always be there."

The Club as an institution is not frequently a leader in city and state affairs, yet it has played a major role throughout its history as a leading member of the civic coalitions that often prove to have the collective weight and authority to make change.

The Club has also been important in giving voice and credibility, even authority, to the civic passions of its members. Sam Witwer and Bob Bergstrom convinced the Club to back them in pursuit of constitutional change. The same for Batko and Stack on their last-minute, last-ditch, and successful effort to undo the political "done deal" over a bad public library idea. Ditto for Bill Nissen and reform of the death penalty.

The Club is a place where a young professional with an interest in public affairs can, like Frank Lowden and Charles Gates Dawes, find a receptive forum and platform for his or her interests, even passions.

SOURCES

Club archives hold the minutes of the public affairs committee from the earliest days. These minutes proved a rich resource for this and other chapters that deal with the public affairs mission of the Club.

Roger Henn's unpublished history of the Club is rich and detailed in describing the Club's public affairs activities, especially in the period when Henn was director of public affairs.

Grant's *Fight for a City* (1955) also covers the public affairs mission for the period 1880 to 1955.

Hutchinson's two-volume *Lowden of Illinois* (University of Chicago Press, 1957) is a fine work that includes numerous references to Lowden's involvement with the Club.

Among my scores of interviews, most touched upon the public affairs mission in one way or another. In particular, the observations and recollections of the following were particularly important to this chapter: Roger Henn, Everett Barlow, Henry Pitts, Hugh Schwartzberg, Ken Meuser, Matt Iverson, John Scully, Frank Whittaker, Bob Bergstrom, and Diana Nelson.

Chicago newspapers are another source of reality checking against the memories of those interviewed, e.g. CITY'S LIONS TOOTHLESS NOW, Basil Talbott, Jr., *Chicago Sun-Times*, January 8, 1980.

The official publication of the Club, *State of the Union* (earlier, *Men & Events*) provides extensive, if sometimes exaggerated, coverage of the Club's role in public affairs.

Chapter 17

THE CLUB AND ITS HOUSE

The Club's house is a giant among its kind—twenty-three floors above ground, three below, 350,000 square feet—a house with many mansions. There are two bars, three restaurants, five floors for fitness, eight of sleeping rooms, elegant meeting rooms large and small, offices for three Club foundations, and more.

Of all this, the Rendezvous Room bar on the fourth floor captures the personality of the Union League Club of Chicago better than any other. Not everyone would like it. It can be noisy and a little smoky. The room reeks of machismo. It's a man's barroom, the kind of bar up-and-coming men enjoyed a hundred years ago. For members who want less energy and some quiet, there is the Heritage Room bar. But if you don't like the ambiance of the Rendezvous, you probably won't like the Club all that much either.

Below an immense painting of a barroom nude, all is dark wood and red leather—the curved box, heavy tables, wainscoting, pegged flooring, and big, comfortable arm chairs.

Until 2002, game trophies shared wall space with the nude—a fourteen-point buck, wild turkey and boar, a buffalo head, a cock pheasant. The room was redecorated that year, the stuffed game pushed aside by the "Seven Lively Arts," bold paintings by seven reputable Chicago artists, which had hung for many years in Riccardo's on Rush Street, another popular watering hole now gone. Each wall table has a brass banker's light with the green glass shade. Phones at several tables. A pool table. Friendly waiters hurry around in white shirts and black slacks and vests, carrying English and German draft beers and sandwiches.

Cheddar cheese and crackers are always available at a side table. Televisions on mute are set to Chicago sports teams or to Chris Matthews and *Hardball* on MSNBC.

Type-A types dominate the room around 4 P.M. That's when commodities brokers from down the street at the Board of Trade stop by to unwind. Four traders are sitting just inside the room. Young, with jutting jaws, one man without socks, cocky, tough-talking—just like the early members of the Club a hundred years ago. Next to the traders are two older couples, the men in blazers, the matronly wives unmindful of the traders, it would seem. The tables are widely spaced.

Six women march in, spot a round table favored by traders, and plop down to catch up over drinks.

A fortyish woman escorts her parents to a table, the couple's awkwardness and wide eyes suggesting the country. Pleased with her role, the lady member points out the nude. A waiter calls her by name and takes their drink order.

Four more traders barge in, one of them East Indian, another African American; one sports a big cigar. There should be a swinging door to herald the cast of characters.

By eight, the traders are gone. Small groups of bankers filter in on this evening. The talk in the main dining room by bank CEO Jamie Dimon is over. Young women bankers are sporting high-hemline business suits. A couple of the men light up cigars. They talk shop and gossip.

Artistes follow to toast the artist whose work is being exhibited at a reception next door in the library. Beards, turtlenecks; slacks for the women. They commandeer several tables. Soon twenty of the artsy crowd are where the traders held forth two hours earlier.

Down the long room at the pool table, three teen girls handle their cues adequately. At a table nearby, a woman lawyer and three male associates go over a brief they are preparing. Legal papers are all over the table, not something tolerated at a stuffy Eastern club. One of the group is parent to one of the teens.

The waiters sometimes shake hands with members as they arrive and chat when time allows. This is not a place for snobs. Egos are a different matter.

The people in the Rendezvous this evening are, in one sense, different from those who sat in the same chairs a few decades earlier—now women, blacks, sockless traders, children at the pool table. In another, the place and the people are the same—high energy, upwardly mobile, relaxed, fun-loving, doing a little business.

The room winds down about eleven this evening. Dining rooms manager Carl Madsen, in that capacity for more than two decades, joins the Higginsons at their favorite table, just inside the Rendezvous. General manager Jonathan McCabe stops to chat for a moment, making his final rounds before heading home to the suburbs.

"It used to be staff serving the members," says one longtime staff member after the Rendezvous closes. "Now, as is often said, it's ladies and gentlemen serving ladies and gentlemen. That's how we see ourselves. Yet we must maintain the professional distance that our members deserve."

There is almost a family feeling that blurs "upstairs-downstairs" class distinctions, at least for members who are in the clubhouse frequently and know the staff well. The membership is now younger than it was a couple of decades ago, and that may engender more relaxed relationships.

Club member Jack Higginson suggests another factor: "The heart and soul of this Club is that a fairly large percentage of us members—me for sure—came from the same 'up by the bootstraps' backgrounds as the staff."

Like the Rendezvous, the clubhouse throughout is a capacious refuge and host. Space—between dining tables, in the silent, deeply carpeted library as well as in the cavernous Main Lounge—precious space provides a luxury that public restaurants and hostelries cannot generally afford.

The space, the respectful elegance, and of course the art, which embraces the members and their guests at every turn, make the clubhouse popular as a meeting place. The week the author wrote this chapter, the clubhouse was the setting for a Transatlantic Conference on Race and Xenophobia cosponsored by the European Union and the University of Illinois. In the same week, the club served as host to Mayor Richard M. Daley, radio personality Paul Harvey, opera star Samuel Ramey, jazz legend Ramsey Lewis, Jr., and more than a score of company and association meetings.

The role of the clubhouse as a setting for civic and public policy meetings is arguably the most important use of the space. The Club is known for its involvement in the public life of the city and state. The public affairs committee and its director welcome civic and policy organizations and their coalitions into the many spaces of the Club, as they have throughout the Club's 125 years.

A police scandal in Chicago in 1960 illustrates the several uses of the clubhouse: as convener, bully pulpit, even hideaway.

Richard Morrison was a petty thief who had several former high school friends among the Chicago police at the Summerdale precinct in Uptown on the north side of the city. These friends asked Morrison to cut them in on the action; he obliged. Morrison and the "burglars in blue" used police cars to haul away tires, television sets, clothing, food, and sundry items prized by these police.

Morrison was arrested and he began talking to aides in the office of state's attorney Benjamin Adamowski, a member of the Club. Knowing he had a hot property on his hands, Adamowski secreted Morrison in rooms at the Club.

The scope of the scandal widened as Morrison's revelations continued. Many police and their superiors were implicated in bribery and protection. Demand for action echoed around the civic organizations.

Club president John Ballman sent out a call to civic leaders for a meeting at the clubhouse. Five hundred civic leaders filled the main dining room to capacity. Ballman appointed three Club members to lead an investigation into the corruption—Virgil Peterson, executive director of the Chicago Crime Commission; Harland Stockwell, staff head of the Civic Federation; and George Mahin, executive director of the Better Government Association.

From that meeting developed the Citizens Action Conference, headed by Club members Graydon Meegan and Barry McCormick. In response to their demands for action, Mayor Richard J. Daley appointed California police expert Orlando W. Wilson to head and clean up the police department. A year later, Meegan wrote members of the citizens' group that their duties had been successfully completed, so he disbanded the coalition.

The space of the clubhouse is also for the enjoyment and fun of the members. "Self-indulgence with missions" is how past president Philip Wicklander describes the Club.

Each fall the Club social season opens with "Homecoming." Fourteen hundred revelers, heavily weighted to the under-fifty crowd, move from floor to floor to sample the cuisine and libations of a theme-party extravaganza. As close as one will get to a Mardi Gras inside a city club.

Before one recent Homecoming, general manager Jonathan McCabe stands to brief his staff. In room 710, ninety Club waiters sit attentively, almost at attention. "You've worked in lots of nice restaurants and clubs," McCabe intones to the men and women, two-thirds of them Hispanic. "The Union League Club is that and a lot more. We operate four of the best Boys and Girls Clubs in the country and we work to shape this city through our public affairs mission. We are different and we are better. And tonight you will show how we can also put on the best party in the country.

"We—you and I—are ladies and gentlemen serving ladies and gentlemen," a term McCabe and Club officers often use.

The waiters march out. They are all real pros. Most have been working all day. Now they will continue until midnight or later.

While McCabe has been briefing staff from floor to floor, the Club is being transformed into the world's largest nightclub. The waiters are changing—black pants, berets, and bistro aprons in the library, that is, the "Moulin Rouge"; T-shirts, hats, and black pants poolside up on floor twenty-one at "Margaritaville," where Jimmy Lynch, the athletic director, is in charge.

The food is as exotic as the cabaret settings. Chef Michael Garbin (everyone calls him "Chef," with the respect accorded to the title of colonel or doctor) has outdone himself. In "Rick's Café Americain," Moroccan braised lamb with raisins and chickpeas are among the offerings; in the "Tropicana," chipotle shrimp with grilled pineapple salsa, and carved suckling pig with mango barbecue sauce are only a part of the groaning board. Cuisine from around the world is served in thirteen different cabaret settings.

Live music from great bands caroms up and down the Club's broad marble and mahogany staircase, which reaches the sixth floor.

On the sixth floor, the main dining room is now the "Flamingo." A believable "Rat Pack" of Frank, Sammy, and Dino are on stage singing.

People are having a great time. Dining rooms manager Carl Madsen, still boyish looking after twenty-seven years at the Club, stands at the door beaming. "Isn't this terrific," he exclaims to no one in particular.

By 11 P.M., the older set begins to depart. The place is still rocking and does so until the morning hours. Two partygoers arise the next morning at 6:30. They head toward the breakfast room on the third floor, expecting a colossal mess, hoping at best for coffee. To their astonishment, the Club is back to normal. Well, almost. In the Wigwam, Lee Ramirez and her associates look beat, not their normal selves.

But they are serving breakfast.

Each had started work the previous morning at 5:45 A.M., had worked straight through until 1:00 A.M. the next day—and were back at work again at 5:45 A.M.

As if it were a huge doll house, one thinks, the clubhouse must have been opened up by giant hands that moved hundreds of tables, ice sculptures, stage props, serving trays, a thousand glasses—whisking all the aftermath away like magic. In fact, the housemen worked all night, rolling tables into their racks, cleaning each room in forty-five minutes. Eddie Mae Henderson's housekeeping staff had also been at work, as had the catering staff. After all, there were two big weddings and a business meeting in the clubhouse that Saturday after Friday's Homecoming!

The Club is an entertainment, social, civic, health, even social service enterprise. It is also a business—three hundred employees and twenty million dollars in annual revenues.

"This is an old building. We have to keep it up," McCabe points out. "The Club has benefited from good governance over the years. We have always invested in our maintenance. We spent 14 million in the past nine years on maintenance—out of cash flow. It cost $2.2 million to put sprinklers on twenty-two floors, took a year and a half."

Michael Petrocelli preceded McCabe as general manager. An imposing Englishman, Petrocelli championed old-world tradition and also over-saw the most extensive renovation in Club history in advance of its centen-nial in 1979. For example, the eight floors of sleeping rooms were stripped to steel and concrete and reconfigured into fewer, larger rooms.

The clubhouse generates six million dollars annually in food business; more than half that revenue is in banquets. Five million dollars in beverage business. McCabe says that typical city clubs generate 32 to 38 percent of total revenues from member dues; at the Union League Club it is 28 percent.

Membership in the Club also brings access to other clubhouses around the world through reciprocal relationships. The Club's list of 190 reciprocal clubs is one of the most extensive to be found. Going to Hong Kong and don't want your host to pay for everything? Call the Club and ask that a let-ter of introduction be faxed to the impeccable American Club there. Take your hosts to either their penthouse club high above Victoria Island or to their country club on Repulse Bay. In London, use the St. James, Lansdowne, Oriental, East India, or Army and Navy clubs. From Nebraska to New York to Jakarta there are clubs that welcome Club members.

In the 1920s, Club leaders designed their new clubhouse with failure in mind. That is, though times were prosperous then, these prudent business-men knew that success forever was not preordained. If the Club failed or had to downsize at some future time, this clubhouse could be sold or leased for use as offices and a hotel.

When the Depression arrived, this foresight became prophetic, at least for some other clubs. The Illinois Women's Club building at the Water Tower just west of Michigan Avenue opened in 1927, was sold a few years later, and is now the main downtown campus building of Loyola University. The Moorish motif of the former Medinah Athletic Club, finished in 1929, can still be seen at the Intercontinental Hotel, just north of the Tribune Tower.

In 1925, the Club issued $2.4 million in bonds to construct its present clubhouse. Half the bonds were purchased by Northwestern Mutual Life Insurance Company, which held the first mortgage, the other half by gen-eral bondholders, mostly members.

The Club decided to build anew on the same site as the first clubhouse at 65 West Jackson. Michigan Avenue with its view of the lake, a favorite setting for Chicago clubs, was apparently not considered.

Designed by the firm of Mundie and Jensen (William Mundie chaired the Club art committee for several years), the clubhouse was to be sheathed completely in Indiana limestone. The Club decided to carry the limestone only to the sixth floor. From that point up, red brick was used.

When completed in 1926, the new clubhouse towered over the south

Loop. Today the clubhouse is in the shadows of more recent skyscraping federal buildings. The new clubhouse boomed in its first years. Six hundred applications for membership were on file, but only 250 vacancies existed within the cap of 2,500 resident members.

The Club magazine declared that "a man may be an outstanding business success, but if he has not shown during his career some interest in his fellow men, he can hardly be relied upon in times of stress to stand by the traditions for which the Union League Club is so well known."

Well and good for successful men, but it proved to be a woman the Club relied upon in times of great stress to see the clubhouse through. Florence Mulholland joined the Club as bookkeeper the same year the new clubhouse opened. She was a young, beautiful Irish lass—a real looker from the Back of the (Stock) Yards neighborhood on the southwest side, according to Roger Henn.

Mulholland never married; she married the Club. In 1933, the year the bottom fell out of Club membership, she was named comptroller, a position she held for more than three decades.

For a Club that had been managing its affairs rather casually, Florence Mulholland set up control systems to track every dollar coming and going from the Club; she could predict a coming year's budget from her head to within a few dollars.

She saw the Club through two bankruptcy reorganizations. The Club tried to deny the Depression. The first mention in the Club *Bulletin* of the great economic collapse did not come until April 1932 with the headline DEPRESSION INCREASES JUVENILE COURT CASES. The Depression also took its toll on the Club. Membership dropped from 2,500 resident members (its self-imposed cap) in 1930 to 2,279 in 1932. Then in 1933 alone, the Club lost 700 more members. The end-of-year total was 1,584. Club revenue dropped from $1.63 million in 1930 to $800,000 in 1933.

In March 1933, the board of directors resolved to pay only taxes and interest on the first mortgage, held by Northwestern Mutual Life, and to defer interest on the general mortgage bonds. "This is the day our troubles began" is scrawled in huge script by an unknown hand across the Club's resolution regarding the mortgage payments.

The Club tried everything to rebuild membership and revenue. Women could occupy sleeping rooms, even attend for the first time the Washington's Birthday celebration. Initiation fees were reduced from five hundred dollars to two hundred to one hundred to nothing. In December 1933, the Club *Bulletin* even clarified that it was not, as many thought, a Republican club.

In a show of gallows humor, the Club wallpapered a million dollars worth of worthless corporate bonds held by members onto its barroom walls. The Associated Press story and photo of the "Million Dollar Room" was reprinted in a thousand newspapers around the world.

Slowly the economy began to improve, but not before 1935, when the Club reorganized its finances in bankruptcy court. Accrued interest on bonds was waived and interest rates were reduced from 6 percent to 3.5 percent, to increase over time to a maximum of 5.5 percent. Still the Club limped along financially. Membership stood at just 1,800 in 1941.

In the early 1940s, Florence Mulholland and Club leadership saw they were not going to be able to meet debt obligations maturing in 1949 and 1950 under the terms of their first reorganization. She worried that in the second reorganization in the late 1940s, the Club could lose control of its own clubhouse. Mulholland took steps to block that possibility.

Club lore holds that a group of "unsavory Loop businessmen, who couldn't gain admission either to the Club or the Standard Club next door," as one member recalls the story, began buying up the Club's bonds for pennies on the dollar. Conceivably, they could hold the fate of the Clubhouse in their hands, forcing foreclosure or takeover of the building.

There is no clear evidence of this in the archives, where the records include complete listings of each bondholder for different periods in the 1940s and 1950s. There was indeed, however, strong interest in buying the bonds at a fraction of their face value. Bond sales transactions were recorded at between twenty and forty cents per dollar of face value.

The Club sought to protect itself by appealing to member bondholders to sell, basically contribute, their bonds to the Club for two dollars per hundred dollars of par value. In this manner, the Club gained control of $218,000 of the $1.2 million in general bondholder instruments. Not enough to control Club destiny.

One major bondholder who refused to sell his bonds to the Club was Harrison B. (H. B.) Barnard, the former Club president and Secret Six vigilante who fought Capone.

True to Mulholland's predictions, in 1950 the Club filed a voluntary petition in bankruptcy court following default on interest payments. UNION LEAGUE CAN'T PAY ITS MORTGAGE, heralded the *Chicago Sun-Times* on February 2, 1950. The Democratic National Committee's newsletter chortled, "The Union League Club of Chicago, a stronghold of Republicanism and a symbol of the Old Guard wing of the GOP, has filed for bankruptcy. The Club states that it is 'amply solvent' but is 'temporarily' unable to meet debts of $2.75 million."

Understandably, the Club proposed a reorganization that would forgive most of the interest owed, cut interest rates, and extend maturities. H. B. Barnard wouldn't buy it.

"These are investments, damn it, not contributions," H. B. shouted into the phone to his lawyer, according to recollections by Barnard's son William. "The Club is worth a lot more than is owed," the senior Barnard wrote to fellow bondholders, "and we have the lowest dues in the city."

In 1950, Barnard held $62,000 worth of bonds at face value. (A nonmember with offices in the Loop owned $67,000 worth, the only individual to own more.) Barnard later increased his position to $116,000 in bonds at face value, just before the second bankruptcy reorganization was approved in court.

Extensive correspondence in the Club archives, from the typewriter used by Barnard's office, indicate that Barnard organized the "Committee for Holders of General Mortgage Bonds of the Union League Club of Chicago." H. B. organized a meeting of bondholders, excluded himself from being a member of the committee leadership itself (in order that it should not be self-appointed), and arranged the hiring of attorney Arnold Shure to represent the committee. The committee represented ownership of bonds having more than one-third of the bonds' face value. As a result, nothing could be approved in court without the committee's consent.

H. B. Barnard held the feet of the Club and of Shure to the fire. "I recall many heated phone conversations between my father and Mr. Shure," said son William Barnard.

H. B. was a tough nut and he was going to get full value for his investment. Florence Mulholland was in and out of court regularly, testifying about Club finances.

In June 1951, a federal court approved a reorganization plan for the Club that provided Barnard everything he sought. Barnard's committee forced the Club to agree to pay all principal and interest owed on the bonds. The court decree also required the Club to increase dues for all classes of membership by about 30 percent.

The mortgage was finally paid off and burned on September 6, 1962. After presenting the final payment to a representative of Northwestern Mutual Life Insurance Company in a ceremony in the clubhouse, Club president Henry Pitts and his board adjourned to the Rendezvous Room for a drink.

H. B. had made a good investment.

Two years later, Florence Mulholland retired from the Club's service. She had never earned more than ten thousand dollars a year. Her pension was seven hundred dollars per month. Upon her retirement, she was given the unprecedented honor of nonmember woman privileges in the Club. Mulholland had no need for the privileges; she and her sister moved to ranch property they owned in the West.

Along with other senior staff and members, Mulholland had also pitched in during the strike against the clubhouse in 1948. In late 1947, Club manager

Taylor Hay recommended giving the nonunion elevator operators a raise to bring the women operators up to the rate of union operators elsewhere. The directors refused and the women decided to organize.

The directors turned the situation over to a hard-nosed member who claimed experience in dealing with unions. Drawing upon any excuse, he had one after another of the elevator operators fired.

Chicago unions took on the challenge. In February, the operators went out on strike, demanding recognition of the elevator operators' union as their bargaining agent. The engineers and other union members in the Club were called out in sympathy. For three months, pickets made life miserable at the Club, sometimes leaving only a foot-wide corridor on Jackson Street for Club members to enter the building.

Florence Mulholland and other female staff members baked pies and made sandwiches for the dining rooms. Meat was delivered by parcel post and coffee came via suitcases. Members who were engineers became licensed to operate the boilers. Coal was the problem; no driver would deliver it.

The situation became desperate. Permanent residents of the clubhouse with medical problems were evacuated to hospitals. All the bathtubs in the clubhouse were filled with water, as it was not known how long pumps might bring water to the upper floors.

Arrangements were made to bring coal in from Hammond, Indiana, in a convoy of nonunion drivers. The first convoy leader got cold feet when confronted by the raging pickets; the trucks drove by and back to Indiana without stopping. The last of the coal dust was swept into the furnaces. The temperature in the Club dropped to fifty degrees. In the dead of night, however, a second convoy of coal trucks made its deliveries.

Temperatures ran high among members. Club archives contain one hundred one letters in support of fighting the strike; two opposed. One longtime Club resident who opposed the Club policy found it necessary to leave the premises because of hostility from others in the Club.

With the Club showing no signs of weakening its resolve to stay open during the dispute, the unions agreed to end the strike without a settlement. Some of the striking elevator operators were allowed to return to work in the Club.

Today, the Club has closed-shop agreements with the hotel and restaurant employees and operating engineers unions.

The president and sixteen-member board of directors operate with thirteen committees. Each is headed by a director who selects his or her committee members; fifteen to forty serve on a committee. These three hundred committee members are the heart of the Club.

Committees and subcommittees meet almost every day in Club meeting rooms on floors seven and eight, at breakfast, over lunch, or after work. Meetings often continue informally in the Rendezvous Room. In this work, leaders identify future directors and presidents. The board meets once a month in late afternoon and has dinner after in the Club.

Bill McDermott, Club president for 1989 to 1990, explains the typical process for vetting prospective Club activists:

> I was a member of another downtown club from 1968 to '78. It was fine, but just a place to eat, nothing else. Frank Covey became my neighbor and told me about this club. I switched and soon I was asked to serve on the finance committee. Committees were looking for some new blood. Somebody must have liked my work because a couple of years later I was nominated for the board.
>
> Fred Ford asked if I would chair the entertainment committee, which shocked me, as I didn't see that as my strong suit. "Would it be much work?" I asked Fred. "No," he smiled.
>
> The first thing Fred asked me to do was increase the committee membership from six to thirty! We had breakfast meetings. Twenty or more members would come in at 7:30. I was amazed.
>
> Again, somebody must have liked what I was doing, as I was put "on the ladder" [second vice president to first vice president, then to president].

The board is not self-perpetuating, nor does it select the president. The board selects a nominating committee of members not on the board, generally chaired by the immediate past president. The nominating committee then presents a slate of new board members and officers for the Club to be elected at the annual dinner meeting in June. The president serves one year only.

Opposition slates of officers are mounted by petition from time to time when there are concerns within the ranks.

For example, in 1920 Dr. John Timothy Stone, pastor of Fourth Presbyterian Church on North Michigan Avenue, was duly nominated for the presidency. Stone was, however, defeated by twelve votes by businessman John Fletcher. The issues of the opposition slate were that Stone had been a member only one year and was a clergy privilege holder rather than a regular resident member. The unspoken issue was apparently that Stone might actually try to enforce Prohibition within the Club.

Election to presidency of the Club is a big deal, certainly for the president. Club presidency signifies civic leadership. In the clubhouse, the president often greets U.S. presidents past and present, Supreme Court justices (Justice John Paul Stevens has been a Club member since 1957), and foreign dignitaries. For a year, the Club presidency becomes almost another full-time job.

"I spent 60 percent of my day at the Club when I was president," recalls Fred Ford. "I attended committee meetings, did a lot of public speaking inside and outside the Club. I was often at the Club for breakfast, lunch, and dinner. At first, I thought I'd let everybody speak his mind at board meetings. Half were lawyers, however, and they will keep talking until the 'judge' raps the gavel. I started rapping the gavel."

Other past presidents estimate as "little" as 30 to 40 percent of their day was devoted to the presidency.

And the year can be frustrating because it's so short. "If you have a big issue you want to accomplish," counsels Fred Ford, "don't wait until you become president. That's not enough time. Start pushing when you're on the board."

Even that may not be enough time. When he was vice president of the Club, Bill McDermott developed a new master plan for renovation, rehabbing, and a sprinkler system. ("My father was a fireman.")

"The board adopted the plan," McDermott recalls, "but when I left office it was put aside. There was a faction that didn't like my plan. They used the 'can't afford it' argument. Some years later, the Club started implementing the plan. But it was a bittersweet experience."

"The best day of the Club presidency," says Ford, "is the day after you leave office." That sentiment was definitely true for at least one president. Don Harnack put the women's issue behind the Club and the Club had a good year to boot. But it was a long, often contentious, just plain miserable year for Harnack.

On the other hand, "It was absolutely the most glorious year of my life," declares the ebullient Everett Barlow. And that's why he continues, as he nears ninety, to be active in any Club group that can use his help. For example, Barlow continues on the boards of the Boys and Girls Clubs and Civic and Arts foundations, which he has headed in the past, and as Club historian and archivist.

Chairing a committee is not always an easy job either. Harnack chaired the house committee, responsible, as the name implies, for the building and much that goes on in the Club. "I hated it. Predecessors had spent five million, then took out loans at 16 percent for another three million. And I was left with a lousy twenty-five thousand bucks in the emergency fund. It's a humbling experience to chair a committee when you have to scramble and patch with no money to keep an old building running."

Service on the board brings few emoluments. There is the annual black-tie holiday dinner for directors and spouses in the Club's elegant French Room. But that's about it, other than the satisfaction and the camaraderie that develops with service.

The Club staff and membership do defer to past Club presidents who represent an informal club within the Club. They dine together from time to time, often in black tie with their wives, and they serve as informal counselors when requested to sitting presidents.

Past presidents and many former board members remain extremely active in the Club. George Sinka has been president of the Club and of all three Club foundations. Several past presidents have also headed one or two of the foundations.

The 300 Club activists could not, however, sustain the Club without the dues and patronage of about 2,400 resident and 1,500 nonresident members. About 10 percent of these members leave the rolls each year to death and relocation as well as for economic and lack-of-usage reasons. That normal membership loss represents one member per working day of each year who has to be replaced. If Club resident membership drops below 2,200, it becomes difficult to maintain the quality and range of services offered by a top club with a big clubhouse.

Maintaining quality and numbers in membership has always been a challenge. More than a dozen Chicago city clubs have closed since the Depression—the Germania, Lake Shore, Covenant, and Illinois Athletic clubs among them. The last, across the street from the Art Institute, is now a dormitory for the School of the Art Institute.

Maintaining membership was especially daunting for city clubs in the 1990s. The factors were many: corporate office moves to the suburbs; elimination or reduction in club membership as perquisites for executives; tax-law changes that reduced deductibility of expenses and dues; and early retirements.

On the other hand, there has been a dramatic increase in urban living by young professionals and also by the not-so-young who move back to the city from the suburbs after their children are out of the nest. Prior to the 1990s, about 70 percent of the resident members lived in the suburbs. In 2003, 70 percent of new Club members reside in the central city. For many, the Club is their country club in the city.

Enrolling one new member a day, every day, puts pressure on admissions director Marsha Pender and her staff, especially when there are some members who think nobody's good enough for the Club.

"I remember," recalled Everett Barlow, who served on the admissions committee for years, "that Austin Fleming didn't think there should be more than a few members in the Club. Back then, each candidate was interviewed separately by the full committee. Austin and a couple others would hold an inquisition, I swear, before a prospect passed muster with them."

Barlow may have brought more new members into the Club than any other member. For prospective new African American members, Everett leaves the varnish off the Club's membership history. "I want them to know that this organization has not always been perfect."

There are several members on the admissions committee who serve as the "conscience of Club quality." They have to walk a line between members who, for example, "don't want any more of those rowdy traders" (who work nearby and comprise a good share of membership, including the president in 2002 to 2003) and the membership office, which has to meet its goals.

"New members don't join because of public affairs or the foundations," says membership director Marsha Pender. "They join because they think they will have fun. They join because they enjoy the energy of the Rendezvous Room, the athletic facilities, the chance to meet new people." Many lawyers belong, says lawyer and past president Don Harnack, because the clubhouse is convenient and a good place to have lunch.

"Like most members," observes past president Jack Wiaduck, "I joined not for the lofty missions of the Club but because the clubhouse is close to my train station. I was also coming up in my bank and was expected to have a club affiliation."

Only later do some of these new members become active in the Club. They hear about a trip to Club 1 for awards night for the boys and girls and decide to go along. Or they attend a glitzy event put on by the Civic and Arts Foundation. A few may even think, "Yeah, I'd like to make a difference in this city," so they attend a meeting of the public affairs committee. Most committee meetings are open to all Club members.

It has been a challenge to attract women members because, well, the Club still looks like a men's club. Women members have softened the place a little; the library now has children's books. But only a little. The Rendezvous Room is still a macho bar.

The Club still suffers, decades after the fact, from its lingering image as a bigoted, racist, sexist place, even though the board in 2002 and 2003 included two African Americans, five women, and at least one Jew.

Prospective members are often invited to the Club for lunch and a tour by a member who wants to show off his Club. But that misses many who might be interested. So, once a month the Club hosts a cocktail party in late afternoon in the Heritage Room. The Club's jazz group (a member activity) provides the background music. Members of the admissions committee serve as hosts. Small-group tours of the facilities are conducted by members and staff. Anyone is welcome, even if he knows not a soul in the membership. Should a person without Club acquaintances be an attractive prospect, a member of the board of directors or the membership committee will be introduced to the guest. This often leads a director or committee member to serve as the sponsor, once they get to know the candidate better.

"Member activities" such as the jazz aficionados' group in the Club are at the heart of the success of a club, according to Jonathan McCabe. "If two or more members want to start an activity, we'll support them. That's what we're all about—meeting the members' interests."

The author walked out of the Rendezvous Room one evening to hear someone belting out "Second-Hand Rose." Maybe it's that extra Bass Ale, the author thinks. But no. The live music is real, coming down the stairwell from a floor up.

The "Way Off Broadway" social group (a member activity) is having final rehearsal for its annual musical review. Twenty middle-aged members, several of them married couples, are hoofing—and huffing—their way through some of the thirty-six tunes they will perform the following evening in a cabaret setting for friends and whoever might be in the Club that evening.

There are forty social and vocational member activity groups within the Club including: "Wind and Wake Watchers" (sailing)," "Fin, Fur, and Feather" (hunting and fishing), camera, jazz, bridge, tap dance, kickboxing (no kidding), chess, faith fellowship, ballroom dancing.

A member describes the last group: "Four or five couples are being led, painfully, through the box step. I predict, in a year's time, the couples will be out on some dance floor, dancing like wooden sticks on a Christmas clock. But they love it."

On the vocational side, there are groups for bankers, lawyers, railway suppliers, securities, insurance, women's networking, and others.

A Club survey in 1960 found that the average age of Club members exceeded sixty. Something had to be done. Young men and women from twenty-one to thirty are offered Club membership for one hundred dollars a month, including athletic fees. It's a little more for the thirty-to-thirty-five group. The dress code has also been relaxed. "Business casual attire" (collared shirt and slacks without jacket or tie) is now acceptable elsewhere throughout the clubhouse, although most men continue to wear jackets.

Older traditionalists in the Club are heard to mutter with disdain about the casualness that younger members insist upon. But as a result, the average age has come down to forty-eight.

After all, this is a big old clubhouse, and energetic new blood is required continually to keep it in mint condition.

SOURCES

The Club archives provided a cornucopia of material for this chapter. For example, the files on the bankruptcy proceedings across three decades are complete and well organized, even to notations by participants, and include all the formal court documents (see Finance Committee Records, #2000-3). In addition, there are copies of letters by Harrison B. Barnard that cast light on this part of the Club's history.

Interviews also proved valuable, including the following: William Barnard, Jonathan McCabe, Carl J. Madsen, Everett Barlow, William McDermott, Jack Wiaduck, Jack and Angeline Higginson, and Marsha Pender.

The unpublished history of the Club by Roger Henn again offered valuable insights as did earlier published histories of the Club, including a supplement to Grant's *Fight for a City,* "Burning the Mortgage," which was published in the Club magazine *Men & Events* (now called *The State of the Union*).

Andrew Yang, a senior at the University of Chicago at the time, wrote his bachelor's thesis on "A Place to Live, to Work and to Play: Private Club Buildings in Chicago, 1890–1929" (University of Chicago, 2001). This was of significant value in providing a context for the development of several club-houses and especially that of the Club, which was among those he studied.

Chapter 18

THE CLUB AND ITS CITY

The Club's values and philosophy throughout its history are best described, the author believes, as "progressive conservatism." Within the Club that has meant, generally, the progressives gravitated to the political action (later, public affairs) committee while the conservatives in the Club tended to their businesses.

Overall, the progressive conservative values have been focused not on economic issues but instead on those of the administrative reform ethic—efficiency, economy, rationality, and honesty in government—and of preparing citizen-voters to sustain these objectives.

Throughout most of the history of the Club, this progressive conservatism has been in conflict with the "politics of opportunity," which has been the hallmark of city politics. Practitioners of opportunity politics consider government a marketplace in which to do business and make one's career, often handsomely, sometimes dishonestly. Efficiency, economy, rationality, and honesty have often been victims of the politics of opportunity, or so Club leadership has believed.

The focus of public affairs in the Club has been upon fighting corruption in government and in reforming administrative procedures to encourage efficiency and constrain dishonesty. The ouster of William Lorimer from the Senate and Edward G. Hines from the Club, and of Charles Yerkes and Al Capone from the city, represent crusades on which progressives and conservatives in the Club could generally agree.

Club involvement in administrative improvements through Chicago charter reform (unsuccessful in 1908), state constitutional reform (unsuccessful in 1920 to 1922, successful in 1970), civil service and election reforms, and a city manager provision are manifestations of values progressives cherish and conservatives can accept.

The progressive spirit was strongest from the 1880s to around 1920. About that time, the progressive urge diminished, according to historian Thomas Pegram, a student of Progressivism in Illinois. In 1920, one-time Club political action committee activist Frank Lowden lost his bid for the presidency. Lowden's campaign was based upon the national acclaim he had received for administrative centralization of government in Illinois during his governorship (1917 to 1921). The reformer lost the nomination in large part because he could not gain the support of those in his own Illinois delegation who practiced the politics of opportunity.

Shortly after, high hopes for a new state constitution in Illinois foundered amidst interest-group bickering and conflict, even among progressives. A convention called in 1920 saw its product overwhelmingly rejected by Illinois voters in 1922.

About the same time, shadows began to dim the glory days of the Club and city. The eminent historian William Cronon wrote of Chicago, "The irony of the World Columbian Exposition is that it marked the climax—and the beginning of the end—of Chicago's role as gateway to the Great West." The city's rapid rise and great size were creating a bottleneck to the transfer of the commerce on which its wealth was based.

The city continued to boom, nevertheless, throughout the 1920s. Skyscrapers rose throughout the Loop, including a new clubhouse for the Club. But the city and the Club were losing some of the "can do anything" swagger.

The Chicago race riot of 1919 revealed a chasm between races that neither city nor Club could understand or bridge. The Club created a committee on the racial problem. So did the state of Illinois, heavily weighted with Club members, but the groups accomplished little.

In 1920, the Club created its first Boys Club in a neighborhood of first-generation Poles and central Europeans. That same year Club activist Julius Rosenwald offered to contribute heavily to a second Boys Club in an African American area but the Boys Club trustees politely tabled the idea. Club members did, however, assist an African American group in setting up their own Boys Club. In 1927, a second Boys Club was established in another white ethnic neighborhood.

The Club eliminated the 2 percent of dues that had been devoted to the purchase of art. Instead, the art committee pleaded with members to donate paintings to the collection, which began to stagnate.

Prohibition helped gangsterism to flourish in Chicago. This deflected the attention of Club leaders who became active in fighting the gangs through the Chicago Crime Commission and the "Secret Six." The Club did hire Dr. Edward Martin as its first professional public affairs director. He kept the coals alive for administrative reform iniatives and the new clubhouse became probably the leading gathering place for civic and reform groups.

In the darkness of the Depression years, the Club struggled to survive while several other clubs closed their doors. The art collection suffered from neglect; plans for a third Boys Club were put on the shelf.

The historic low point in the Club came later, in 1951, when the Club manager declared that distinguished Chicago scientist and African American Percy Julian would not be permitted to enter the clubhouse for a luncheon with other scientists.

Two years later, the Club embarked on a drive to boost membership, which had been declining. The initiation fee was waived for several months and old members encouraged younger men at their banks and law firms to join. More than eight hundred new members joined in 1953, including many younger men who became directors and presidents a decade or so later.

A good case can be made, according to interviews with men who recall that period in the Club, that this spurt of new blood changed the chemistry of the Club leadership over the ensuing two decades, from old and very conservative to progressive though still conservative.

Half the officers and board of the Union League Club in 2003—Jews, blacks, women—would have been either ineligible or unacceptable for membership in the Club in 1953. Until at least 1960, almost all officers and directors in the Club were white Anglo-Saxon Protestants. In the 1940s and 1950s, religious affiliation was a prominent question on the application for membership. Archival records reveal that the Club officers and directors for 1950 and 1960 (a few records are missing) were all Episcopalian, Presbyterian, Congregationalist, or Methodist, with one Christian Scientist and a nondenominational Protestant.

Since the 1950s, haltingly and sometimes grudgingly, the Club has been transforming itself. Club leaders had to flout Club processes and bylaws, respectively, to enroll a black member in 1969 and women as of 1987. These issues evaporated within the Club almost as soon as the color and gender lines were breached. Subsequently, the Club elected both an African American and a female to the Club presidency. The Club now actively recruits qualified black and women members.

In 2003, when religious affiliation is no longer asked on the application, there are Jews, Catholics, and Protestants among Club officers and directors, with a Greek Orthodox as Club president.

The central city of Chicago has become a remarkably vibrant, rapidly expanding center for business, the theater, and performing arts—and residents. Once-seedy third-class business buildings have been resurrected as loft-style condominiums; new high-rise condo complexes appear as frequently near the central city as business buildings did in the Loop in the 1920s.

Mayor Richard M. Daley (son of mayor Richard J.) has taken on some of the swagger that business leaders showed in the glory days before 1920. Unfortunately, there are now far fewer independent business leaders of great wealth than there were a century ago.

Chicago is still living on the legacy of its golden age in the late nineteenth century. In that era, a relatively few men could gather at the Chicago or Union League clubs to make big plans. Over lunch they would raise the capital to build an Art Institute, create a Chicago Symphony, hold a world's fair, launch a whole campus of great museums, and promote a grand design of parks and living space throughout the city—a plan named for Commercial Club, Chicago Club, and Union League Club member Daniel Burnham.

Independent civic magnates such as Field, Higinbotham, Armour, even Yerkes and Insull have been replaced by corporate leaders who report to a headquarters far away. Who today, like Higinbotham, could or would willingly take two years away from a rapidly growing young business—his sole livelihood—to run a world's fair?

Will clubs—can clubs—like this one, with its collective strength, fill the gap left by the city's builders?

The Club is slowly regaining its reputation as a place where progressive conservatives can try to make a difference in the city. This image was badly tarnished during the controversies over black and women membership. From the 1950s to the 1980s, the Club became better known for its resistance to blacks and, especially, for its stubborn resistance to women than for crusades against corruption.

Civic leaders once thought of the Club first when putting together a "good-government" coalition. During the membership controversies, many civic groups stopped meeting in the Club and pointedly kept the Club off their coalition letterheads.

Some things never change. The Chicago Club is still the club de rigueur for major company CEOs. The Standard Club is still predominantly Jewish although it is open to all. And the Union League, University, and Chicago Athletic clubs are still the clubs for ambitious, energetic, often younger men and women who aspire to success.

Public corruption has not been rooted out over the past 125 years. Most of Chicago's governmental and political leaders have tolerated corruption, possibly as a cost of leadership in a fragmented society where for many the dictum "Where's mine?" is more important than "Thou shall not steal."

In the 1980s, for example, a scandal of appalling breadth found more than one hundred judges, attorneys, and court personnel guilty of bribery—and even price-setting for favorable judicial decisions—in the Greylord scandal.

Government is still for many a place to do well rather than do good. Progressive conservatives can win battles now and then but will not likely win the war for rationality and purity in a fragmented, polyglot society where corruption has always been a part of the politics of opportunity.

The conservatives have generally kept an eye on the public affairs committee to keep it from jumping into roiling political waters. This happened in the 1960s when Roger Henn and the public affairs committee were reined in from their crusade against the sanitary district. On the other hand, in the battle to prevent the new Chicago public library from locating in a former department store, Club officers and directors stood shoulder to shoulder with their crusaders.

Progressive conservatives are still active in the Club—Tony Batko, Paul Stack, and Fred Ford (the library), Bob Bergstrom (constitutional reform), Bill Rylowicz and Don Harnack (women membership), and Bill Nissen (death penalty moratorium), among others. They are the counterparts to Victor Lawson, George Cole, William Kent, Frank Lowden, and others of the nineteenth century and Harry Kelly, H. B. Barnard, and Frank Loesch in the 1920s.

But the refrain is heard, "Where are the 'giants' of old in the Club today?" or anywhere in Chicago, for that matter? Like Frank Lowden, they may be in the Club but undiscovered as yet. Lowden was an unknown but energetic, ambitious lawyer when he was active in the Club. By self-description, George Cole was a second-class businessman before he found himself thrust into the leadership of the Municipal Voters' League when nobody of stature would take the job.

Reform Republican Charles Deneen was a member of the Club long before he was elected governor in 1908. So were Richard Ogilvie and Jim Thompson before their governorships in 1969 to 1973 and 1977 to 1991, respectively.

This Club is much more than this writer expected. Far from perfect, the Club is still today a vivid proponent of the American model that honors both the individual pursuit of success and the obligations of citizenship.

According to past Club presidents to a man and woman, the soul of the Club lies, first, in its civic commitment to public affairs and then with the work of the Boys and Girls Clubs and Civic and Arts foundations. This, they say, is what puts the Club above any other in the country.

ARTICLES OF ASSOCIATION

The Chicago Club of the Union League of America, December 19, 1879 (name changed to the Union League Club of Chicago on January 17, 1882)

The condition of membership shall be absolute and unqualified loyalty to the Government of the United States of America.

The primary objects of this association shall be:

1ST. To encourage and promote, by moral, social, and political influence, unconditioned loyalty to the federal government, and to defend and protect the integrity and perpetuity of this nation.

2ND. To inculcate a higher appreciation of the value and sacred obligations of American citizenship; to maintain the civil and political equality of all citizens in every section of our common country, and to aid in the enforcement of all laws enacted to preserve the purity of the ballot box.

3RD. To resist and expose corruption and promote economy in office, and to secure honesty and efficiency in the administration of national, state, and municipal affairs.

UNION LEAGUE CLUB OF CHICAGO: A REPRESENTATIVE CHRONOLOGY

1879	Union League Club incorporates December 19 and establishes four committees: political action, membership, library, and audit.
1880–99	Club proposes legislation creating Chicago Sanitary District and later runs successful slate of candidates for sanitary district board.
1881	Restaurant opens and ladies admitted to "Thursday dinners."
1886	First clubhouse constructed on present site. First artwork "of merit" acquired, *Cologne Cathedral* by Ross Turner, a gift from a member.
1887-88	Club art association formed.
1887	Club initiates annual celebration of George Washington's birthday.
1889	Reception at Club for President Benjamin Harrison and Vice President Levi Morton as part of dedication of the Auditorium Theatre.
1890s	Club vigorously opposes election fraud, graft, and corruption in local government.
1890	Membership reaches one thousand. Stockholders of Columbian Exposition hold first meeting in clubhouse, April 10; Club endorses World's Fair, July 22.
1891	Club amends by-laws to provide for three-member art committee and for allocation of 2 percent of the annual dues of members for the purchase of art.

1899	First catalog of the collection published. Club agrees to patronize local artists by purchasing works from the Art Institute's Annual Exhibition of Works by Artists of Chicago and Vicinity.
1907	Club discusses "A Rational Method of Dealing with Delinquents." Favors extension of sanitary district channel to Joliet.
1916	Athletic department opens.
1919	Club merges Committee on Political Action and War Committee into Public Affairs Committee; advocates reorganization of Chicago government; endorses Constitutional Convention plan; endorses legislation for "citizen army" and "system of universal training of young men."
1920	Club promotes Illinois Constitutional Convention, hosts meetings of delegates. Club funds provided for researching issues and background research. Union League Boys Club 1 dedicated. Governor Frank O. Lowden appoints Club members on Chicago Commission on Race Relations.
1926	Construction of present clubhouse completed. Club commissions Edwin H. Blashfield to create the mural *Patria* in main lounge.
1927	Union League Boys Club 2 opens. Boys Club conducts competition among young Chicago artists.
1929	Club by-laws amended to delete provision for allocation of 2 percent of members' dues for purchase of art.
1930	"Secret Six" vigilante group formed by Club leaders to fight Al Capone.
1930–31	Contributes to fund to finance study of citizenship training; urges calling of Illinois Constitutional Convention.
1933–34	Special fund raised for "honest ballot."
1934	Union League Club of Chicago Post 758 of the American Legion established within clubhouse. Club raises special fund to prosecute vote fraud and convict offenders; resulting publicity helped to enact Permanent Registration Act for Chicago.
1935	Club seeks bankruptcy protection; mortgage bonds refinanced.
1939	Club urges adoption of City Manager Enabling Act.
1942	Rendezvous Room bar opens.

1949	Union League Civic and Arts Foundation incorporated.
1951	Distinguished Chicago African American chemist Percy Julian denied admittance to attend a function for scientists. Clubhouse mortgage bonds refinanced a second time.
1953	Civic and Arts Foundation purchases forty-one paintings from Municipal Art League collection. Club endorses proposals to amend the Judicial Article and reapportionment provisions of the Illinois State Constitution as well as a plan to create Chicago Metropolitan Services Commission and a commission to reorganize the Illinois merit system.
1956	Air-conditioning of clubhouse completed.
1959–60	Summerdale Police Scandal. Club leads call for reform of Police Department and organizes Citizen Action Conference for that purpose. State's attorney hides "Babbling Burglar" in clubhouse.
1961	Club becomes first civic organization to endorse proposed amendment to Illinois Constitution to provide for judicial reform. Sophomore Leadership Conference expands to include four students from each of the fifty Chicago public high schools.
1962	Club pays off mortgage bonds issued originally in 1925. Governor Otto Kerner addresses Club membership on state personnel problems and credits Club with initiative in creating a modern personnel administration in Illinois. Judicial reform approved by Illinois voters.
1962–63	Club undertakes basic redrafting of reform legislation covering Metropolitan Sanitary District of Greater Chicago.
1964	Club invites election officials to review developments in electronic voting devices and opens campaign for law to permit such devices to be used in Illinois. Club undertakes a round-table forum program on foreign affairs called "Great Decisions," repeated in 1965 and 1966.
1967	Sanitary district scandal. Following attempt on the life of sanitary district chairman, Club organizes and leads drive to reform district's management and personnel code.
1968	Club participates in drive for State Constitutional Convention; commissions, publishes, and distributes research papers on issues that were likely to come before the convention. Union League Club hosts meetings for the delegates.

1969	Fred Ford becomes first African American elected to membership in Club.
1970s	Major renovation of clubhouse in advance of 1979 centennial.
1972	Club rescinds rule that women must enter via the side door.
1977	Club membership vote rejects women as members: 178 opposed, 104 in favor.
1980	Club membership rejects women membership a second time: 721 opposed, 349 in favor. Traveling show of fifty of its paintings, with exhibition catalog, mounted by the Club to celebrate its centennial. First curator of the collection hired.
1985	Fred Ford elected president of Club. Union League Boys Clubs become Boys and Girls Clubs.
1986	Club leads drive against use of Goldblatt's building as a new central Chicago Public Library.
1987 *(March)*	Club membership rejects women membership for a third time: 1183 in favor, 658 opposed, just shy of the two-thirds majority required in by-laws. (July) Under threat of loss of liquor license from Chicago City Council, Club board votes to begin accepting proposals for membership without regard to sex.
1989	Club arranges for design of election process for local school councils of Chicago public schools and provides funds for printing of sample ballots.
1995	Board of directors provides for monthly allocation of one-half of 1 percent of membership dues for an art acquisition fund.
1996	Club establishes Distinguished Artists Membership Program.
1997	Club is site for dinner celebrating the fiftieth anniversary of establishment of Israel.
1998	Laura Hagen elected president of Club. First full-time paintings conservator hired.
2002	Club opens its fourth Boys and Girls Club at LaFayette Elementary School. Rendezvous Room redecorated; most wild game trophies replaced by "Seven Muses" paintings. Club and the Civic and Arts Foundation honored by Chicago Children's Choir.
2003	Club publishes first scholarly catalog of art collection.

CLUB PRESIDENTS

1880	Lewis L. Coburn	1908	Leroy A. Goddard
1881–82	John C. Coonley	1909	Jesse Holdom
1883	Elbridge G. Keith	1910	John E. Wilder
1884–86	J. McGregor Adams	1911	William P. Sidley
1887	George W. Smith	1912–13	Abram W. Harris††
1888	John L. Thompson*	1913–14	William H. McSurely
1888	Franklin H. Head†	1914–15	Clarence S. Pellet
1889	George F. Bissell	1915–16	William F. Hypes
1890	Cyrus D. Roys	1916–17	Frank J. Loesch
1891	Franklin H. Head	1917–18	Howard G. Hetzler
1892	George A. Adams	1918–19	Frank H. Scott
1893	Ferdinand W. Peck	1919–20	Charles W. Folds
1894	John P. Wilson	1920–21	John Fletcher
1895	John H. Hamline	1921–22	George T. Buckingham
1896	Christian C. Kohlsaat	1922–24	Wyllys W. Baird
1897	Thomas B. Bryan	1924–26	William J. Jackson
1898	Alexander H. Revell	1926–27	Harry Eugene Kelly
1899	John S. Miller	1927–28	Harrison B. Barnard
1900	Eugene Cary	1928–29	Benjamin F. Affleck
1901	Volney W. Foster	1929–30	Charles M. Moderwell
1902	Robert Mather	1930–31	John R. Montgomery
1903	Edgar A. Bancroft	1931–32	Guy A. Richardson
1904	Wallace Heckman	1932–33	Henry P. Chandler
1905	Alexander A. McCormick	1933–35	John McKinlay
1906	Frederic A. Delano	1935–36	Edwin C. Austin
1907	Charles S. Cutting	1936–37	Ernest L. Hartig**

1937–39	Nicholas J. Conrad	1972–73	Kenneth L. Block
1939–40	John L. Clarkson	1973–74	John J. McEnerney
1940–41	Kenneth E. Rice	1974–75	John A. Mattmiller
1941–42	Ferre C. Watkins	1975–76	Charles L. Strobeck
1942–43	Albion C. Cronkhite	1976–77	John S. Pennell
1943–44	George I. Haight	1977–78	Herbert C. Brook
1944–45	Thomas E. Bond	1978–80	Grover J. Hansen
1945–46	Claude F. Baker	1980–81	N. P. Crockett
1946–47	Charles Z. Henkle	1981–82	Richard H. McKay
1947–49	Frank C. Rathje	1982–83	Terence F. MacCarthy
1949–51	George Hyde Redding	1983–84	Edward Bernardi
1951–52	Joseph Allen Matter	1984–85	Everett J. Barlow
1952–53	Vernon R. Loucks	1985–86	Frederick C. Ford
1953–54	Russell L. Peters	1986–87	Robert A. Rylowicz
1954–55	Alex D. Bailey	1987–88	Don S. Harnack
1955–56	Abe R. Peterson	1988–89	Richard G. Walker
1956–57	George R. Bailey	1989–90	William J. McDermott
1957–58	James G. Badger	1990–91	Frank M. Covey, Jr.
1958–59	William M. Edens	1991–92	George O. Sinka
1959–60	John P. Ballman	1992–93	Frank R. Patton
1960–61	Joseph J. Snyder	1993–94	Harold J. Wiaduck, Jr.
1961–62	Thomas A. Harwood	1994–95	Anthony J. Batko
1962–63	Henry L. Pitts	1995–96	Philip J. Wicklander
1963–64	Charles B. Weaver	1996–97	Richard A. Rauch
1964–65	Frederick W. Wendnagel	1997–98	David B. Whitehurst
1965–66	L. Raymond Billett	1998–99	Laura J. Hagen
1966–67	E. Douglas Schwantes	1999–2000	John E. Scully
1967–68	David Ferguson	2000–1	Robert M. Fitzgerald
1968–69	Milton F. Darr, Jr.	2001–2	Mark A. Lies II
1969–70	Warren A. Logelin	2002–3	Robert J. Pierce
1970–71	Clifford D. Cherry	2003–4	Michael J. Chioros
1971–72	Robert W. Bergstrom		

* Elected President January 24, 1888, died on 31st day of same month.

† Elected to fill vacancy after death of President Thompson.

†† Fiscal year changed to end last day of February instead of last day of December.

** Fiscal year changed to end April 30 instead of last day of February.

MISSION OF THE CIVIC AND ARTS FOUNDATION

With Illustrations of Activities
Prepared by the Foundation

The mission of the Civic & Arts Foundation is to develop and promote programs that support education, civic responsibility, and the arts for children and young adults in the Chicago metropolitan area. The foundation has been nurturing civic, cultural, educational, and artistic programs for more than fifty years. Armed with a rich history, Civic & Arts is, in many ways, a new foundation: programs are being rebuilt while new ones are being developed to carry forward its mission.

The Civic & Arts Foundation is particularly proud of its unique scholarship competitions. These programs award young artists for their artistic talent and encourage them to develop their gifts and pursue their artistic goals. Scholarships are awarded in the fields of music, visual arts, and fiction writing.

The foundation also facilitates Chicago's oldest and most respected music scholarship program. This competition's young awardees include some of the most talented pre-professional up-and-coming musicians in the Chicago area. The Music Composition Competition and Jazz Improvisation Contest are two of the newer musical programs and are a testament to the foundation's development. At recent foundation and Club functions, heads have been bouncing and fingers snapping as young jazz musicians perform with the ULCC Jazz Band.

The Visual Arts Competition, Chicago's largest, provides combined scholarships of over twenty thousand dollars to young painters, sculptors, and photographers. This blind competition is judged by some of the most respectable figures in the Chicago art community, such as James Rondeau, associate curator of twentieth century art at the Art Institute of Chicago, Greg Knight, curator at the Chicago Cultural Center, and Marianne Richter, Union League art curator. The young people are given the opportunity to meet some of Chicago's finest artists and to have their work publicly celebrated when their works are exhibited at a large reception at the Club.

The Civic & Arts Foundation's Fiction Competition for Young Writers is unique to our city. A distinguished panel of judges, including renowned writers and Golden Apple recipients, awards young writers between the ages of sixteen and twenty-six, then publishes their stories in an anthology. Following are the insightful words of one of the foundation's 2003 fiction awardees:

> It [was] an honor to have my fiction recognized by such an important organization in Chicago. I would like to thank the Union League Civic & Arts Foundation for their kindness and support of young people. I am confident that as long as writers are encouraged by their society, they will continue to uncover truth, beauty, and merit in their surroundings.

The Civic & Art Foundation's participation in the Young Chicago Authors' annual poetry program provides additional support to emerging young writers. The foundation also encourages Chicago's young people to make positive contributions to society by supporting programs with the Boys & Girls Clubs Speech Competition, Chicago Children's Choir, and the Chicago Youth Symphony Orchestra.

The members of the Civic & Arts Foundation are dedicated to improving society and believe that the foundation's civic programs address societal needs in a direct and effectual way. In 2004, the foundation will be developing a program with the Center for Professional Development, Illinois Institute of Technology, to provide opportunities for inner-city high school students to enter military and college programs. This unique program will offer inner city JROTC students the opportunity to receive necessary education and skills training that would be otherwise unavailable.

Also under development is a family court brochure, which will be distributed free of charge by the Circuit Court of Cook County to middle- and low-income divorcing parents with minor children who have limited access to, and general unfamiliarity with, legal services and family law disputes. The brochure is designed to help parents support their children during the divorce process, a time of great emotional crisis for adults and children. Cook County has the highest divorce rate in the nation.

Over the last year, the Union League Civic & Arts Foundation has planted the seeds for growth in all of its programs in order to expand its reach within Chicago's educational and artistic community. Rooted in a rich history, this foundation continues to move into the future by providing resources that cultivate the talents, opportunities, and dreams of its young beneficiaries.

BIBLIOGRAPHY

Books

Addams, Jane. *Twenty Years at Hull-House.* New York: Macmillan, 1910.

Allsop, Kenneth. *The Bootleggers: The Story of Chicago's Prohibition Era.* New Rochelle, N.Y.: Arlington House, 1961.

Andreas, A. T. *History of Chicago.* Chicago: A. T. Andreas Co., 1886.

Andrews, Wayne. *Battle for Chicago.* New York: Harcourt, Brace and Company, 1946.

Angle, Paul M., ed. *Prairie State: Impressions of Illinois, 1673–1967, by Travelers and Other Observers.* Chicago: University of Chicago Press, 1968.

Appelbaum, Stanley. *The Chicago World's Fair of 1893: A Photographic Record.* New York: Dover Publications Inc., 1980.

Asbury, Herbert. *Gem of the Prairie: An Informal History of the Chicago Underworld.* Garden City, N.Y.: Garden City Publishing Co., 1940.

Aylesworth, Thomas G., and Virginia Aylesworth. *Chicago: The Glamour Years (1919–1941).* New York: Gallery Books, 1986.

Badger, Reid. *The Great American Fair.* Chicago: Nelson-Hall, 1979.

Barnard, Harry. *Eagle Forgotten: The Life of John Peter Altgeld.* N.J.: Lyle Stuart, Inc., 1973.

Barnhart, Bill, and Gene Schlickman. *Kerner: The Conflict of Intangible Rights.* Urbana: University of Illinois Press, 1999.

Bellows, Henry W. *Historical Sketch of the Union League Club of New York.* New York: G.P. Putnam's Sons, 1879.

Berger, Miles L. *They Built Chicago: Entrepreneurs Who Shaped a Great City's Architecture.* Chicago: Bonus Books, 1992.

Bergreen, Laurence. *Capone: The Man and the Era.* New York: Simon and Schuster, 1994.

Berkin, Carol Ruth, and Mary Beth Norton, eds. *Women of America: A History.* Boston: Houghton Mifflin, 1979.

Bishop, Glenn A., and Paul T. Gilbert, compilers. *Chicago's Accomplishments and Leaders.* Chicago: Bishop Publishing Co., 1932.

Birmingham, Stephen. *The Rest of Us.* Boston: Little, Brown and Company, 1984.

Bliss, E. R. *Beginning of the Union League Club of Chicago.* Chicago: E. R. Bliss, 1916.

Bolotin, Norman, and Christine Laing. *The World's Columbian Exposition: The Chicago World's Fair of 1893.* Washington, D.C.: The Preservation Press, 1992.

Browne, Waldo Ralph. *Altgeld of Illinois: A Record of His Life and Work.* New York: B. W. Huebsch, Inc., 1924.

Buckmaster, Henrietta. *Let My People Go: The Story of the Underground Railroad and the Growth of the Abolitionist Movement.* New York: Harper and Brothers, 1941.

Buenker, John D. *Urban Liberalism and Progressive Reform.* New York: Charles Scribner's Sons, 1973.

Burg, David F. *Chicago's White City of 1893.* Lexington: University of Kentucky Press, 1976.

Bukowski, Douglas. *Big Bill Thompson, Chicago, and the Politics of Image.* Urbana: University of Illinois Press, 1998.

Busch, Francis X. *Enemies of the State.* Indianapolis: Bobbs-Merrill, 1954.

Cameron, William E. *The World's Fair.* Chicago: Chicago Publication & Lithograph Co., 1893.

The Chicago Blue Book of Selected Names, 1911. Chicago: Chicago Directory Co., 1910.

The Chicago Blue Book of Selected Names of Chicago and Suburban Towns. Chicago: Chicago Directory Co., 1898.

Chicago Civic Agencies: A Directory of Associations of Citizens of Chicago Interested in Civic Welfare, 1927. Chicago: University of Chicago Press for the Public Affairs Council of the Union League of Chicago, 1927.

Ciccone, F. Richard. *Daley: Power and Presidential Politics.* Chicago: Contemporary Books, 1996.

———. *Chicago and the American Century: The 100 Most Significant Chicagoans of the Twentieth Century.* Chicago: Contemporary Books, 1999.

Clark, Herma. *The Elegant Eighties: When Chicago Was Young.* Chicago: A.C. McClurg & Co., 1941.

Cook, John A. *The Union League Club.* Chicago: Union League Club of Chicago, 1998.

Craven, Wayne. *American Art: History and Culture.* New York: Harry N. Abrams, Inc., 1994.

Cronon, William. *Nature's Metropolis: Chicago and the Great West.* New York: W. W. Norton & Co., 1991.

Dawkins, Richard. *The Selfish Gene.* New York: Oxford University Press, 1976.

Dean, C. *The World's Fair City.* Chicago: United Publishing Co., 1892.

Dedmon, Emmett. *Fabulous Chicago.* New York: Random House, 1953.

Dedmon, Emmett and Edward T. Blair. *A History of the Chicago Club.* Chicago: Chicago Club, 1960.

Demaris, Ovid. *Captive City.* New York: Lyle Stuart, Inc., 1969.

Dennis, Charles H. *Victor Lawson: His Time and His Work.* Chicago: University of Chicago Press, 1935.

Dinnerstein, Leonard. *Antisemitism in America.* New York: Oxford University Press, 1994.

Dreiser, Theodore. *The Titan.* New York: Boni & Liveright, 1914.

———. *The Financier.* New York: Harper Bros., 1912.

Duis, Perry. *Chicago: Creating New Traditions.* Chicago: Chicago Historical Society, 1976.

———. *Challenging Chicago: Coping with Everyday Life, 1857–1920.* Urbana: University of Illinois Press, 1998.

Duncan, Hugh Dalziel. *The Rise of Chicago as a Literary Center from 1885 to 1920: A Sociological Essay in American Culture.* Totowa, N.J.: The Bedminster Press, 1964.

Duncan-Clark, S. J. *The Progressive Movement: Its Principles and Its Programme.* Boston: Small, Maynard & Co., 1913.

Farr, Finis. *Chicago: A Personal History of America's Most American City.* New Rochelle, N.Y.: Arlington House, 1923.

Fehrenbacher, Don E. *Chicago Giant: A Biography of "Long John" Wentworth.* Madison, Wis.: The American History Research Center, 1957.

Flinn, John J. *Hand-book of Chicago Biography.* Chicago: Standard Guide Co., 1893.

Fuller, Henry Blake. *The Cliff-Dwellers, A Novel.* New York: Harper & Bros., 1893.

Gardner, Helen. *Art through the Ages.* New York: Harcourt Brace, 1926 (often updated).

Gilbert, James. *Perfect Cities: Chicago's Utopias of 1893.* Chicago: University of Chicago Press, 1991.

Ginger, Ray. *Altgeld's America: The Lincoln Ideal versus Changing Realities.* New York: Funk & Wagnalls Co., 1958.

Gove, Samuel K., and James D. Nowlan. *Illinois Politics & Government: The*

Expanding Metropolitan Frontier. Lincoln: University of Nebraska Press, 1996.

Granger, Bill. *Fighting Jane: Mayor Jane Byrne and the Chicago Machine.* New York: Dial Press, 1980.

Granger, Bill, and Lori Granger. *Lords of the Last Machine: The Story of Politics in Chicago.* New York: Random House, 1987.

Grant, Bruce. *Fight for a City: The Story of the Union League Club of Chicago and Its Times, 1880–1955.* Chicago: Rand McNally & Co., 1955.

Greeley, Andrew M. *Andrew Greeley's Chicago.* Chicago: Contemporary Books, 1989.

Green, Paul M., and Melvin G. Holli, eds. *The Mayors: The Chicago Political Tradition.* Carbondale: Southern Illinois University Press, 1975.

Harrison, Carter H. *Stormy Years: The Autobiography of Carter H. Harrison.* Indianapolis: Bobbs-Merrill Co., 1935.

Hartman, Donald K., ed. *Fairground Fiction: Detective Stories of the World's Columbian Exposition.* New York: Motif Press, 1992.

Hayes, Dorsha B. *Chicago: Crossroads of American Enterprise.* New York: Julian Messner Inc., 1944.

Herrick, Robert. *Memoirs of an American Citizen.* Cambridge: Harvard University Press, 1963.

———. *The Web of Life.* New York: Garrett Press, 1970.

Higinbotham, Harlow N. *The Making of a Merchant.* Chicago: Forbes & Co., 1915.

Hirsch, David Einhorn. *Rabbi Emil G. Hirsch: The Reform Advocate.* Chicago: Whitehall Company, 1968.

Hoffmann, John, ed. *A Guide to the History of Illinois.* New York: Greenwood Press, 1991.

Horowitz, Helen Lefkowitz. *Culture and the City: Cultural Philanthropy in Chicago from the 1880s to 1917.* Chicago: University of Chicago Press, 1989.

Howard, Robert P. *Illinois: A History of the Prairie State.* Grand Rapids, Mich.: William B. Eerdmans Publishing Co., 1972.

———. *Mostly Good and Competent Men: Illinois Governors, 1818–1988.* Springfield: *Illinois Issues* and Illinois State Historical Society, 1988.

Hutchinson, William T. *Lowden of Illinois: The Life of Frank O. Lowden.* 2 vols. Chicago: University of Chicago Press, 1957.

Illinois Secretary of State, *Illinois Blue Book 1971–1972.* Springfield: State of Illinois, 1973.

Jacobs, Jane. *The Death and Life of Great American Cities.* New York: Random House, 1961. Reprint, New York: Modern Library, 1993.

Irwin, Willard, Earl Chapin May, and Joseph Hotchkiss. *A History of the*

Union League Club of New York. New York: Dodd, Mead, and Company, 1952.

Jaher, Frederick Cople. *A Scapegoat in the New Wilderness: The Origins and Rise of Anti-Semitism in America*. Cambridge: Harvard University Press, 1994.

Karamanski, Theodore J. *Rally 'Round the Flag: Chicago and the Civil War*. Chicago: Nelson-Hall Publishers, 1993.

Kellman, Jerold L. *The First One Hundred Years*. Chicago: Union League Club of Chicago, 1984.

Kennedy, David M. *Freedom from Fear: The American People in Depression and War, 1929–45*. New York: Oxford University Press, 1999.

Kerber, Linda K., and Jane Sherron De Hart, eds. *Women's America: Refocusing the Past*. 2nd ed. New York: Oxford University Press, 1987.

Kilian, Michael, Connie Fletcher, and F. Richard Ciccone. *Who Runs Chicago?* New York: St. Martin's Press, 1979.

Kimball, Milton Frederick, ed. *100th Anniversary Celebration: The Union Club of Boston, Inc.* Boston: Union Club of Boston, 1964.

King, Hoyt. *Citizen Cole of Chicago*. Chicago: Horders, 1931.

Kobler, John. *Capone: The Life and World of Al Capone*. New York: G. P. Putnam's Sons, 1971.

Kogan, Bernard, ed. *The Chicago Haymarket Riot: Anarchy on Trial*. Boston: D.C. Heath & Co., 1959.

Landesco, John. *Organized Crime in Chicago*. Chicago: University of Chicago Press, 1929.

Lawson, Melinda. *Patriot Fires: Forging a New American Nationalism in the Civil War North*. Lawrence: University Press of Kansas, 2002.

Leach, Paul R. *That Man Dawes*. Chicago: The Reilly and Lee Co., 1930.

LeJeune, Anthony. *The Gentlemen's Clubs of London*. New York: Mayflower Books, 1979.

Leonard, John W., ed. *The Book of Chicagoans: A Biographical Directory of Leading Living Men of the City of Chicago*. Chicago: A. N. Marquis & Co., 1905.

Levy, George. *To Die in Chicago: Confederate Prisoners at Camp Douglas 1862–1865*. Evanston, Ill.: Evanston Publishing, Inc., 1994.

Loy, Dennis J., and Caroline Honig. *One Hundred Years: 1887–1987*. Catalog of the collection. Chicago: Union League Club, 1987.

Lyle, Judge John H. *The Dry and Lawless Years*. Englewood Cliffs, N.J.: Prentice-Hall, Inc., 1960.

Malone, Dumas, ed. *Dictionary of American Biography*. New York: Charles Scribner's Sons, 1932.

Martin, Edward M. *The Role of the Bar in Electing the Bench in Chicago*. The University of Chicago Press, 1936.

Masters, Edgar Lee. *Levy Mayer and the New Industrial Era.* New Haven: [Yale University Press] 1927.

———. *The Tale of Chicago.* New York: G. P. Putnam's Sons, 1933.

Mayer, Harold M. *Chicago: City of Decisions.* Chicago: Geographic Society of Chicago, 1955.

Mayer, Harold M., and Richard Dade. *Chicago: Birth of a Metropolis.* Chicago: University of Chicago Press, 1969.

McAdams, Benton. *Rebels at Rock Island: The Story of a Civil War Prison.* DeKalb: Northern Illinois University Press, 2000.

McDonald, Forrest. *Insull.* Chicago: University of Chicago Press, 1962.

McElvaine, Robert S. *The Great Depression.* New York: Times Books, 1984.

McPhaul, John J. *Deadlines & Monkeyshines: The Fabled World of Chicago Journalism.* Englewood Cliffs, N.J.: Prentice-Hall, 1962.

Merriam, Charles Edward. *Chicago: A More Intimate View of Urban Politics.* New York: MacMillan & Co., 1929.

Miller, Donald L. *City of the Century: The Epic of Chicago and the Making of America.* New York: Simon & Schuster, 1996.

Monroe, Harriet. *Harlow Niles Higinbotham: A Memoir with Brief Autobiography.* Chicago, 1920.

Morrison, Hugh. *Louis Sullivan, Prophet of Modern Architecture.* New York: W. W. Norton, 1935.

Ness, Eliot. *The Untouchables.* New York: Julian Messner, Inc., 1957.

Nord, David Paul. *Newspapers and New Politics: Midwestern Municipal Reform, 1890–1900.* Ann Arbor, Mich.: UMI Research Press, 1981.

Otis, Philo Adams. *The Chicago Symphony Orchestra: Its Organization, Growth, and Development.* Chicago: Clayton F. Summy, 1924.

Pease, Theodore Calvin. *The Story of Illinois.* Chicago: University of Chicago Press, 1949.

Pensoneau, Taylor. *Governor Richard Ogilvie: In the Interest of the State.* Carbondale: Southern Illinois University Press, 1997.

Perdue, Joe, ed. *Contemporary Club Management.* East Lansing, Mich.: Educational Institute, American Hotel and Motel Association, 1997.

Peterson, Virgil W. *Barbarians in Our Midst: A History of Chicago Crime and Politics.* Boston: Little, Brown & Co., 1952.

Pierce, Bessie Louise. *The Rise of a Modern City, 1871–93.* Vol. 3 of *A History of Chicago.* New York: Alfred A Knopf, 1952.

Randall, Frank A. *History of the Development of Building Construction in Chicago.* 2nd ed. Urbana: University of Illinois Press, 1999.

Roberts, Sidney I. "Businessmen in Revolt: Chicago 1874–1900." Ph.D. diss., Northwestern University, 1960.

Russo, Gus. *The Outfit: The Role of Chicago's Underworld in the Shaping of Modern America.* New York: Bloomsbury, 2001.

Schaaf, Barbara C. *Mr. Dooley's Chicago.* Garden City, N.Y.: Anchor Press/ Doubleday, 1977.

Schiesl, Martin J. *The Politics of Efficiency: Municipal Administration and Reform in America, 1800–1920.* Berkeley: University of California Press, 1977.

Schneirov, Richard. *Labor and Urban Politics: Class Conflict and the Origins of Modern Liberalism in Chicago, 1864–97.* Urbana: University of Illinois Press, 1998.

Schoenberg, Robert J. *Mr. Capone: The Real—and Complete—Story of Al Capone.* New York: Perennial, 1992.

Simpson, Dick. *Rogues, Rebels, and Rubber Stamps: The Politics of the Chicago City Council from 1863 to the Present.* Boulder, Colo.: Westview Press, 2001.

Sinclair, Upton. *The Jungle.* 1906. Reprint, Urbana: University of Illinois Press, 1988.

Smith, Carl S. *Chicago and the American Literary Imagination 1880–1920.* Chicago: University of Chicago Press, 1984.

Smith, Page. *The Rise of Industrial America.* Vol. 6. New York: McGraw-Hill, 1984.

Spinney, Robert G. *City of Big Shoulders: A History of Chicago.* DeKalb: Northern Illinois University Press, 2000.

The Spirit of the Union League Club 1879–1926. Chicago: Union League Club, May 21, 1926.

The Standard Club of Chicago, 1869–1969. Chicago: Standard Club, 1969.

Steffens, Lincoln. *The Shame of the Cities.* New York: Hill & Wang, 1904.

———. *The Autobiography of Lincoln Steffens.* New York: Harcourt, Brace and Co., 1931.

Stoddard, William O., Jr., ed. *Lincoln's Third Secretary: The Memoirs of William O. Stoddard.* New York: Exposition Press, 1955.

Sullivan, Edward D. *Rattling the Cup on Chicago Crime.* New York: Vanguard Press, 1929.

Sutherland, Douglas. *Fifty Years on the Civic Front 1893–1943: A Report on the Achievements of the Civic Federation of Chicago.* Chicago: Civic Federation, 1943.

Tarr, Joel Arthur. *A Study in Boss Politics: William Lorimer of Chicago.* Urbana: University of Illinois Press, 1971.

Tuohy, James, and Rob Warden. *Greylord: Justice, Chicago Style.* New York: G. P. Putnam's Sons, 1989.

Union League Club Art Collection. Chicago: Union League Club of Chicago, 2003.

The Union League Club of Philadelphia Celebrates 125 Years: 1862–1987.
Philadelphia: The Union League of Philadelphia, 1987.

Veblen, Thorstein. *The Theory of the Leisure Class.* New York: MacMillan &
Co., 1899; New York: New American Library, 1953.

Waldrop, Frank C. *McCormick of Chicago: An Unconventional Portrait of a
Controversial Figure.* Englewood Cliffs, N.J.: Prentice-Hall, Inc.,
1966.

Watkins, T. H. *The Great Depression.* Boston: Little, Brown & Co., 1993.

Weber, Max. *The Protestant Ethic and the Spirit of Capitalism.* New York:
Scribner, 1930; New York: Charles Scribner's & Sons, 1958.

Wendt, Lloyd, and Herman Kogan. *Bosses in Lusty Chicago: The Story of
Bathhouse John and Hinky Dink.* Bloomington: Indiana University
Press, 1943.

———. *Give the Lady What She Wants!* Chicago: Rand McNally & Co.,
1952.

Werner, M. R. *Julius Rosenwald: The Life of a Practical Humanitarian.* New
York: Harper & Brothers, 1939.

Wille, Lois. *Forever Open, Clear, and Free: The Struggle for Chicago's Lakefront.* Chicago: Henry Regnery, 1972.

Winik, Jay. *April 1865: The Month That Saved America.* New York: Harper,
Collins, 2001.

Periodicals

Bachmann, Lawrence P. "Julius Rosenwald." *American Jewish Historical
Quarterly* 66, September 1976.

Bateman, Newton, and Paul Selby. "Secret Treasonable Organizations."
Reprint, *Men & Events,* Union League Club of Chicago, April 1962.

Baumann, Edward. "The Haymarket Bomber." *Chicago Tribune Magazine,*
April 27, 1986.

Baylen, Joseph O. "A Victorian's 'Crusade' in Chicago, 1893–1894." *Journal
of American History* 51, December 1964.

Benton, Elbert J. "The Movement for Peace without a Victory during the
Civil War." *Collections of the Western Reserve Historical Society,* 1918.

Bryant, George T. "The Gripman Wore a Sheepskin Coat." *Chicago
History* 1:1, Spring 1970.

Buckingham, Colonel George T. "The Projected Sack of Chicago." 1939.
Reprint, *Men & Events,* Union League Club of Chicago, April 1962.

Buenker, John D. "Chicago's Ethnics and the Politics of Accommodation."
Chicago History, Fall 1974.

Bushnell, George D. "Chicago's Leading Men's Clubs." *Chicago History,*
Summer 1982.

Clayton, John. "How They Tinkered with a River." *Chicago History* 1:1,
    Spring 1970.
Cochran, William C. "The Dream of a Northwest Confederacy." State
    Historical Society of Wisconsin, Separate No. 175, from the *Proceed-
    ings of the Society for 1916.*
Collins, Charles. "The Funk Case: A Plot That Failed." *Chicago Tribune
    Sunday Magazine,* May 2, 1954.
Duis, Perry. "Whose City? Part Two." *Chicago History,* Summer 1983.
Field Museum News 14:9–10, September-October 1943.
Grosch, Anthony R. "Social Issues in Early Chicago Novels." *Chicago
    History* 4:2, Summer 1975.
Hamilton, E. Bentley. "The Union League: Its Origin and Achievements
    in the Civil War." *Transactions of the Illinois State Historical Society,*
    1921 (Springfield, 1922).
Henn, Roger. "Constitutional Revision in Illinois: The Union League
    Role." *National Civic Review* 60:8, September 1971.
Hofer, J. M. "Development of the Peace Movement in Illinois during the
    Civil War." *Journal of the Illinois State Historical Society* 24:1 (April
    1931): 79–83.
Horowitz, Helen Lefkowitz. "The Art Institute of Chicago: The First
    Forty Years." *Chicago History,* Spring 1979.
Keyes, Jonathan J. "The Forgotten Fire." *Chicago History,* Fall 1997.
Kogan, Herman. "Myra Bradwell: Crusader at Law." *Chicago History* 3:3,
    Winter 1974–75.
Loesch, Frank J. "Personal Experiences during the Chicago Fire." *Chicago
    History* 1:4, Fall 1971.
———. "Long Range Plans Report." *Men & Events,* Union League Club
    of Chicago, July 1975.
Marcus, Jacob Rader. "Background for the History of American Jewry."
    Chapter 1, in Oscar I. Janowsky. *The American Jew.* Philadelphia:
    Jewish Publications Society of America, 1965.
Men & Events. Union League Club of Chicago, 1925–1979.
Roberts, Sidney I. "The Municipal Voters' League and Chicago's
    Boodlers." *Journal of the Illinois State Historical Society,* Summer 1960.
———. "Portrait of a Robber Baron: Charles T. Yerkes." *Business History
    Review,* Autumn 1961.
Saltzstein, Joan W. "Dankmar Adler, the Man, the Architect, the Author."
    Wisconsin Architect, July-August 1967.
Schneirov, Richard. "Chicago's Great Upheaval of 1877." *Chicago History*
    9:1, Spring 1980.
Scriabine, Christine. "Upton Sinclair and the Writing of *The Jungle.*"
    Chicago History, Spring 1981.

Siry, Joseph M. "Chicago's Auditorium Building: Opera or Anarchy." *Journal of the Society of Architectural Historians* 57:2, June 1998.

Tarr, Joel A. "William Kent to Lincoln Steffens: Origins of Progressive Reform in Chicago." *Mid-America,* January 1965.

———. "The Urban Politician as Entrepreneur." *Mid-America,* January 1967.

———. "The Expulsion of Chicago's 'Blond Boss' from the United States Senate." *Chicago History,* Fall 1972.

Miscellaneous Sources

The Union League Club Archives is a comprehensive collection of records pertaining to the Club and its role in Chicago history from the Club's founding in 1879 to the present. Included in the archives holdings are board minutes and annual reports; committee minutes and reports; pamphlets, books, periodicals, and directories published by the Club; membership records; photographs; subject files; and audio tapes. Of particular note are records of public affairs projects the club has promoted over the years.

Most of the records are fully processed and have automated finding aides. The archives are open to staff, members, and the public by appointment.

Adams, Frederick Upham (presumed author). "Edward Hines to the Union League Club, A Statement of Facts Relative to Charges Considered by its Board of Directors." June 17, 1912. ULCC archives. See Edward Hines Collection, #2001-13, Box 1.

Adams, Frederick Upham. *The Plot That Failed: A Startling Exposure of a Deliberate Conspiracy against William Lorimer & Edward Hines.* Union League Club of Chicago archives, n.d.

Adler, Dankmar. Newberry papers. Newberry Library, Chicago.

Aldrich, James Frank. "Letterbooks." Vol. 2, 1853–1933. Chicago Historical Society Collection.

———. "Reminiscences." *Union League Club Bulletin,* monthly series, 1926.

Ashley, Frederick J. *Chicago's Union League—75 Years Young.* Reprint, Sexton Desk Diary, 1956. ULCC archives. In General Historical Files, 1999-2002, Box 5.

Boys and Girls Clubs, Union League Club of Chicago. *Minutes.* 1919 to present.

Bushnell, George. "Union League Club Centennial Book." ULCC archives, n.d.

Citizens' Association of Chicago. *Annual Reports,* 1874–1925. General Historical Information, Box 11, ULCC archives.

Cook, John A. "The Union League." Paper presented to the Chicago
    Literary Club, January 12, 1998. ULCC Library.

Dinwiddie, Oscar. Reminiscences. ULCC archives, 1925.

Gibson, Guy James. "Lincoln's League: The Union League Movement
    during the Civil War." M.A. thesis, University of Illinois at Urbana-
    Champaign, 1957.

Grant, Bruce. *Fight for a City: A Supplemental History of the Union League
    Club of Chicago from 1955 to 1965.* ULCC archives.

———. "Burning the Mortgage," supplement to *Fight for a City,* n.d.

Haight, George I. "History of the Union League of America." Chap. 1 in
    History of the ULA. ULCC archives. N.p., circa 1946, , #2001–18.

Henn, Roger. "Lincoln's Loyal Legions." June 24, 1971. Union League of
    America, History, Box 1, FF6, ULCC archives.

———. "History of the Union League Club of Chicago." 1980. ULCC
    archives.

———. "The Union and the Union League Club." Memorandum. ULCC
    Archives, #1999–44, Shelf 40-B.

Hirsch, Emil G. "Dankmar Adler." Funeral eulogy, Temple K.A.M.,
    Chicago, April 13, 1900.

Martin, Dr. Edward M. "Statement of Col. William H. Bates." March 3,
    1928. ULCC archives.

McIlvaine, Caroline. Newberry papers. Newberry Library, Chicago.

Miller, Joan S. "The Politics of Municipal Reform in Chicago during the
    Progressive Era: The Municipal Voters League as a Test Case, 1896–
    1920." M.A. thesis, Roosevelt University, 1966.

Pitts, Henry L. *My Life.* 1999. A copy is located in ULCC library.

"Record of the Trail of Edward Hines before the Union League Club of
    Chicago," June 11, 1911–February 23, 1912. Located in the Gallagher
    Law Library, University of Washington, Seattle.

Sachdev, Rohit. *The Founding Years of the Union League Club of Chicago: Its
    Origins and Early Development, 1879–1900.* Chicago, 1996. Located in
    ULCC library.

Starrett, Julius. Reminiscences. ULCC archives, 1925.

Wagner, Joan. *A History of the Art Collection of the Union League Club of
    Chicago.* Chicago: Union League Club, June 2000. Located in the
    office of the art curator.

Interviews

Arthur, Ardelle. June 20 and July 17, 2001.

Barlow, Everett. December 20, 2000, and numerous subsequent dates.

Barnard, William, Burton Barnard, and James Barnard. December 14, 2001.

Batko, Anthony. November 5, 2001.

Bergstrom, Robert. ULCC president. March 5, 2001.

Carstedt, Nancy. September 29, 2001

Castillo, Edwin. Education Director, Barreto Boys and Girls Club. August 30, 2001.

Darr, Milton F., Jr. September 29, 2001.

Ford, Fred. November 6, 2001.

Gersey, Gerry. July 20, 2001.

Grundman, Rose Ann. June 20 and July 18, 2001.

Harnack, Donald. November 20, 2001.

Henn, Roger. Former ULCC director of public affairs. March 9, 2001.

Iverson, Matt. June 20, 2001.

Kreston, Jeanette. September 29, 2001.

Lee, Josephine. September 29, 2001.

Lynch, Jim. ULCC athletic director. December 14, 2001.

Markle, J. A. Former executive director, Union League Boys Clubs. June 20, 2001.

McCabe, Jonathan. December 19, 2000, and July 19, 2001.

McCullagh, Lois. June 20 and October 22, 2001.

McDermott, Bill. June 12, 2001.

McKay, Dick. November 6, 2001.

Meuser, Ken. Chairman, ULCC public affairs committee. August 30 and October 22, 2001.

Pitts, Henry. ULCC president. March 2, 2001.

Richter, Marianne. July 11 and 27, 2001.

Rylowicz, Robert. October 3, 2002.

Schwartzberg, Hugh. September 12 and 29, 2001.

Scully, John. July 17, 2001.

Stack, Paul. November 15, 2001.

Swindall, Bart. Tour and interview, Chicago Auditorium Theatre, July 17, 2001.

Thomas, Doreen. Secretary to Club manager Taylor Hay from 1956 to 1974. August 23, 2001.

Wagner, Clark and Joan. October 4, 2002.

Wiaduck, Jack. October 3, 2002.

Whittaker, Frank. November 14, 2000.

INDEX